THE PERFECT PATSY

THE PERFECT PATSY

The Winger Murders

Edward Cunningham

Library of Congress Control Number:		2013918517
ISBN:	Hardcover	978-1-4931-1271-5
	Softcover	978-1-4931-1270-8
	eBook	978-1-4931-1272-2

This book was printed in the United States of America.

Rev. date: 01/16/2014

To order additional copies of this book, contact:
Xlibris LLC
1-888-795-4274
www.Xlibris.com
Orders@Xlibris.com
126639

CONTENTS

Part V: The Defense

JACKET

A Perfect Patsy

This is the story of Mark Winger, a man with a near-genius IQ. He graduated from VMI as a nuclear engineer. He joined the service as an officer, but because of his failure to take responsibility for his troops, he was denied a promotion. On discharge, he was employed in Miami, Florida, and then in Champaign, Illinois. While in Florida, he was introduced to Donnah Winger by his brother, who worked with her at the hospital. Donnah was a happy, effervescent young lady who made you feel good about yourself. She was a medical technician, having finished high school and then went on to tech school in Hollywood, Florida.

After a brief courtship, Donnah and Mark were married in 1987 in Hollywood, Florida. In 1989, they came to Springfield, Illinois, where Donnah obtained a job at a hospital as a medical technician and Mark as a nuclear engineer working for the state of Illinois.

Mark Winger was a smart guy—arrogant, manipulative, and macho. He could be funny and a stand-up comic. He talked about his ambitions and was enamored with himself; he thought he was smarter than everyone else. He could be charming and engaging. Underneath this personality there was a self-centered mentality.

All who knew Donnah and Mark—the neighbors, friends, and their family—thought they had a near-perfect marriage. In June of 1995, they started adoption proceedings, as Donnah could not maintain a pregnancy.

In late August of 1995, Donnah Winger was bludgeoned to death, allegedly by a van driver who had taken her from St. Louis, Missouri, to Springfield, Illinois, six days earlier. Mark shot the van driver and killed him. The initial investigation showed that this was justifiable homicide—Mark had killed the killer of his wife.

A year later, Mark married a nanny whom he had hired to take care of his young adopted daughter. They had three subsequent children. He continued to work for the Illinois Department of Nuclear Safety.

In June 2002 Mark Winger was convicted for the double murder of his wife, Donnah, and the van driver, Roger Harrington, and is now spending his time in a maximum-security prison in Tamms, Illinois. NBD, ABC and the Discovery Channel have featured these murders on their programs.

This is a story of how justice prevailed because of the perseverance of the police, the state's attorney, and the courage of a witness in coming forward.

AUTHOR'S NOTES

This book is based upon actual events surrounding the murder of Donnah Winger. The events described herein are accurate, but much of the dialogue and conversations have been reconstructed, as I obviously was not present when these conversations took place. I tried to capture the events and keep the book flowing and dramatize the events; I have therefore created the conversations, and they are fiction.

The actual events have been described both in the police reports, interviews, depositions, and the transcripts of the trial. The courtroom scenes have been abbreviated, hopefully to portray effectively the testimony of this trial without getting tedious. I have therefore summarized this testimony.

With any situation such as this, there are always gaps and loose ends. Only in fiction can everything be tied up neatly. What I tried to do was capture the events. The conversations have therefore been constructed by me. The names of certain individuals have been changed because they have started new lives, and there is no desire to refer to them with their real names.

I wish to thank the cooperation of the state's attorneys, John Schmidt, and others in the State's Attorney's Office in helping me locate and review documents and records pertaining to this trial and in providing information regarding this case. I also want to thank the clerks of the appellate court, Fourth District, and the Sangamon County Court Clerk's Office for their aid in letting me review records in their offices. I have interviewed a number of people, but many of these individuals desire to remain anonymous, so I am not going to mention their names. I also want to give a particular thanks to Charles Cox for his help.

I also want to thank Abby Southerland for typing multiple drafts and especially Wendy Mytar for putting the book in final form and her suggestions.

I also want to thank Ira Drescher for his helpful insights into the case; he was instrumental in providing information to the police and prosecutors to help reopen the case and to secure the eventual conviction.

Certain individuals have declined to discuss the case with me, including but not limited to, Mark Winger, DeAnn Schultz, Rabbi Mark Datz and his wife, and Doug Williamson. I have therefore used the police reports and other records, including court documents, to portray their activities surrounding this case. I, of course, would have preferred to interview them. Certain other individuals were prohibited by attorney-client privileges and confidentiality rules from talking to me, including Dr. John Lauer and Attorney Breen. Similarly the conversations with Dr. Lauer are fictional as they are privileged. I have abbreviated much of the testimony as it is sometimes tedious. The cross-examination is partially mine and partially the attorneys trying the case. Case was well tried on both sides, and the judge was fair in his rulings. The jury decided on the facts as presented in court. This is how the justice system should work.

PROLOGUE

August 29, 1995, was a hot and humid day in Springfield, Illinois. August is always the worst month for the heat. The heat becomes suffocating, especially when there is no breeze. There was very little rain, but it was perfect for growing corn in the Midwest. The heat brings out the worst in people. Drivers are short-tempered. Domestic disputes keep the police department busy, and barroom brawls fill up the Sangamon County Jail.

Besides the domestic disputes and barroom fights, there had been three murders in August. August 29 added three new murders. The police department was busy. Everybody was blaming the suffocating heat and the lack of relief for a monthlong period of hot and humid days.

This was not so for Donnah Winger. She had been in Florida the previous week visiting her mother, Sarah Jane, and her stepdad, Ira Drescher. She had taken a three-month-old child to meet them. She and her husband, Mark, were in the process of adopting the child. Donnah was ecstatic. She wanted a family of her own but had been unable to conceive. They had started the adoption proceedings in late May. She went down to Florida while Mark was taking a course in Chattanooga, Tennessee. Donnah wanted to show her child to her mom, stepdad, and also to her two sisters, who were living there while Mark was out of town. It was a good time to go for a visit.

When in Florida, Donnah's mom, stepdad, and two sisters could not get enough of the little baby. She was their first grandchild. Cindy was a cute baby girl, smiling and cooing. Donnah was all smiles. Donnah and the baby came back on August 23, as her husband's course was finished on August 25, and she wanted to be home when he came back.

On her husband's return on Saturday they had a cookout at their house with their best friends, DeAnn and John Schultz. On Sunday they cooked at the Schultzes. Donnah had taken vacation days from her job as a medical technician. She did not go to work on Monday or Tuesday and stayed at home with her child. She did not want to be separated from her new baby. Mark returned to work on Monday.

On Tuesday, August 29, 1995, she and Mark decided to take Cindy to Mark's office. As proud parents they wanted to show her off to Mark's co-workers and friends. This was somewhat of a close-knit group who had visited each other at their homes, etc. Mark suggested that Donnah come at noon, when there wouldn't be too much of a disruption of the office, and afterward they would have lunch together.

After Cindy took her morning nap, Donnah brought her to Mark's office. As she entered the office, the receptionist called Mark, and the office virtually emptied out as employees surrounded him and Donnah. All of the women wanted to hold the baby. Cindy was passed around one to the other, people putting her fingers in her small hands. No work was done.

Finally Mark said, "Let's go out to lunch." Donnah said, "Yes, I need to go! I have an appointment to get Cindy's three-month pictures."

No one in the office had ever seen Donnah so happy, smiling, nonstop talking, and full of energy. She could barely stand still.

After lunch Mark went back to work, and Donnah took Cindy to Sears to have her pictures taken. Donnah wanted to be satisfied so she made sure the pictures were just right. After the photo session, Donnah and Cindy went home at around 4:00 p.m. Cindy was sleeping after being exhausted from all the day's activities. When she arrived, Mark was already at home working out in the basement on his treadmill. Mark left the door unlocked because Donnah was coming in later.

At 4:15 p.m. it was still hot and humid. There was no breeze, and the leaves on the trees were absolutely still. The heat radiated from the roads, and the lights shimmered, reflecting how hot it was. Donnah could hardly wait to get home and into the cool, air-conditioned house at 4305 Westview. She had had a near-perfect day—lunch with her husband and showing the baby to his co-workers. She was happy, but Cindy was hot and was starting to get fussy. She needed to be changed. Once she got into the house with the air-conditioning, she could then relax.

As Donnah pulled in the driveway, she noticed a red car parked across the street from her house facing the wrong direction. No one was in the vehicle. She didn't think anything of it. Upon getting Cindy out of the car, she walked into the cool house and took Cindy into the master bedroom, right off the entryway. She laid Cindy on the bed and was about to change her diaper after she changed her blue jean cutoffs. She heard some strange noise in the kitchen and dining area. She did not know what it was and went in to investigate. She left Cindy in the middle of the bed and went into the hallway leading into the dining room.

As Donnah entered the dining room, someone grabbed her from behind. She tried to resist the strong arms, but she was unable to. A voice then said, "Get on your knees." And she refused, asking why. "Do what I tell you and shut up," he responded. She felt someone pushing her down onto her knees; she fell onto her knees and screamed, "What are you doing?" The voice answered, "I said shut up." And he pushed her to her knees. "Why are you doing this?" He was pushing her forward. There was no response. "Please, what's going on? What are you doing?"

All of a sudden she felt a sharp, intense pain in the back of her head. She cried out in pain. Six more blows struck the back of her head, crushing her skull. She faded into unconsciousness, saying to herself, "Why? Why me?" as she lost consciousness and fell forward into an ever-widening pool of blood.

This is how Donnah Winger, a new mother, someone who brought sunshine into the life of many people, died on the floor in her own home at 4:30 p.m. on August 29, 1995.

CHAPTER 1

The 911 Call
August 29, 4:27 p.m.

The 911 operator could not have been more surprised when the 911 call came in from 4305 Westview Drive in Springfield on the west side of town. The male caller was in a panic and speaking fast. He would gasp and start up again. It was a true emergency.

DISPATCHER: 911 Emergency, what's your emergency?

CALLER: Emergency, emergency . . . this man, just . . . he beat my wife . . . I shot him . . . please help me. My god . . . my wife's not breathing.

DISPATCHER: Okay, do you need an ambulance?

CALLER: I need everything . . . I need everything.

DISPATCHER: Springfield Police.

CALLER: Help me.

DISPATCHER: What's the problem?

CALLER: I just shot this man in my house.

DISPATCHER: He's inside your house right now?

CALLER: He's inside my house. He beat my wife.

DISPATCHER: Is he there right now?

CALLER: Yes, they're both . . .

DISPATCHER: Does he have a gun?

CALLER: Her brains are everywhere.

DISPATCHER: Where's the man at?

CALLER: He's lying on the floor. (*Man can be heard moaning.*)

DISPATCHER: Is he dead?

CALLER: I don't know . . . he's making weird sounds. Please . . .

DISPATCHER: Okay, sir, slow down. I can't understand you . . . slow down.

CALLER: I'm at 2305 Westview, Westview Drive

DISPATCHER: Slow down, I can't understand you. Is the man still in your house?

CALLER: Yes. He's lying there on the floor with a bullet in his head.

DISPATCHER: Did you shoot him?

CALLER: Yes, I shot him. He was killing my wife. (*Man can be heard moaning.*) Please . . . my baby's crying . . . my baby's crying. I've got to go. I'll call you right back. (*Caller hangs up phone*).

DISPATCHER: Fuck! (*Springfield Police Department calls back*).

ANSWERER: Yes. Yes. What?

DISPATCHER: Are you Mark Winger?

ANSWERER: Yes, yes.

DISPATCHER: This is the police department. We've got officers in route. I need to know what's going on there.

ANSWERER: My wife is dying on the floor.

DISPATCHER: Okay. Is she still alive?

ANSWERER: I think so.

DISPATCHER: We've got an ambulance en route, and we've got police officers en route. Where is the gun?

ANSWERER: It's on the table . . . it's on the table . . . Please, God. Please come here.

DISPATCHER: Okay. We've got people on the way.

ANSWERER: Okay.

DISPATCHER: Who is this man?

ANSWERER: I don't, I don't know who he is.

DISPATCHER: Is he still inside the house?

ANSWERER: Yes. He's lying on the floor. Okay. I've got to hold my wife. I've got to get to my wife.

DISPATCHER: Are you Mark Winger?

ANSWERER: Yes, I am. Yes, I am.

DISPATCHER: Okay. And your wife is Donnah?

ANSWERER: Yes, she is.

DISPATCHER: When did the man come there?

ANSWERER: I, I don't . . . a few minutes ago. I've got to get to my wife. Please just let me get to my wife. I won't hang up . . . okay?

DISPATCHER: The officers are en route.

ANSWERER: My door's open. (*Man can be heard moaning.*) (*In the background.*) Oh, Donnah, oh, Donnah, oh, Donnah.

DISPATCHER: (*Radioing to EMS.*) He thinks his wife is still alive. (*Man can be heard moaning.*)

ANSWERER: (*In the background.*) Oh Donnah, oh Donnah, oh baby, baby, baby. Please don't die, Donnah, please, Donnah, please, Donnah.

DISPATCHER: Okay, I can't hear you. No, I mean we're en route. No, they're not 1060 yet. Okay. We're not there yet.

ANSWERER: (*In the background.*) Oh, Donnah, Donnah, Donnah, Donnah, please, Donnah, please, Donnah.

DISPATCHER: Oh god. Did you look at the premises, Jerry?

DISPATCHER: We're there. (*Tape cuts out . . .*)

ANSWERER: (*In the background.*) Please, Donnah, please, Donnah, please, Donnah. (*Tape cuts out . . .*)

ANSWERER: (*In the background.*) Please, Donnah, please, Donnah, please, Donnah. She's not breathing. Help me . . . help me . . . Don't stop breathing. Don't stop breathing, Donnah. Oh, baby. Oh, baby. (*Background noises heard.*) Pumpkin, you're going to be okay. I promise. You're going to be okay. You're going to be okay. (*Moaning can be heard in the background.*)

DISPATCHER:	We don't know where they are at. We've got . . . Lincoln 10 is there.
ANSWERER:	(*Background noise is heard.*) Hang in there, baby. Don't stop breathing on me. Don't stop breathing. Don't stop breathing, honey . . . honey, honey, honey . . .
DISPATCHER:	Where are they at?
DISPATCHER TO POLICE:	The gun is on the table. The other people are in the living room. The guy said he left the front door open. The husband is in the living room on the floor with his wife. The husband is on the phone with us. He's on the floor with his wife. He's got the phone lying on the floor. He's laid the phone down now. The suspect is on the ground.
	(*Background noise is heard as the police enter the house.*)
ANSWERER:	Come here, help me . . . help me.
POLICE:	Put the gun down!
ANSWERER:	My gun's up there . . . it's right there . . . help my wife.

CHAPTER 2

Background

Mark Winger and Donnah Winger were married in 1987 at a Jewish temple in Hollywood, Florida. The wedding was followed by a large reception. It was a storybook wedding, with Donnah beautiful in her long, white wedding gown and Mark handsome in a black tuxedo.

Donnah had completed vocational school and became a medical technician. She started working at a Hollywood hospital. As a medical technician, she would scrub in on surgeries and aid physicians in setting up the surgical suite and handing them instruments during surgery. She was twenty-five at the time, small (five feet and 105 pounds), lively, and beautiful. Donnah was very close to her family and, in particular, to Sarah Jane Drescher, her mother, and to her stepdad, Ira Drescher. She was the oldest of three sisters.

Her husband, Mark Winger, was from Elyria, Ohio. He had an older sister and an older brother. His father was very successful. Mark was accepted at West Point but decided to go to Virginia Military Institute. He graduated in 1986 with a degree in nuclear physics. Mark, although only five foot eight, was regarded as bright, a near genius, and macho and was muscular in build. After graduating he spent a year as a lieutenant in Korea but had difficulties there and had a reputation for being arrogant and had tried to shift blame to others for an accident when a vehicle turned over. He also started hitting on female NCOs, who, in turn, complained to his superiors about his conduct. His officer denied him a promotion to captain because he liked "to push enlisted personnel around." He was relieved of duty in Korea, and he came back to the United States for a second year of service in Georgia. Mark could be charming and engaging, but female NCOs wanted nothing to do with him.

Donnah and Mark were introduced to each other through Mark's older brother, who worked at a hospital in Hollywood, Florida, where Donnah was employed. Her parents, who did not approve of her past relationships, were relieved when she started dating Mark. Mark was well educated and came from a good Jewish family. After a brief courtship they were married in Florida in a formal wedding. After the wedding they went on a honeymoon and returned to Florida, where Mark had obtained a job in an engineering firm. He then moved to Champaign, Illinois, with another engineering firm and, in 1991, was hired as a nuclear safety engineer in the Department of Nuclear Safety for the State of Illinois in Springfield. Donnah obtained a job at Memorial Medical Center as a medical technician, where she was well liked. She was happy, outgoing, and made friends easily. Once they settled down and felt comfortable in their jobs and community, they decided to purchase a home. They bought a house at 4305 South Westview, Springfield, Illinois.

When Mark and Donnah moved to Springfield, they joined the Temple Brith Shalom, and Donnah became active in a program for young women. She kept herself busy in the temple by working with this group and by having an active social life, both with the rabbi and his wife, Mike and Jo Datz, DeAnn Shultz and her husband, John, and Gary May and his wife and other friends, including Barbara and Dennis Rendleman, who were their neighbors.

Their house was always open to friends and neighbors. A friend, Amy Jaffee, who grew up with Donnah in Connecticut, came to Springfield to get a master's degree in social work. While getting this degree she stayed with the Wingers. They basically put her up with free room and board. When Amy graduated, she got her own apartment, and Mark came over and helped lay the carpet of the apartment for her.

While employed at Memorial, Donnah met DeAnn Shultz. DeAnn worked as a nurse in the operating room, and because of working together, they became close friends. They went to the FitClub together to work out at least three times a week. They talked weekly, if not daily. They would go out to eat with their husbands or went to each other's houses to watch movies or play fantasy football, have cookouts together, etc. DeAnn was a nurse, bright and attractive with dark hair and a slender build. Their husbands became friends through their wives.

DeAnn Shultz and John Shultz were married in Brentwood, Missouri. It was John's first marriage and DeAnn's second. DeAnn had married at seventeen, while in high school. She was a registered nurse; John had a BS and an MBA in information technology. DeAnn was outgoing but seemed to need attention and reassurance. John and DeAnn lived initially in Hannibal, Missouri, where John was finishing his master's degree. DeAnn found her niche there; she worked in a small hospital, was a school nurse, and had a lot of contact with students, teachers, and parents. She wrote articles on health for the school newspaper and the local newspaper and was a popular figure at school games and other school functions. She was happy in her job and was well-liked and well-known in the community. She was very high-strung. John was very quiet and reserved, bright, and very laid back. DeAnn was plagued by migraine headaches.

John, unlike DeAnn, found the small town atmosphere limiting; and after finishing his degree John and DeAnn moved to Springfield in 1990, where there would be more opportunities for John. In 1993 DeAnn started working for St. John's Hospital in Springfield. Prior to that, she had been working at Memorial Medical Center in the operating rooms, where she met Donnah. At St. John's she was a visiting nurse in the psychiatric area. She would visit outpatients, check on their medications and their psychiatric status, and report to the hospital what she found. It didn't involve a lot of interaction with other people but tons of paperwork. The paperwork never seemed to end. After visiting patients she would go home and complete the reports on the computer. About that time the Schultzes adopted a second child. They had an older one who was in her early teens. They then decided to adopt a baby boy.

Donnah and Mark wanted to have a family. However, in late 1994 or early 1995, Donnah found out she was unable to conceive; both were disappointed. Mark and Donnah started a private adoption through a physician she knew. On June 1, they obtained a baby girl, Cindy, who had been born three days earlier. This was a happy time for Donnah. She was walking on clouds. Donnah's life was now centered on her new baby.

Neighbors and friends of Donnah and Mark were ecstatic, along with Donnah's parents. Everyone knew how badly Donnah had wanted to have a family. Donnah's parents, Sarah Jane and her stepdad, Ira Drescher, visited

Springfield numerous times prior to and after the adoption. Donnah had said that this was just the beginning—she wanted to adopt "many more."

The friendship between the Schultzes and the Wingers became stronger. Mark and Donnah included them in monthly get-togethers. Although not Jewish, the Schultzes were invited by the Wingers to the temple to attend a Seder and bar mitzvah. They had become almost inseparable as friends.

In 1994 DeAnn began feeling the strain of her job, children, and marriage. She had migraine headaches, and these also seemed to be getting worse and more frequent. DeAnn talked about having left Hannibal, Missouri, and how much she missed it. She talked to her husband about returning. She did not feel that she had the support of her husband and complained about his lack of attention. John got tired of her complaints and stopped listening. She would call Donnah. Donnah also was getting tired of these constant complaints. She told Donnah that John took her for granted. Donnah began to feel that her relationship with DeAnn was becoming suffocating.

It was easy for DeAnn to confide in Donnah. She needed to talk to someone. She had a narcissist personality and an underlying insecurity. She was feeling stressed from working full time and caring for her two-year-old son and a fifteen-year-old daughter.

In July of 1995, Donnah mentioned to Mark the possibility of DeAnn moving and leaving her husband to go to Minnesota. Donnah asked Mark to not talk about it, because she thought that DeAnn had told her this in confidence.

During this period of time Mark was traveling to Chattanooga, Tennessee, to get additional training. There were two two-week sessions, the first session in July and the second in August. He completed the first two-week session and came back to Springfield in late July. On August 10, he returned for his second session in Chattanooga.

Donnah called her parents, Ira and Sara Jane Drescher, and said that since Mark was going to be out of town again, would they like to have her visit and bring the new baby to visit with them. Sarah Jane jumped at the opportunity and said, "I will send you the ticket."

Donnah and Cindy went to Hollywood, Florida, for a five-day visit with Sarah Jane and Ira Drescher. She was walking on clouds; it was the happiest her family had ever seen her. One morning, just before Ira and Sarah Jane woke up, Donnah had snuck into their bedroom and placed Cindy between them. When they woke, there was Cindy in bed with them and Donnah at the end of the bed, just laughing and smiling with joy.

Donnah left Hollywood to return home on August 23, as Mark was returning home Saturday from his course in Chattanooga. Her mom and stepdad drove her to the airport. On the way to the airport they played with the baby and hugged and kissed Donnah while waiting for the flight to St. Louis, telling her, as Sarah Jane always did, "Drive safely."

They did not know that this was the last time they would see her alive.

PART I

The Murder

Whoever slayeth Cain, vengeance shall be taken on him sevenfold.

~Wordsworth~

CHAPTER 3

The Ride from St. Louis to Springfield

The airplane ride from Miami to St. Louis was uneventful, and the plane arrived on time. Springfield, Illinois, is about an hour and a half away from the St. Louis airport, and a shuttle service was hired to pick up Donnah and Cindy to take them home from the St. Louis airport. The van driver, named Roger, held up a card saying "Donnah Winger" at the baggage counter. Donnah asked if he was the driver from BART, and Roger said, "Yes." He helped her with her suitcase, and they went to the van in the parking lot. Donnah got in the front seat with him and put the baby in front of her on the floor in the carrier. Roger asked her to put Cindy in a car seat with a seat belt, and Donnah said that she was too small, and she would hold her if she got fussy. Roger replied, "You have to use the car seat because I could get a ticket if she is not in a car seat."

Donnah said, "No one will know, and I really want to hold her if she gets fussy." This appeared to upset Roger because had an annoyed look on his face as they left the airport.

Trying to pacify him, Donnah said, "I have a muffin from the airplane. Would you like to share that?"

Roger replied, "No. I am not eating today."

Donnah inquired, "Why not?"

Roger replied, "I am anorexic and I don't feel hungry. Today is one of the days I am not eating."

Once they left St. Louis and got on Interstate 55 to Springfield, Roger began driving erratically and at a speed of 75-80 mph. He came up behind cars and honked repeatedly until they got out of his way. At the same time, he beat on the wheel with his hands.

"Please slow down," Donnah asked. "You are making me nervous and you are scaring me. You are going over seventy-five miles per hour."

Roger replied, "I drive this route all the time. Don't worry, I need to get moving. I am in a hurry."

Donnah started playing with Cindy and looked up at the vehicle right in front of the van. Roger was honking and tailgating and pounding on the steering wheel. She was frightened.

Donnah said, "What do you mean by you are in a hurry?"

"I want to get home," Roger replied.

"Please, slow down." But Roger continued tailgating and speeding, saying, "I am a good driver, don't worry. I have never gotten a ticket or had an accident." Her requests seemed to anger him.

Hoping to distract him, Donnah asked, "How long have you been a van driver?"

Roger replied, "Not long, six months. I have been a phlebotomist, someone that takes blood. I have been a truck driver and done jobs like that. Where do you work?"

Donnah answered, "I work in Springfield at Memorial Medical Center."

"What job do you do?"

Donnah replied, "I am a medical technician."

"Do you like it?"

Donnah replied, "Very much. I enjoy working with the doctors."

Roger said, "I did not like being a phlebotomist."

Roger started speeding again and pounded his hands on the steering wheel.

"Where do you live?" Donnah asked.

"In the country." And then Roger asked, "Do you believe in spirits?"

"I just don't know," Donnah replied. "My mother and I used to play with Ouija boards."

"I do too. It is not a game. The spirits are real. I have a spirit that protects me when I drive and at home and everywhere. He has been with me for ten years. His name is Dahm. He is a dragon. He sucks blood. I keep him in my bedroom, but sometimes he gets out. He tells me to do bad things. He liked me working as a phlebotomist. He likes blood. When I quit he got mad and would not let me eat."

"What does he tell you to do?" Donnah asked.

"He sometimes tells me to kill people. When I tell my psychiatrist about it, Dahm gets mad. Once he told me to go down the Mississippi in a canoe with some explosives to blow up some buildings. I told my psychiatrist about that, and he put me in the hospital. Dahm got real mad and wouldn't let me eat. He punishes me if I tell my psychiatrist what my plans are. He won't let me eat. He won't let me sleep."

"Please slow down. You are making me very nervous."

"Dahm tells me to do things. Sometimes he takes me out of my body and makes me fly over treetops. After that he comes down to my body."

"That is scary," Donnah replied.

"I can tell when he is coming. My hands start shaking. Like now," Roger continued.

"Please slow down," Donnah asked again.

"Dahm tells me to drive fast."

Donnah replied, "Can we talk about something else?"

"Sure."

"Where do you live?" Donnah asked.

"I live in a trailer in the country that I share with an older woman. I like older women. I used to be married to one, but it did not last."

He continued, "You are older. Do you ever smoke pot?"

Donnah replied, "No!"

"I do. We have these marijuana parties where I live. We have great parties and run around naked and smoke pot and get high. The next day you really don't feel very good, but you sure have a good time. I had some pot this morning. If you want some, I can get you some."

"No."

"Are you sure? It makes you feel good."

Donnah added, "I am sure."

"Did you ever use a Ouija board?" Roger asked.

Donnah replied, "I sometimes do, but it is just a game."

"No, it isn't. It's real. You can talk to spirits. Do you think I am crazy?"

Donnah paused. "No, just a little different."

Roger said, "You are really nice. Most people think I am weird and don't want to talk to me."

Donnah said, "Oh, but you scare me when you talk like the way you are."

Roger continued, "Would you like to come to one of our parties? We all talk to the spirits and smoke pot. You would have a great time."

Donnah, not wanting to confront him, said, "I'll think about it."

After they arrived at 2304 Westview Drive in Springfield, Donnah went into the house with Cindy, locked the doors, and called her friend DeAnn. She told DeAnn about her ride and asked her what she thought. DeAnn responded, "You know, he could be a schizophrenic. He must be off of his meds."

"Could he be dangerous? He talks to this spirit Dahm, who tells him to kill people."

"I don't know. I would be worried. Do you think he was high?" DeAnn asked.

"He could be," Donnah said.

"These types are unpredictable and particularly if he is on marijuana," DeAnn added.

"The way he drove was scary. He pounded the steering wheel, tailgated at 75-80 mph, honked his horn if people did not get out of his way—he was really scary. He knows where I live."

"I will come over and stay with you tomorrow until Mark comes home. I can't come over now because John is out of town," DeAnn said.

"I would appreciate it. Thanks."

The next day, Thursday, DeAnn came over in the evening. DeAnn asked, "Have you called Mark?"

"No."

"Don't you think we should tell Mark about this?" DeAnn said.

Donnah's Notes Of Her Trip With The Van Driver

August 23rd

We entered the van, and he introduced himself
me as Roger. After stopping for a coke,
we proceded onto the highway. I asked him if
wanted to share a blueberry muffin that I had
saved from the plane. He told me no thank-you —
also told me he has this disease called anorexia.
We talked about that for a period of time. Meanwhile
felt as if we were speeding, so I peeked at th
speedometer — we were going 75 miles per hour. It made
me somewhat nervous that we were traveling, that
t. Also, when Roger was wanting to pass another
ars, he would drive up very closely behind them, until
the car moved over. I noticed him keeping his hands
on the steering wheel nervously as if he was
aggrivated at waiting to pass another car. That, too
made me feel uneasy.
    Now, getting back to his eating disorder condition
told me he's had this problem for many years. He
said sometimes he doesn't eat for days. (3 days in a
row) We talked about many previous jobs that he ha
held (truck driving, phlebotomist.)
    Somehow, he talked to me about being spiritua
and started telling me about his spirt, "Dahm." He told
me that Dahm has been around for 10 years, and has
vampire background (found out from a weejee board),
although he looks like a dragon. However, reveal
himself in a form of a dragon. He told me
things Dahm makes him do things — some bad
things — like sets car bombs + killing people. He said
when this happens, he confides in his psychiatrist bec
it makes him mad. If he doesn't do these things,
he said Dahm does bad things to his body. He —
not eating. He also told me of some experiences
when Dahm appears when he is driving. I was very
nervous at this point. He said sometimes Dahm takes
         of his body when he's driving, and makes

isn't know where he is — He said he can tell when
him is coming because his hands begin to shake
uncontrollably. I felt very nervous because as he's
telling me all of this, he was spending excessivly.
He also told me about nude parties at the home
which he shares with an older women. They have
parties all the time, and he said he gets drunk about
once/ month. He also said that people who he hangs
out with have spirits, too. They all have there own
Weejee boards. (+blood crystals)
    This experience made me feel very nervous
and extremely uncomfortable. I felt as if my
life and the life of my daughter were in the hands of
a nut.

CHAPTER 4

August 25, 1995 to August 29, 1995

On August 25, after Mark completed his course, he received a phone call from Donnah and she sounded distressed. She told him about the ride. Mark reacted. "The driver had endangered you and our child. He should not be driving." He was concerned about Donnah being by herself. "Are you going to be safe?"

"DeAnn stayed over on Thursday and will stay over Friday night until you get home. She is here now, her lunch break. I think I'll be okay."

"That makes me feel a lot better, but still, I want you to take care and lock the doors. Let me talk to DeAnn."

Donnah gives the telephone to DeAnn. "Hi, Mark. It is DeAnn."

Mark asked, "Did Donnah talk to you about this ride?"

"She sure did. She is concerned, and I agreed to stay with her."

"You have got some psychiatric background. What do you think is wrong with this guy?"

"I haven't the slightest idea. He could be schizophrenic and could be off his meds."

"Do you think he could be dangerous?"

"You don't know with these kinds of people. They could act out and are unpredictable. If he is not on his medicine, I haven't the slightest idea how he would react. You know these are the types of people you see walking down the street talking to themselves. They can be delusional and think something is happening that really isn't."

"Do you think Donnah's safe?"

"Yeah, I think so, but as I said, I will be with her."

"Do me a favor and call the police. Let them know about this ride. I don't know if anything can be done, but at least we should put them on notice."

"I did that already. When are you coming back?"

"The exam was over about noon. However, I'm bushed, and we're going to try to start back on Saturday."

"Okay."

"Could you put Donnah back on?"

Donnah picks up the phone. "Make sure you have the doors locked. Do you feel safe?"

Donnah replied, "Yes, as long as DeAnn's here. I think we're okay. I'll keep the doors locked."

"Okay, as I told DeAnn, I am going to start back early Saturday morning because I'm pretty well bushed now."

"I'll look forward to seeing you on Saturday. Remember, I love you."

Mark hung up.

DeAnn had called the police. She had talked to the desk officer and described the ride and expressed concern for Donnah's safety. The desk sergeant had told her, "We'll make extra patrols around the house, but we don't know this guy's name, and besides, that he hasn't really committed any crime yet. He sure sounds a little bit off, but that's not a crime. We can't pick him up for that. We'll make sure the police do extra patrols around the house."

DeAnn replied, "Thanks. I appreciate the help."

On Friday afternoon, DeAnn went out and checked on some of her patients and then went back to Donnah's house. While Donnah was changing Cindy's diaper, there was a call and DeAnn picked it up.

"Hello, Winger residence."

In a halting and monotone voice, a male asked for Mr. or Mrs. Winger. DeAnn responds, "Donnah is busy. Can I take a message?"

The caller hung up.

"Who was that?" Donnah asked.

"Some creep. He just asked for you, and when I said you were busy he hung up. He didn't leave a message. He sounded like he was slurring his words and speaking in a monotone. He might have been on something."

Donnah replied, "That's weird."

Donnah and DeAnn didn't think anything more about it; they talked about a baby shower on Saturday at Jo Datz's house for her new baby. They discussed what they were going to bring.

Donnah said, "Do you think I should bring Cindy?"

DeAnn said, "No, we can get my daughter, Susan, to come over and babysit. Mark should be back on Saturday afternoon."

On Saturday, DeAnn's fifteen-year-old daughter Susan came over to babysit Cindy while they went to the baby shower. Susan played with Cindy after Donnah and DeAnn left. The telephone rang. She picked up the phone and a male voice asked in a monotone voice, sort of slurring his words, "Is Mrs. or Mr. Winger there?"

Susan replied, "No, they are unavailable. Is there a message?"

Click.

The caller hung up.

Mark started home early on Saturday morning with his co-worker Candice Boulton. Candice and Mark were friends from work, and both had to attend training in Chattanooga. They had about a ten-hour drive back home, and although Candice was with him, Mark drove the entire way because Candice preferred not to.

Candice and Mark talked about their training and what they had learned on the trip back from Chattanooga. They talked about their jobs, what they did for fun, and chatted about things they were interested in. Mark mentioned Donnah's ride and said it really upset him and his wife. Candice knew Donnah and had been over to their house several times. Mark said, "This guy shouldn't be driving. He's dangerous."

"It doesn't sound like he should be dealing with the public."

Mark asked, "What do you think would happen to Cindy if Donnah died? Do you think I would still be able to adopt her? You know, we just started the process."

Candice replied, "Well, that's a little strange question. Do you really think the guy is that dangerous?"

Mark responded, "I don't know."

"I know a lot of single dads who have custody of their children. I don't think that would be a problem. You, of course, have to make some arrangements to take care of her."

Mark replied, "Yeah, I'm just a little worried."

They stopped several times for coffee, and Mark paid for that. He paid for a couple tolls and tossed the change in the car. He got home, and Candice took the car back to her house to return to the carpool on Monday.

When DeAnn and Donnah returned home from the shower, DeAnn and Susan told Mark about the telephone calls. "Did you get the guy's number?" Mark asked.

Both of them answered, "No, he just hung up."

Susan added, "He sounded a little creepy."

Mark said, "I wonder if it's this driver. He knows where we live and our number."

Donnah said, "I have no idea."

DeAnn and Susan left to go home. Mark asked Donnah for more details about the ride. "The ride was scary, the guy drove fast, was hammering on the steering wheel, talking about marijuana and the spirit of Dahm. I was glad to get home."

Mark said, "I called Duffy on Friday, and I'm going to call him again and tell him this guy shouldn't be on the road. He's dangerous. Write down what happened during ride."

When Mark called the owner of Bart Transportation, Ray Duffy, on Saturday, he was angry. He wanted Roger's last name; he wanted to tell him to quit calling the house. He wanted to tell him to stop bothering Donnah. He didn't think a van driver like that should be working with the public. "He endangered my wife and child." Duffy listened. Duffy was hesitant to give the number to Mark. He said he would call Roger and get his. Mark threatened to call the police and file a police report. Duffy said he would call Mark back.

Over the weekend, Donnah, Mark, DeAnn, and John had a cookout at the Wingers' house on Saturday night. Mark talked about his training experiences in Chattanooga; they watched some TV, grilled, and generally just hung out together.

On Sunday night they did the same at the Schultzes' house. They grilled dinner, drank some wine, and played some fantasy football.

Duffy was unable to reach Roger over the weekend. When Duffy reached him on Monday, he told him of the accusations that Mark had made.

Roger replied, "There was no big problem. I thought she was nice. We just talked. I remember I was a little upset because she didn't want to put the baby in the car seat. We talked a lot. She said her mom, or her stepmom, was a psychic or that sort of thing and had visions or heard voices. I told her that I played around with Ouija boards and tarot cards."

"Did you tell her that you were seeing a psychiatrist or that you lived in the country with an older woman and smoked marijuana?"

"I told her I was living with an older woman and that we lived in the country, and it was pretty casual. You can go around without clothes. I didn't tell her I saw a psychiatrist. I've never had a psychiatrist. I did not talk about marijuana."

Duffy asked, "Did you talk about spirits?"

"Not really. We did talk about tarot cards and that sort of thing and that I had a spirit Dahm that would help me, that's all. I didn't think she was scared. She didn't act scared."

"I'll give him your number, and he'll give you a call. You have got to just get this straightened out or you will not get any more rides."

"I will. I like my job. I need to get some more rides. I did not mean to frighten her."

On Monday Mark went back to work. Duffy reached him on Monday and gave him Roger's telephone number. Mark was looking distracted. Mike Parker, his boss, saw that and asked, "What's going on? You don't seem your normal self."

"My wife had a ride back from St. Louis. The guy was a weirdo. He frightened Donnah. I am going to get his number to call him and tell him to leave us alone."

"You sure that's a good idea? Maybe you should just forget about it."

"Can't. We have gotten two hang-up calls. I think it is him."

"Your decision."

"Yeah, yeah."

On August 29, about 9:00 a.m., Mark called Roger Harrington.

"Roger Harrington, this is Mark Winger."

Roger replied, "I was expecting your call."

"You know you scared the hell out of my wife, talking about spirits and driving fast, smoking marijuana, and whatever. You know you shouldn't be dealing with the public if you do that. I want to talk to you about this when I get off work."

Roger replied, "I didn't do any of those things. I didn't scare your wife. She didn't act scared, but I want my job back." According to Mark, he seemed upset. He started talking weird, like he was talking to third parties, and Mark got concerned and said forget it and hung up.

Mark went to his boss.

"I just talked with him."

Parker said, "I told you that was not a good idea. The guy sounds like he is nuts. You press guys like that to the wall and you never know how they are going to react."

"Well, maybe he is, but I wanted to try to straighten it out with him, but he started talking to someone else—like he was talking to a third party and not me. So I just hung up on him."

About lunchtime on the twenty-ninth, Donnah came into the office and wanted to show Cindy to the women in Mark's office. No work was done for about a half an hour as the offices emptied. They all wanted to hold the baby and to pass her around.

Finally, Donnah said, "I have an appointment to get her three-month-old pictures taken at Sears."

Mark responded, "You ready to go to lunch? We better get going."

She said, "Sure."

They went to lunch, and after lunch Donnah went off to Sears to get the three-month-old pictures, and Mark went back to work. He left work and got home around three thirty, his normal time. He left the door unlocked because he knew Donnah would be coming in a little later and will have her hands full with the baby, so he didn't want to make her fish for her keys. He changed his clothes and went to the basement to run on the treadmill.

In the meantime, Candice Boulton had taken the car back to the car pool and discovered that some change was left in the car. She knew the money was Mark's, and she wanted to return it to him. Candice called Mark around 4:00 p.m. on Tuesday but did not get an answer.

CHAPTER 5

The 911 Response

The dispatcher who received the call listened in shock. She knew the area. It was a residential street in a quiet neighborhood on the west side of town. It was a neighborhood where the kids played in the streets and the residents cared for their own yards, mowed their own grass, and trimmed their own bushes. Kids would ride bikes and play catch. The neighbors knew each other. They would have block parties and attend baseball and soccer games, which were played at a nearby park. It was a quiet neighborhood.

The 911 operator immediately transferred the call to the police and fire departments. She kept the telephone line open. She said it was an emergency and that someone had been shot and a lady had been beaten. The caller did not know whether they were alive. The call was made at 4:27 p.m. Immediately Captain Cunningham, a fireman, and his driver left the nearby firehouse. The firemen were trained as paramedics. He replied to the dispatcher, "We're on our way." He then sped off with his sirens blaring; they arrived at four thirty.

As they passed by the house, Cunningham said, "That's the house, but it's quiet. I don't see anything going on. There were gun shots fired. We better wait for the police."

The driver said, "Yeah, let's go by and then come back and wait."

They turned around and came back and parked in front of the house. They stood between the truck and the house. The door appeared to be closed. They were waiting for the police to arrive.

At 4:32 p.m. Officer Jones arrived in his squad car with lights and sirens. He had heard that there was a shooting; he was in the general vicinity. He pulled up behind the fire truck and got out and called out.

"What's up?"

Cunningham replied, "No idea. We are waiting for you to clear the house so we can go in. We understand there are two casualties. We don't know if it's safe."

At that time, Sergeant Filburn arrived. Both he and Jones drew their service revolvers from their holsters. Jones said, "We don't know what to expect."

Sergeant Filburn replied, "Let's go slow. Someone has a gun inside, and we don't want anyone else shot."

Filburn and Jones cautiously walked around the outside of the house and, seeing nothing, entered through the front door. It was unlocked. They went down the hallway with their guns out. They saw a female body lying face down in a pool of blood with a male kneeling over her. They shouted, "Where's the gun?"

"On the table."

On the dining room table there was a semiautomatic. Filburn quickly unloaded it. They looked over to the side and saw a male figure, about six feet from the female. He was lying on his back with a pool of blood under his head. There was blood on the walls and on the floor. Filburn shouted out the door to the firemen, "Get in here! They need your help! The place is clear!"

The firemen rushed in, bringing their equipment.

Jones asked the man leaning over the female, "Are you Mark Winger?"

Gasping, he replied, "Yes." Sobbing and highly emotional, he screamed, "This is my wife. You've got to help her."

She appeared to be breathing.

In the meantime, Officer Young had come in. Young said to Winger, "We need you to leave her so the paramedics and the firemen can treat her. Get up and come with me, please."

Winger was hesitant and said, "This is my wife. I don't want to leave her."

Young responded, "The paramedics need to start treating her. They can't treat her with you kneeling over her."

With that, Winger started crawling toward the police and was helped up by Filburn. They led Winger into the back bedroom, where the baby was on the bed.

By that time, Sergeant Murphy had arrived and asked Filburn to take the baby outside and to see if there was a neighbor who could take care of her while they figured out what happened; he gave the three-month child to Barbara Rendleman, a neighbor and a friend.

Two ambulances had arrived. The police directed the paramedics into the house. Both Donnah Winger and the male were still breathing. They had pulses, but they were weak. The firemen started providing oxygen to Donnah. Mark Winger could be heard sobbing in the bedroom.

The paramedics, working feverishly, started IV. Donnah Winger was rolled over and oxygen was put on her and placed over her mouth and nose. They cut off her blouse for monitors and threw it in a corner. A bloody towel was also thrown aside.

With the male, they cut his shirt off and put monitors on him. They brought in a defibrillator and other emergency equipment. They also started an IV on him. He had lost a lot of blood, as had Donnah. Charles Cox and Doug Williamson arrived, the detectives assigned to the case; they talked to the fireman and paramedics and looked over the scene before talking to Mark Winger.

The pulses were weakening, and their breathing was becoming shallow.

A paramedic said, "We are losing them. We have got to get going to the hospital."

Another paramedic said, "I think if we move the male he will probably go into cardiac arrest."

"We don't have a choice. He is going to die here or we have to get him to the hospital to try to save him."

They moved them to stretchers. One ambulance took the male and another took the female. As the male was being taken into the ambulance he went into cardiac arrest and they started performing CPR. Murphy and Young hopped in the ambulance with the male. They arrived at the hospital a little after five. The male was pronounced dead by the emergency room doctors.

Donnah Winger lived about fifteen minutes at the hospital. She then was pronounced dead after staff did CPR and tried to shock her heart back into beating. She had lost too much blood.

CHAPTER 6

August 29, 1995, 4:30 p.m.,
Springfield Police Station

Detectives Cox and Williamson were at their desk filling out reports, typing notes, etc. Cox was a veteran detective who was known and respected for his ability and instincts. Williamson was a veteran police officer who had been assigned recently to the detective unit; he was regarded as an up-and-coming officer.

Cox said, "What a month and we're not quite over with it yet. Three murders, numerous robberies, rapes—I can hardly wait until this month is over."

Williamson replied, "Yeah, you know at this rate we'll be in running with Chicago. August always brings out the worst in people with the heat. I don't know what it is, but it's almost like it's a full moon. At least John Day was not assigned to us."

Cox responded, "Yeah, we are lucky. He was shot and killed about 1:00 p.m. on the north end. I wonder if it was gang related—might be random. He apparently was a good kid, honor student, Sunday school teacher, lettered in three sports at Lanphier. It's just nuts. I can hardly wait to get home, relax, and get some rest. This month hasn't been fun."

As both started putting their files away, the dispatcher called them on the radio.

"Gunshots fired at 4305 Westview in Springfield. 911 call reported a shooting and a woman bludgeoned. All units to respond."

Cox said to Williamson, "Oh shit, I thought I was going to get home at a reasonable hour. This is going to screw up the evening. We are not so lucky after all."

Williamson, "Let's go."

They jumped into their car and sped off to 4305 Westview and got there fifteen minutes later. Upon approaching their area, they saw police cars, fire trucks, and a couple of ambulances. The police crime scene van was there, and the home was being cordoned off with the yellow police tape.

As they went into the small dining area, they saw the female on her back with the paramedics working over her. She is still breathing. She was young and dark haired with a pool of blood under her head. She had no shoes on and was dressed in shorts and blouse with her blouse cut off. The paramedic was working over her, giving her oxygen and checking her airway.

"How's she doing?" Cox inquired.

A paramedic replied, "She's in bad shape. There are multiple injuries to her head. She is breathing, but the lady has apparently been hit in the head multiple times. We're doing what we can. We have her on monitors and are going to intubate her. It doesn't look good."

Looking over the room they saw a male lying on his back, about five to six feet to the north and west with a pool of blood under his head and another pool of blood a foot or so from his head. He was similarly dressed in shorts and a T-shirt. He was groaning and had shallow breaths. On his right hand and wrist were a ring and a watch. He was being worked on by a couple of paramedics.

They saw Cunningham. "What happened, Tom?"

"We don't know. When we got here the husband of this lady was bending over her, holding her. She was on her stomach. The paramedics rolled her over. Murphy and Young took her husband into the back bedroom. There is a male victim too. He was shot in the head."

Cunningham continued, "The paramedics are trying to keep him alive. He lost a lot of blood. I don't think he will make it."

A paramedic replied, "We're going to have to transfer him to the hospital, but he will probably go into cardiac arrest once we move him. We've got oxygen on him and we got his airway clear, but he's got two bullet holes in the head. If he does survive, it's not going to be much of a survival."

Cox said, "Oh shit."

They looked around the room and found blood splatter on the south wall and the ceiling and footprints in a couple pools of blood; stretchers were brought in by the paramedics. They notice a couple .45 shells and the crime scene technician, Norval Morton is videotaping and photographing the scene.

Taking a closer look, they noticed a male who was on his back; he was about six feet from the female, with his feet facing the same direction as the female's feet. There is a pool of blood about a foot from the male in the same area of his head. The blood is seeping out into the carpet from his head.

Cox asked, "Who is this female?"

A paramedic replied, "Donnah Winger. This is her home."

Cox then asked, "Who is this guy?"

The paramedic replied, "No clue."

Cox reached into the back pocket, pulled out the wallet, and checked the driver's license. The driver's license showed "Roger Harrington." He has a couple of credit cards, but that's about all. They then saw a gun on the table. After looking at the blood spatter, Cox said to Williamson, "Well, we have seen enough. Let's go to the bedroom and talk to the husband."

In the bedroom they saw a male sitting on the bed; Young was asking questions. This male has his shirt off. He has blood on his shoulders, his hands. He has his T-shirt off and all wadded up; he appeared to be sobbing. He was rocking back and forth. Cox and Williamson took over the questioning.

Sergeant Murphy and Young went out to question the neighbors and canvas the neighborhood.

CHAPTER 7

The Investigation

As Cox came into the bedroom, Winger asked, "How is my wife? Is she alive? Please help her."

Cox said, "They are taking her to the hospital. We can only hope for the best. They will do everything they can."

Winger wanted to call Mike Datz, his rabbi, but Cox said, "Datz will have to wait. I want to get your statement first."

Winger was sitting on the bed and rocking back and forth. He had his shirt off; it was balled up and bloody. He had blood on his hands and his chest. He appeared to be sobbing and hysterical.

Cox tried to be gentle. "I know this is difficult, but we have to figure out what happened. Are you up to it?"

"I don't know. I'll do my best."

"Go slow, just tell me what happened."

In a halting voice punctuated by sobs, he told Cox, "We were just adopting a baby. I had gone to lunch with Donnah. After lunch she was going to take the baby for photographs at Sears. I got off work and came home and started working out in the basement. I have a treadmill down there. I left the front door unlocked. I knew Donnah would be coming in after me. She would be carrying the baby, and I didn't want to have her fumble with her keys. She must have come in a few minutes after me."

Winger broke down and started sobbing. After a few minutes he continued, "I heard some noise upstairs. I heard what sounded like a scream. I thought maybe someone had fallen. I heard Cindy crying. I slowed the treadmill. The baby was crying again. I heard some more noise. I shut off the treadmill and ran upstairs because I thought maybe the baby had fallen and gotten hurt. I ran into the bedroom. The baby was all alone on the bed. Donnah wouldn't do that. Then I heard some more noise in the kitchen area, the dining area. I didn't know what it was, but I was concerned because of the scary ride that Donnah had from the St. Louis airport. I got my gun from the bedside table. I ran into the hallway towards the kitchen and dining area. I saw this guy bending over Donnah. He had a hammer in his hand and he was hitting her."

He started sobbing and gasping again. Cox said, "Just go slow." After a moment, Winger continued, "I saw this guy beating my wife. I shot at him. I think I hit him because he sort of fell and rolled off Donnah. I saw some blood on his forehead. Donnah was lying face down on the floor. I continued running down the hall, and this guy started to get up. Then I shot him again in the forehead. I told Donnah, 'I'm here, I'm here. Don't die. I'll get help.' I grabbed the telephone off the kitchen wall and called 911. I told them I needed help, I needed an ambulance, I needed the police, please hurry, that there was an intruder and I shot him. That's what I told them.

"Then I heard the baby crying again, so I hung up the phone and went and made sure the baby hadn't fallen off the bed. She was okay, and I came back and 911 had called me back and asked me what was happening. I told them my wife was being hit over the head and that I shot the man that was hitting her. This guy continued groaning, so I picked up the hammer and hit him in the chest to shut him up. I was angry."

Winger asked, "Who was that guy?"

Cox said, "It is Roger Harrington."

He started sobbing again and became hysterical. He asked Cox, "Can I go get cleaned up and put on a clean shirt?"

Cox says, "Sure."

He also asked for a soda. Williamson got it for him and came back with a handwritten note that described the trip from St. Louis.

About that time Murphy and Young returned. They had just gone out with some neighbors to see what information they could add. Murphy said, "The paramedics are transferring to the hospital, and Young and I are going to go out with them."

Cox said, "See what information you can dig up on Harrington."

Young said to Cox, "Let's get him to show us what happened."

Cox then asked Winger if he is capable of showing them what happened. Winger replied, "I think so."

With that, he got himself up off the bed and showed them where his .45 was kept in the bedside table. He then showed them where he took the first shot and where he took the second shot. He showed them how Harrington was hitting Donnah and, after the first shot, how Harrington fell.

He again asked to speak to Rabbi Datz. Rabbi Datz had been called by the neighbors and was outside. They took him outside the house to Rabbi Datz, and Rabbi Datz tried to console him.

While outside, Cox received a call from the hospital that Donnah Winger had died. He pulled Rabbi Datz aside and told him that Donnah had died. Datz responded, "I know Mark and his wife. They are friends. Donnah was particularly close to my wife. I think I should be the one to break the news to him."

Cox looked at Datz. "That's okay with me, but I want to be present when you talk to him."

Both Rabbi Datz and Detective Cox went over to where Mark Winger was standing and told him that Donnah had died. Mark fell to his knees and started sobbing. Datz put his arms around him and helped him up. With Cox's permission they left to go to Datz's house. Datz told Cox that he knows Donnah's parents, and he would like to make the call to them.

Williamson had gone outside and checked the car that was parked in front of the house. He found a note in the car, handwritten in both ink and pencil, on the front seat, that said, "Mark Winger, 2305 W-view, 4:30 p.m." He retrieved the note and put it in an evidence bag. He also searched the car and found that there was a homemade blackjack and an overnight bag that contained a sheath knife.

Neighbors were still gathering, and police officers were interviewing them. They had left the child with a neighbor and friend, Barbara Rendleman. She was asked by the police how well she knew the Wingers.

"We attended the synagogue together. We were neighbors and we were friends. I babysat for them."

"Were there any marital problems between the Wingers?"

"None that I ever heard of. They were just adopting a baby, and their marriage was rock solid."

"Did you know anything about this ride from St. Louis?"

"Donnah had talked to me about that. She told me that there was a crazy driver who talked about spirits, smoking marijuana, and parties. She was afraid of him. She thought he was crazy. DeAnn Schultz, one of her friends, came over and stayed with her because Mark was out of town. That's how concerned she was."

Police officers continued to canvass the neighborhood. Not a single neighbor had anything negative to say about the marriage. Cox and Williamson went over to Datz's house, where Mark had gone. DeAnn Schultz was there; she had seen a newscast of the murders and came over.

DeAnn was visibly upset and crying. She said, "Donnah was my best friend. Donnah told me about this ride she had on Wednesday, and she was scared because Mark was out of town. We talked about it, and I stayed over at her house until Mark got back. We talked to Mark on Thursday, and he asked that we call the police, and I told him I already had done so. They said they couldn't do anything because there was no crime committed, but they would do a premises check.

"While I was at her house, I think it was Friday, we had a strange call from a male who talked in monotone, and when I said Donnah was unavailable he just hung up. He did not leave a message. He had a strange voice, like he was either on drugs or something else. That concerned us."

"Did you stay over again?"

"I stayed overnight on Friday night, and we had been invited to go to a shower at Jo Datz's on Saturday morning for her baby. Both of us were invited. Mark hadn't come home yet, so I got my daughter, Susan, to babysit. She got one of those strange calls also, and she said that the Wingers were not available. The guy just hung up again and didn't leave any message. She said it was a monotone voice. As soon as Mark got home we told him about this. He was really upset, and he wanted to call the owner of Bart Transportation and get Roger's last name. I think he did so." When questioned about the marriage she said that they were happy and just adopting a baby.

Cox interviewed both Jo Datz and Rabbi Datz, "It was a solid marriage." Jo Datz continued, "Donnah was one of my closest friends. She never complained about Mark or her marriage. She was ecstatic that they were adopting. She wanted to adopt more."

Rabbi Datz had called Donnah's parents in Hollywood, Florida. Ira Drescher answered. The conversation went something like this:

"Ira, this is Mike Datz."

"Hi, Mike, how are you doing? Why are you calling this time of night?"

"This isn't a fun call. I've got some bad news. Please sit down."

"What do you mean?"

"Are you sitting down, Ira?"

"What is the problem?"

"Donnah has just been murdered."

"You are kidding, aren't you?" replied Ira.

"No, I'm sorry to break it to you, but I didn't know how else."

"What happened?" Ira asked. He could not believe what he was hearing

"We don't know all the facts, but we know there was an intruder who broke into the house and was bludgeoning Donnah on her head, and Mark shot and killed him. Donnah died from the head wounds."

"Oh my god, oh my god," Ira replied. "How am I going to tell Sara Jane?"

"Do you want me to?" asked Datz.

"No, I have to do that myself."

Ira hung up. He went into the study area, where Sara Jane was reading a book. She looked up and asked, "Ira, are you okay? You are pale. Who was that on the phone?"

He went over to Sara Jane. "That was Rabbi Datz from Springfield. I don't' know how to tell you . . . Donnah was murdered."

Sara Jane responded, "This has got to be a joke, a nasty joke."

"No, it isn't. Mike would never do that."

"Oh my god," said Sara Jane.

She started shaking. "What happened?"

"I don't know a lot. Apparently an intruder came into the house and was hitting Donnah over the head with a hammer. Mark shot and killed him."

The two could barely continue talking. Ira got himself together and said, "Sara Jane, we've just got to get to Springfield."

Sara Jane was numb and in a fog. They got the first available flight from Miami to St. Louis. They packed suitcases. They called a friend to pick them up in St. Louis and drive them to Springfield. They both were going through the motions but had no sense of reality.

Cox and other officers were continuing to investigate and check with neighbors and friends. They checked on Roger Harrington. Cox had prior experience with him when Harrington tried to kill his wife. They found that he had a psychiatric condition and a record of domestic violence.

Cox got a call from a former passenger who had flown to St. Louis and taken a Bart Transportation van back to Springfield. She was alone in the van with the driver called Roger. "The guy drove like a madman. He would come up on cars and honk. He would tailgate. He talked to himself. I got scared. If I could have gotten out I would have. If I could find another way to get back to Springfield, I would have done so. I was really upset."

"Did you ever make a complaint?"

"No, I didn't. I was concerned that if I did, he knew where I lived, but I was awfully happy to get home. I heard about the murder on the news, and I wanted to call you to tell you because this sounds like the same guy."

Cox responded, "Thanks for the call. That's helpful."

After assigning officers to canvass the neighborhood, Murphy and Young went to Memorial Medical Center to talk to Coroner Norman Richter. They met with Roger Harrington's parents.

"When did you last see Roger?" they asked.

"It was at the time of the state fair in early August. We talked to him last night on the telephone."

"Where was he living?"

"He was staying with a friend, Susan Collins. He had been there a month. She rented him a room in her trailer."

"When you talked to him on the telephone did he seem to have any problems?"

"No, he hasn't had any more problems. He had a traffic accident some time ago but nothing since then. He was happy working for Bart."

"Did he have any other problems?"

"No."

"Did he have any mental or emotional problems?"

"We have not been close in the last couple of years. He may have been admitted to McFarland Zone Center four to five years ago, but that was voluntary."

Upon further inquiry, the Harringtons became defensive, so the officers asked about his background.

"He had some problems in the past. He did not graduate from high school. He tried to join the National Guard but did not get through the training. He worked for a short time as a truck driver."

They were too upset to continue. They did not want to identify the body and asked that the detectives call Susan Collins.

"Do you have the telephone number of Susan?"

"Yes," they responded.

They gave the officers her number and they called her. She came to the hospital and identified Roger Harrington. She told them that he had been paying her $200 a week for room and board.

"When was the last time you talked to him?" Young asked.

"He had received a call from someone at work. It was a complaint. Someone had called his boss and said there was a complaint from a female passenger. The husband wanted to talk to him. They asked for his okay to give the husband his name. He said go ahead. Roger was told that he would not get any further rides until he straightened this out. About three or so he said he had to go meet the husband."

"What kind of person was he?" Murphy asked.

"I have known him for three years. We got along real well. He was laid back and very kind."

"Did he have any psychiatric problems?"

"Not really. He was a little different. He had a guardian angel he called Dahm. He spoke to him sometimes. He had a psychiatrist."

"Did he drink or use drugs?"

"No hard stuff. He and I smoked marijuana. Sometimes he would drink. He had no hang-up on drugs."

"Could we go to look at his room?"

"Sure."

Collins left to go to her trailer and they followed; once in the trailer, Collins showed them Roger's room. Pointing to a mask of a dragon in the chair, she said, "That's Dahm, his guardian angel. It is a good spirit and Roger was very close to this spirit."

"Did Dahm ever tell him to kill people?"

"No, Dahm was a good spirit. I have one also that I keep in a box."

The officers looked over the room and took a picture of the mask.

"Did he get any telephone calls today?"

"Yes, a call from work, and then he got a call from the husband. The call from work was longer. The call from the husband was shorter. I did not hear the conversation because he went into his room. He said the husband wanted to meet with him about four thirty. He wrote down the name and address on a slip of paper."

"When was the call made?"

"I have caller ID."

They all looked at the caller ID and saw that the call was made at 9:07 a.m. in the morning. They wrote down the number but did not write down any other numbers.

Susan Collins said that Sandra Ray was in the trailer, and the officers talked to her.

"I was sleeping in the morning, so I did not hear the call from the husband," Ray said. "In the afternoon I remember he got a call from someone at work. He went to his room to talk to him. I did not hear what was said, but I knew that he was not going to get any more rides until this was straightened out."

Meanwhile, other officers continued to canvass the neighborhood. A neighbor reported seeing Donnah on the porch on Friday looking worried; he did not know why.

Another neighbor, Lauralee Smith, stated that she had babysat for the Wingers on occasion and was unaware of any problems in the marriage. She lived next door, and on the twenty-ninth she had picked up her children from a babysitter and was unloading the car around 4:30 p.m. She heard what she thought was a shot but did not think anything of it because nothing happened after that. She continued unloading the car and went into her house.

Cox, Williamson, and Murphy met together.

Murphy said, "Where are we?"

Cox replied, "We ought to get everyone together for a roundtable to see what we have. Right now it looks to me like Roger Harrington killed Donnah Winger, and Mark shot him in self-defense." Murphy and Williamson agreed, and they called the investigation officers in for a roundtable.

Williamson said, "Maybe this is a little too soon. Shouldn't we check out those suspicious telephone calls?"

Cox replied, "Let's see what the roundtable says."

Crime Scene Photographs

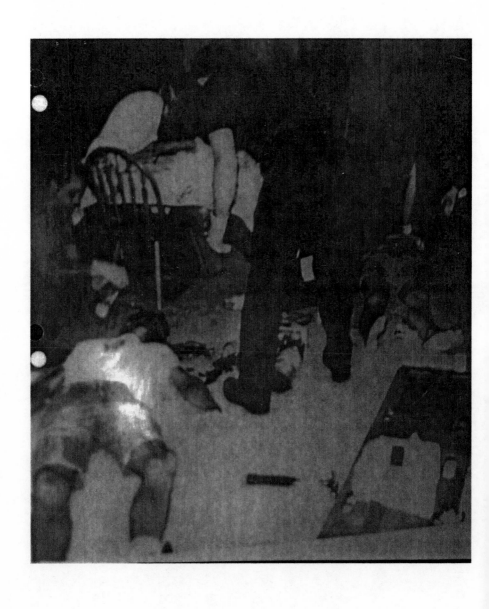

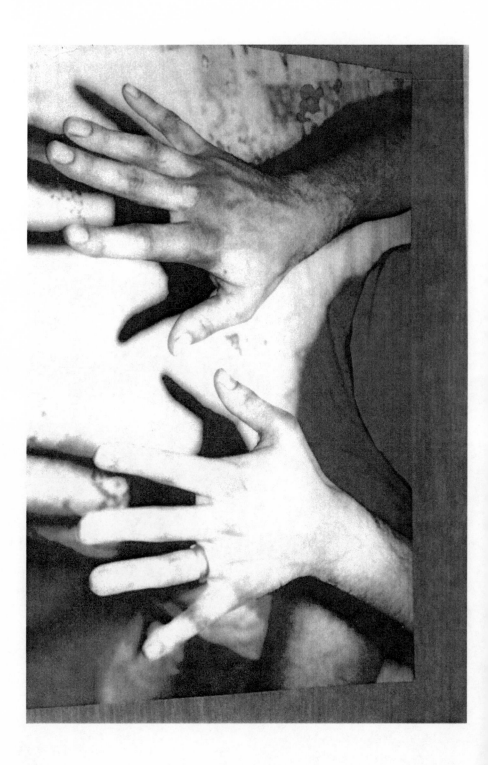

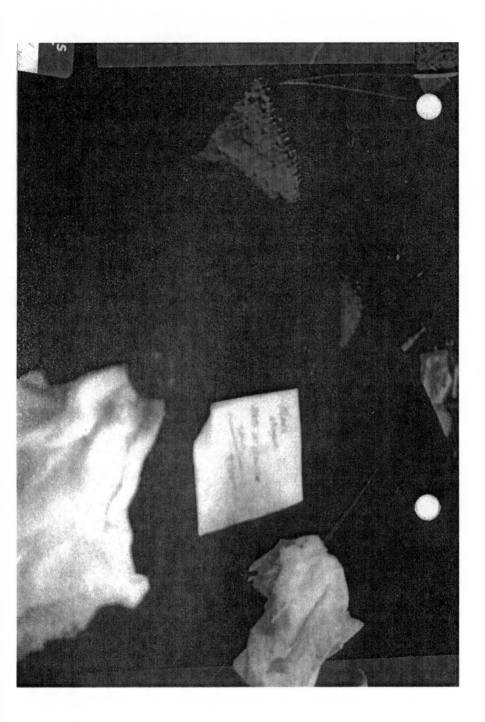

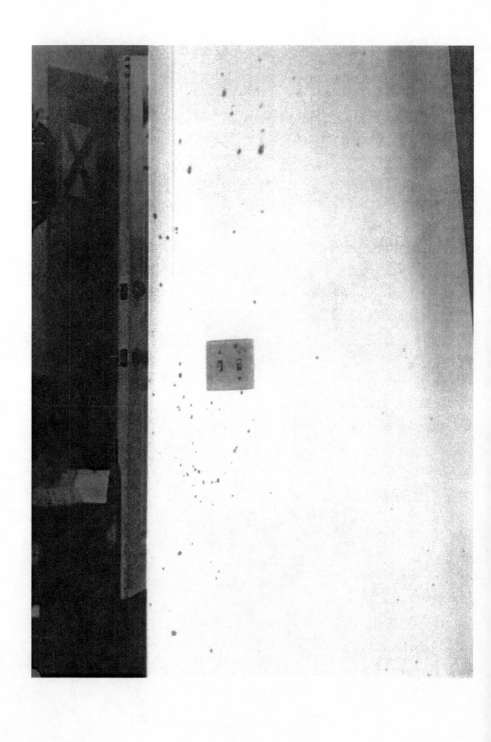

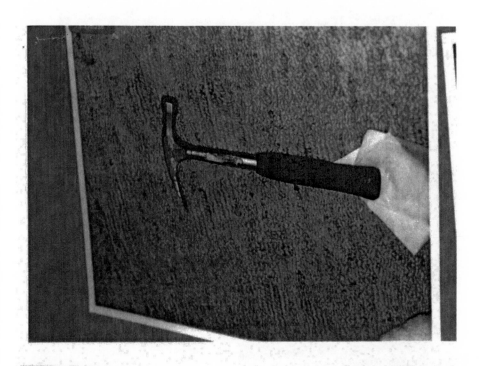

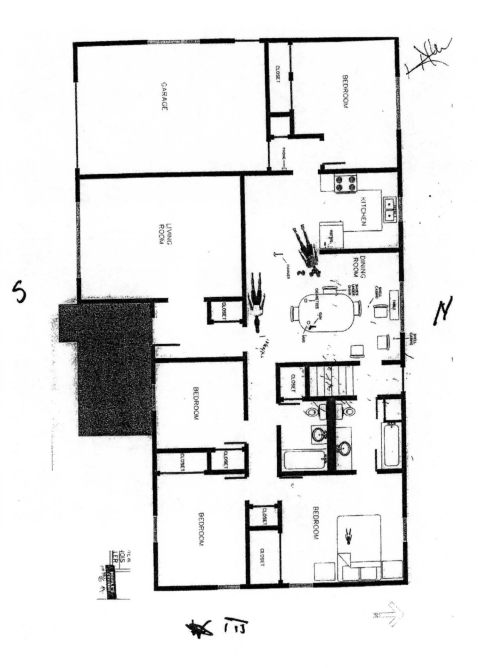

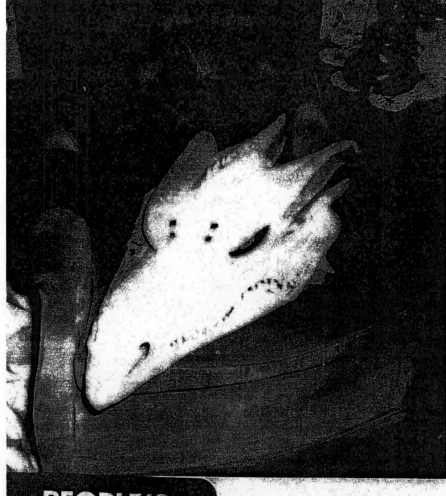

126 01-C7
798

CHAPTER 8

The Police Roundtable

On August 31, 1995, at the police station in Springfield, acting chief Murphy, the head of the major crimes unit, brought together the investigating officers. There were some ten officers—Investigators Young, Jones, Murphy, and Filburn; Detectives Cox and Williamson; and the crime scene technicians.

The chief started the meeting. "Okay, let's get this show on the road. With these two included we have six murders during August. There were also ten other major crimes. This had been one hell of a month. None of these have been resolved."

"This death here looks like a murder, and then the husband shoots Roger Harrington. Let's be thorough about it."

Murphy continued, "On the death of the wife, Donnah Winger, only two people could have done that, Roger Harrington or her husband. Let's talk about her husband first. Charlie, what have you learned? You and Doug should start it off and tell us your thoughts."

Cox responded, "The crime scene was a mess when we got there. There were at least eight or more people milling around in the dining room. Blood on the walls, on the floor. There were three pools of blood on the floor. It looked like someone had spilled a bucket of red paint. There were two bodies on the floor."

Cox described what he observed and the location of the bodies. Then Cox described his interviews with Winger and described his emotional state.

"He was very emotional. He had his shirt off and it was bloody. His shoulders and arms and hands were also bloody. He had been found cradling his wife. He had made the 911 call."

Murphy said, "As to the marriage, we checked with the neighbors. The baby was given to Barbara Rendleman, who was a neighbor, and both she and Dennis, her husband, said there were no problems. They said it was rock solid. We canvassed the neighborhood. No arguments, no complaints."

Cox said, "I was asked by Mark to call his rabbi, Datz. He came over right away. Donnah and Mark were good friends of his and his wife, Jo Datz. He said they would see them frequently, and Donnah was very active in the temple. He never heard any complaints from them or anyone about their marriage."

Cox said, "Mark had no criminal record. Harrington had been arrested several times for hitting his ex-wife and for tearing up the house of his sister's ex-boyfriend. He had cut up the house with a knife with several friends. He also pointed a gun at his ex-wife, handcuffed her, etc."

Williamson then added, "Donnah's mom, Sara Jane Drescher, and Ira Drescher, Donnah's stepdad. We questioned both of them. Donnah had visited them about five days. She was happy, floating on clouds about the adoption. She had no complaints about Mark Winger. There was no evidence of abuse."

"What else do we know about this guy Roger Harrington?"

Murphy and Young said, "He had a couple different jobs, dropped out of Lanphier. He had joined the army but was discharged shortly afterward. He was a truck driver and was fired. He was a phlebotomist for a while, then Bart Transportation, and that was his longest job. He had been working there for about six months. They finally did say that he had been at McFarland for a psychiatric condition several times. We knew he had been on drugs in the past."

"We went out to see where he lived and looked through the trailer." Murphy and Young continued, "We went to Harrington's room in the trailer.

It had a mattress on the floor and a chair with a mask of a dragon. Murphy asked Collins, 'What is that?'

"Collins told us, 'That's the spirit of Dahm. Roger sometimes talks to Dahm. You know it's a spirit. I have a spirit too. I talk to spirits. Sometimes Dahm tells him what to do. There is nothing wrong with that.'

"Young asked her, 'Did Dahm ever tell him to hurt people?' She said, 'No, Dahm is a good spirit.'"

Williamson said, "Winger did call Harrington, and we know that Harrington was going to lose his job if he didn't straighten this out."

Cox added, "I have some past experience with this guy. I owned a trailer court. I was out there a year or so ago, and Harrington was in the trailer that his ex-wife rented. I heard some noise, went in there, and he was on her, hitting her. I pulled him off of her. He has been in the hospital for psychiatric conditions. We know he smokes marijuana."

"Does anyone know what the pathologist found?"

Cox replied, "Yeah, I talked to the pathologist. He said that Donnah Winger had been hit in the head with a hammer about seven times. The blows came from behind. They crushed the skull in seven places. It was violent, like someone was consumed with rage. It wasn't just one or two blows—it was seven, and they were struck with such force that the actual skull was crushed."

"Looks like this was done by someone who was angry."

Cox responded, "Hammering someone to death shows anger or rage. It is up front and personal. The blows were violent."

"Anything at all indicating that this marriage was in trouble?" The officers shook their heads.

Murphy added, "It does not look like a case against Mark Winger. He had good marriage, new baby. This weird ride with this guy who has a psychiatric condition and a record of violence—it fits with Mark Winger's story."

Williamson said, "I still have some problems about this note. It looks like the meeting could have been set up. We should check the telephone calls, maybe take a little more time."

Murphy replied, "Collins she said that on Monday or Tuesday Harrington got a call from work. He was told to straighten it out with Winger. The note was probably written out that time."

Williamson said, "The note had four thirty on it."

"Yeah, but that could have been written after the second call."

Cox said, "There always are loose ends in these things, but we don't have anything contradicting what Winger said. No motive, a good marriage, adopting a baby, no record of violence. Nothing points to him."

It was self-defense and a justifiable homicide of Harrington. Donnah was killed by Harrington and Harrington by Winger. The police reported this to the state's attorney, and the case was closed to any further investigation.

CHAPTER 9

The Inquest

In suspicious deaths or deaths where the cause of death is not readily apparent, the coroner has jurisdiction to hold an inquest to determine the cause of death. A six-person jury is selected by the coroner, and usually the jurors serve on multiple cases. The coroner may subpoena hospital medical records and other documents and may call witnesses and present hearsay testimony. These are not criminal proceedings but can lead to criminal prosecution if the result of the inquest suggests that a criminal act was involved. Witnesses have the right to plead the Fifth Amendment against self-incrimination; and in almost all coroners' inquests, hearsay evidence is used, and cross-examination is rare. The hearing is usually a perfunctory proceeding, but the record may be used for subsequent criminal proceedings or civil proceedings.

Coroner Richter called an inquest on September 15, 1995, to formally determine the cause of death of Donnah Winger and Roger Harrington. Although the cause of death was evident, the official cause of death is established by this inquest. In Illinois, the coroner himself or herself is normally not a physician and will have an autopsy done by a pathologist who will either make a written report or, in some cases, testify at the inquest. The coroner can summarize the autopsy findings.

Coroner Richter obtained a report from Travis Hindman, the pathologist who performed the autopsy. He reported, "Dr. Hindman did an autopsy of both Roger Harrington and Donnah Winger. Roger Harrington had two gunshot wounds to the head from which he died from about five pm on August 29, 1995. The toxicology screening revealed that there were marijuana metabolites in his urine."

Richter then reported, "Donnah Winger died on August 29, 1995, about five minutes after Roger Harrington. She was thirty-one and died of massive trauma to the brain due to blunt force injury caused by multiple blows by an assailant using a hammer, causing massive destruction of brain tissue."

"She was struck seven times in the head." Hindman's conclusion was, "The blows were from behind with the assailant behind the victim. The number of blows, the violence of the blows, would indicate that the assailant was enraged or angry."

Richter then called Detective Cox. "On August 29, 1995, at about 4:30 p.m., myself and Detective Williamson got a call from dispatch to go immediately to 4305 Westview because there had been gunshots fired, and there reportedly was a bludgeoning of a woman."

Cox described the investigation, the interview with Mark Winger, and the crime scene.

Cox said, "We investigated all the angles of this case, trying to prove or disprove what he said. There is nothing that came to light at all that would have brought into the question the statement about the husband. Everything fit with the evidence of the scene."

Richter asked about Roger Harrington.

Cox replied, "The police have dealt with Harrington numerous times for violent behavior. He has been violent with handguns as well as knives, where the police had to take them out of his hands. He has threatened to kill police officers and himself on several occasions. He barricaded himself in a house with suicidal intent. He had psychiatric help at different times of his life, and he actually was committed to McFarland. The police department knew him to be a potentially violent person. All of the evidence lead to the husband's justifiable shooting of this individual."

The coroner did not call Mark Winger.

The coroner's jury ruled that the killing of Roger Harrington was justifiable homicide. They further concluded that the death of Donnah Winger was the result of injuries received from Roger Harrington and that it was a homicide committed by him.

Autopsy Photographs

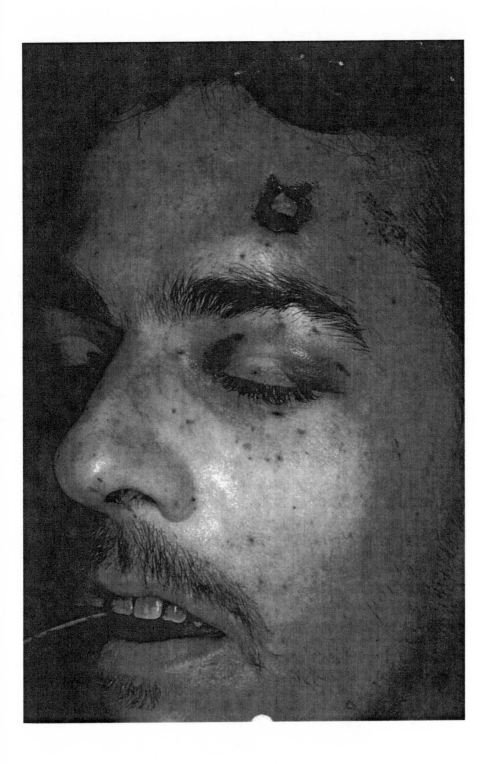

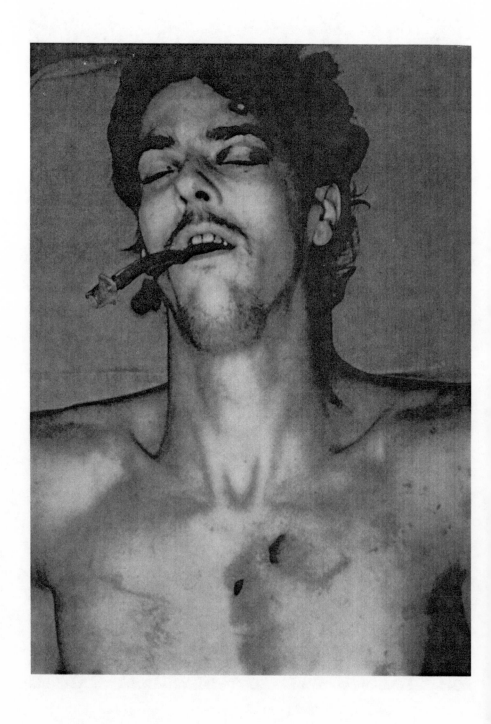

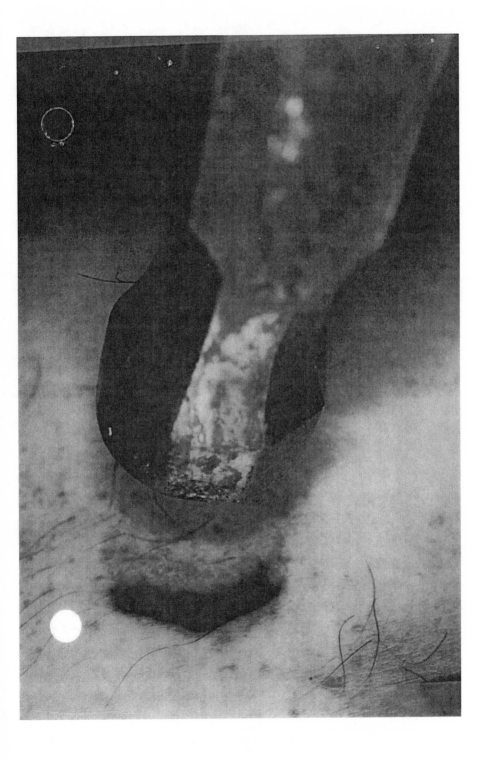

PART II

Arrogance

The truest characteristics of ignorance are vanity, pride, and arrogance.

~Samuel Brittan

CHAPTER 10

The Civil Suit

Michael Metnick, a Springfield attorney who a highly regarded reputation for handling personal injury cases and criminal matters, remembered watching television in August. He saw a news report about a double murder at 4305 Westview Drive. He saw the home roped off with all the police cars in the area. It was a gruesome crime. He didn't think any more of it. The next day he went to his office, picked up a file, and headed to Jacksonville, Illinois, about forty-five minutes west of Springfield. He had a hearing scheduled at ten thirty.

While going to Jacksonville on August 30, 1995, he received a call on his cell phone. Only two people knew his cell phone number, his secretary and his wife. He noticed that it was not from either of them. This was unusual. He picked up the call, and it was from Rabbi Datz. Mike attended the Temple B'rith Shalom, where Rabbi Datz was the rabbi. He wondered how Datz had gotten his number. He picked up the call and Rabbi Datz said, "Mike, I got an urgent matter. I need to talk to you right away."

Mike replied, "How'd you get my telephone number, my cell phone?"

"I called your office and persuaded your secretary to give it to me. I need to talk to you. This is urgent."

"Well, I'm on my way to Jacksonville to a hearing, and I can't meet with you right now. What is the problem?"

Datz said, "Look, I can't talk to you about it over the telephone. You know cell phones are notorious for being intercepted. I need to meet with you at my house. I have some people I want to you to meet, and it is urgent."

Mike said, "Give me a clue."

Datz replies, "I can't do that on a cell phone."

"Okay, I'll get there as soon as I can. I have this hearing at ten thirty. It will probably take about an hour. Then I will be on my way back."

"Thanks, Mike. Get here as soon as you can."

He went to his hearing in Jacksonville and finished up the matters there. He was wondering what Rabbi Datz thought was so urgent that he had to talk to him right away. He called his office, and his secretary said that she gave him the cell phone number, but he didn't tell her what it was about; he just stressed how urgent it was.

He skipped lunch and drove directly to Rabbi Datz's house on Cherry Road in Springfield. Rabbi Datz and his wife, Jo Datz, met him at the door. They were visibly upset, and there were a number of people sitting in the living room. They were emotional, and some had obviously been crying.

Off the living room he saw a thirty-year-old man who looked shaken up. He was staring off into space; he was sitting by himself. Rabbi Datz introduced him to Mark Winger. Mike had never met Mark, but he knew of Donnah.

Rabbi Datz said, "Someone broke into Mark's home and started bludgeoning Mark's wife to death, and Mark shot him and killed him. His wife later died. I thought you should talk to him to see if you could do anything for him.*"

"I saw the report on TV last night. What a tragedy. I will do anything I can," Mike said.

---

* The conversations herein are fiction but are based on the sequence of events, court records, and from interviews. Mike Metnick, who was interviewed, could not reveal his conversation with Mark Winger because of attorney-client privileges.

They sat down with Mark. Mark was upset but coherent. He repeated again what had happened—this guy beating his wife with a hammer. He had shot and killed him. He told Mike about the ride from St. Louis to Springfield. He said the guy was a psycho and shouldn't have been driving. Mike listened. Mark was gasping as he told the story.

"You have my heartfelt sympathy. I have seen a lot of bad stuff in my practice, but this has got to be the worst. I don't know that there is anything I can do for you at this stage. Once you get through with the funeral, give me a call. We can talk about it."

Mark said, "Cindy's mother has been killed. My wife, someone I loved dearly, was hammered to death."

Mark had many conversations with friends and family. All were upset with Bart for hiring this "psycho." He was encouraged to file a civil suit against Bart. Toward the end of November, Mark called up Mike Metnick.

"Mike, do you remember me? This is Mark Winger."

"Sure, I do. How's it going?"

"Not so good. I went back to work. That's going fine, but I still can't put this behind me. We had just adopted a child, and Donnah was happier than I had ever seen her. Then all of a sudden the bottom dropped out."

"Mark, no one can understand how this affects a person. Are you seeing a psychiatrist or anyone to help?"

Mark replied, "No, I just went back to work. That's probably the best therapy I can have. I also have some friends I can talk to. That helps. But sooner or later I've got to come to grips with this."

"Well, what can I do for you?"

"Bart never should have had this guy driving people around. He would be driving people like Donnah and others. They should screen their people. Check them out and make sure they are safe and not psychos. I want to sue them"

Mike replied, "I understand your anger. You know the difference between a civil suit and a criminal suit is that a civil suit seeks damages. We could sue Harrington, but then we couldn't get damages. He doesn't have anything. We have to get to Bart. I'll have someone check it out to see about a claim against Bart, and then let's get together and talk about it."

"He put my wife and baby in danger. He was dangerous and nuts. They should have never let anyone like that drive people around."

"I'll give you a ring in a month or so after we have done some research on it. I know there are some cases that might support a theory of negligent hiring. I'll go get the coroner's inquest records, and I'll call you back."

"Okay, thanks," Mark replied.

Mike checked the police records and the coroner's inquest and did some research.

In December, Mike called Mark Winger, and they got together. Mark seemed composed. Mike said, "I have good news and bad news. The bad news first."

Mark said, "Well, let's have it."

"The bad news is that there are a whole bunch of cases where a deliveryman delivering a stove, refrigerator, or whatnot assaults a female. The cases all say that's outside the scope of agency, and there is no liability on behalf of the employer unless the employer knew about his prior record. The employers get off scot-free unless they have some kind of notice that the guy has a criminal record. Perhaps we can distinguish these cases."

Mark then asked, "Well, what's the good news?"

"There is a developing theory, though I can't say how far it's gone. The theory is negligent hiring. For instance, there are statutes that require checking out nursery school workers, schoolteachers, nurses, health-care workers, and school bus drivers to see if they have any criminal background or any history that would make them dangerous to the public. In particular, there are cases where there is an assault on a school kid by a teacher or school bus driver. Those cases are growing."

Mark asked, "What about Bart hiring this psycho?"

"Most of the cases are based upon the statutory duty to investigate the person's background. There aren't a whole lot of cases dealing with a duty imposed by common law. However, some of the appellate cases give us hope that we could extend that duty. The question is going to be whether there was a duty by Bart to investigate whether Harrington had any criminal or any psychiatric record. It's worth pursuing."

"They deprived Cindy of a mother, and they deprived me of a wife. All you have to do is read Donnah's notes, and you know that he wasn't fit to deal with the public. They should have checked him out."

Mike replied, "I agree. There are a number of claims. One would be for the survival action, for the pain and suffering before Donnah died, and the other would be for wrongful death for you and Cindy. We can get a judgment against Harrington, but that would be worthless. A judgment against Bart is a little bit more *iffy*. We would have to show negligence in hiring him. We have a claim by Cindy for the loss of her mother for affection and support in bringing up the baby. From what I have heard, Donnah was just a wonderful young lady. The loss to Cindy and the brutality of the crime could mean a substantial verdict."

Mike continued, "We also have a cause of action for loss of consortium for you."

Mark asked, "What is that?"

"This is your loss of companionship, sex, your relationship with each other. It is mainly for the love and affection you had for each other that you are deprived of."

"I told you I was devastated. She was the love of my life. I am having a hard time adjusting to this. I can function on the job, but emotionally I'm having a hard time."

An eight-count complaint was filed in the end of December 1995, alleging negligent hiring.

Civil suits take three to four years before they are resolved. Defendants and plaintiffs file requests to produce, interrogatories, take depositions, etc.; it takes a long time for their suits to get resolved. Metnick went over to the police station and obtained the evidence that the police had collected from the crime scene and receipted for it, including pictures, clothes worn by the parties, videotapes, and other matters that had been collected during the course of the investigation.

Defendants are not anxious to press the cases, so they take their time. However, in April 1997, Mark Winger had his deposition taken by the defendants. Winger stated that after Donnah's death, he married Barbara, a young lady who was Cindy's nanny, and she also joined in the adoption proceedings. Mark dropped out of the Jewish religion and joined a fundamentalist church Barbara was attending. He taught Sunday school and read to his children at night. He testified Barbara was "a model mother" for Cindy and their other children.

The defendant's attorneys then questioned the note found in the car saying "M. Winger W. View Drive 4:30."

"I didn't set up the meeting with him," Mark said. "I called him, but when he started talking strange I just hung up on him. He must have written it down at the first part of the conversation. I had told him I would be back about four thirty from work. He said he wasn't going to get any more rides until he straightened this out, so he wanted to meet with me."

Mark Winger again stated what he told the police—that he was working out in the basement, heard a noise, saw his wife being beaten, and then shot Harrington.

"Donnah and I had a great relationship. She couldn't carry a child, so we started to adopt a child. I have never seen my wife so happy. I think of how much Donnah would have loved Cindy if she lived. Cindy's got a lot of grandparents now. She's got Donnah's parents, she's got my parents, and she's got my wife's parents."

When questioned about his wife Barbara, he said, "She was Cindy's nanny. We got married in September 1996. She is a great mother and wife; we have two natural children. She takes care of them and Cindy. She adopted Cindy. We have a very good marriage. I dropped out of the Jewish religion and joined her church. I love her greatly."

At times the deposition had to be halted so that Mark could compose himself.

"I've had a lot of sleepless nights. I've lost twenty-five pounds. Donnah was what held us together. Everyone loved her."

Mark Winger had remarried and Cindy had a new mom. Winger had continued with his work, and he got promoted, and they had children together. Barbara had adopted Cindy. There could well be liability, but they did not think it was not going to be a "bell ringer."

Unfortunately, the suit caused the downfall of Mark Winger.

CHAPTER 11

Donnah, Mark, and DeAnn

In early summer 1994, DeAnn called up Donnah. "Donnah, I need to talk to someone about my marriage."

Donnah was not surprised because DeAnn had been unhappy for some period of time. They talked frequently on the telephone. Donnah was a good listener who loved to talk on the telephone and so did DeAnn. DeAnn felt comfortable with Donnah.

"What's going on?"

"John and I are not getting along."

"I sensed some of that, but I didn't know it was serious."

"It is serious."

"What's the problem?"

"Lack of intimacy, you know what I mean. We don't seem to relate together. We are like two strangers living in a house. It is tense. I don't know what caused this. I guess the stress of the children, the stress of the jobs. I don't know. We seem to have drifted apart."

"Does he ever say he loves you?"

"No. At home we hardly talk."

"Sounds like the pressures are getting you down."

"You are right. Both John and I don't have a relationship anymore. My job is very stressful. The kids are great, but they add to the stress. I try to talk to John and he does not listen."

"Maybe you need to get away."

"I wish I could."

"I'm going to go visit my parents in Florida for a couple of weeks. Would you like to come with me? It could give you a break."

"I don't know. Let me think about it. I'll check with my job and John."

"Okay, call me back. It will be a couple weeks during June. It will be good for you."

Donnah had planned to visit her mom and stepdad for a couple of weeks to Florida. It had been some time since they had been together. Donnah asked if it would be okay if she brought a friend from Springfield who was having a rough time with her marriage. Sarah Jane replied, "Of course that would be okay."

DeAnn and Donnah talked again, and Donnah said, "DeAnn, what about it?"

DeAnn replied, "I talked to John, and he thinks that it might be a good idea. He wants to take care of the kids. We are having a rough time, and he thinks that this might help."

Donnah and DeAnn left in late June to go to Florida for two weeks. They sat on the beaches and spent time together. DeAnn, upon coming back, said to Donnah, "Thanks, I needed that. I feel that this has helped me a great deal." She acted more relaxed.

DeAnn went back to her normal routine, working as an outpatient for psychiatric patients—lots of paperwork and visiting patients. It was a lonely job with no contact with other nurses doing outpatient work. John and DeAnn thought they had gotten things back together. The stresses of working full time and having two children, one very young and one a teenager, created tensions. DeAnn kept saying, "John, why did we ever leave Havana?"

He said, "There are more opportunities here."

DeAnn replied, "I was really happy in Havana, and now I am miserable here. I want to move back." John didn't know what to say. His job was in Springfield. In the meantime Donnah and DeAnn continued to visit.

In July 1995, DeAnn called Donnah. "I am thinking of leaving John."

"What is going on?" Donnah asked.

"Well, the same old issues, the lack of intimacy. We are two strangers living in the same house. We don't talk, we argue, no affection—I can't handle it."

Donnah replied, "Is there anything I could do?"

"No. I have contacted an old boyfriend of mine in the Minneapolis/St. Paul area. I told him that I am having real problems with my marriage, and I was thinking of leaving John. We started talking and it was like old times. He said he was going to be in St. Louis for a performance and asked if I would come have lunch or dinner with him. I told him I would and went down to St. Louis and met with him."

"You're kidding."

"No," DeAnn said. "He said I had an open invitation to come back anytime I wanted to."

"Are you going to?"

"I think so. I have never been so unhappy my whole life."

Mark came home that evening and noticed that Donnah was upset and asked her what was going on. Donnah said, "You know the problems with DeAnn and John? Well, its back on again. DeAnn says there is a lack of intimacy, they don't talk, they act like strangers, etc. I don't know what she means by that, but I'm sure it's inability to relate to each other to talk, lack of sex, etc."

"Well, what else is new? They have been having this problem ever since we've known them," replied Mark.

"DeAnn is thinking of leaving and hooking up with an old boyfriend of hers."

"Is she really serious about this?"

"I think so. I hate to see her move, but not much we can do about it."

Donnah asked Mark to keep this confidential.

When Mark was at a training course in Chattanooga on July 20, he gave DeAnn a ring at her home.

"DeAnn, this is Mark Winger."

"What are you calling about, Mark? You are out of town."

"I know. That is why I am calling you."

"What do you mean?"

"I talked with Donnah. She said that you are having a rough time. She said that you are thinking of moving."

"I told that to Donnah in confidence. That's upsetting. I am surprised that she told you this."

"Well, we're both very concerned about you moving. I don't want you to move. You know, I have always felt something special towards you."

"What do you mean?"

"Well, I don't quite know how to say this, but I have been attracted to you, and you know, Donnah and I have been having trouble in our marriage too. We have problems in our relationship."

"What do you mean? It seems pretty good to me."

"That's only on the surface. We have our problems. Perhaps it's been brewing for a while—ever since she learned that she could not get pregnant. I had hoped that by adopting that might change, but it seems to have gotten worse. The new baby is the focus of her life—she seems to have forgotten about me."

"What's this all leading to?"

"Well, I have been thinking of leaving Donnah."

"You're kidding."

"Nope. I hate to see you move, but I do have real feelings for you. You are attractive, bright, and I enjoy your company."

"Mark, I feel the same about you, but we're married."

"Well, you leaving John . . . I'm going to leave Donnah . . . why don't we get together and talk?"

"What do you mean?"

"Get together. I have this weekend free and we could talk it out. We can meet in Mount Vernon. Maybe we can help each other out."

DeAnn replied, "Mark, this is awfully sudden for me."

"I've wanted to get together with you for a long time. You're very attractive. I like being with you."

DeAnn replied, "Are you thinking of us spending the weekend together? Having an affair?"

Mark answered, "Yes."

"I don't know. Let me think about it."

Mark then added, "I think it was a mistake for me to marry Donnah. Give me a call back after you think about this."

"Okay."

Two days later DeAnn calls back. "Mark, I've decided to take you up on this."

Mark replied, "That's great. Over the weekend I'll have a car, and then I'll drive up to Mount Vernon. Why don't we meet at the Comfort Inn?"

"I don't know how to get there."

"It's very easy. Just take the interstate down to Mount Vernon. The Comfort Inn is just off the interstate."

"I will tell John I need to get away for the weekend," DeAnn replied.

DeAnn checked into the Comfort Inn on July 22. She paid for the room. Mark was waiting for her. They had dinner together, talked about their problems with their marriages, their families, and talked about the lack of intimacy. Mark told DeAnn how much he liked her. She talked about her family and growing up and how unhappy she was. He listened to her. Someone was finally listening to her. They drank some wine and went to her room. That's how the affair started.

CHAPTER 12

Changing Relationships
September 30, 1995 to December 31, 1998

A. Mark Winger, the Schultzes, Dreschers, and Datzes

In late September 1995, Mark Winger returned to Springfield after spending three weeks in Ohio with his family. He went back to his job. He told people that the best therapy was to work. The community felt sorry for Mark, and he enjoyed the outpouring of good will.

Ira and Sarah Jane Drescher remained very close to Mark. Ira had developed a very strong relationship with him. Sarah Jane would visit and babysit Cindy. She regarded Cindy as her granddaughter.

During the fall of 1995, Mark went on a spending spree, purchasing a new truck, a temperature-controlled wine cabinet, and an expensive computer system. Some thought this was his way of grieving and trying to forget about what happened. Ira came to Springfield and helped him put together the wine cabinet.

Upon Mark's return from Ohio, he brought with him a nanny. She was a nice, quiet young lady. The arrangement was that she would take care of Cindy during the day, and Mark would take care of her during the evenings and weekends. She was hired for a forty-hour week. Mark would come home; the nanny would go to her room or watch television. It didn't last long. Frequently Mark would come home from work and then leave. He wouldn't get home until eleven or so in the evening. She didn't know where he went. Weekly, if not more than once a week, the Schultzes would come over and drink wine with Mark. The Schultzes never brought a bottle of wine, and they would drink sometimes two or more bottles in the evening. They would talk, watch TV, play fantasy football, and just visit. No one thought anything of this because they were good friends trying to come to grips with Donnah's death.

One evening in November the nanny got a call from John Schultz around 11:00 p.m. He had just gotten home from work, and he asked if his wife was there. The nanny looked in the driveway and saw DeAnn Schultz's car parked there. She looked around for DeAnn but couldn't find her. She knocked on the bedroom door, and after a period of time, DeAnn came to the door, dressed in some of Mark's clothes. She went to the telephone and then left.

One time the nanny was sleeping downstairs and Mark came down the stairs. She opened her eyes and saw Mark looking at her. She pretended to be asleep, and Mark just stood looking at her. Another time, as she was getting out of the shower and had a towel wrapped around her, Mark came down looking at her and then said he was getting a beer. This made her uneasy.

Mark went to Ohio for Christmas. Prior to leaving he told the nanny that he would no longer need her. She was not given any reason. Her dad then came and picked her up and drove her back to Ohio. She was crestfallen; this was her first job. When Mark came back to Springfield in January 1996, he brought with him a new nanny. Her name was Barbara.

During this period of time, Mark would complain to various female friends about how he missed a female touch, a woman's touch; he said he missed having sex with Donnah. Some of these friends began to feel uneasy and felt he was making a pass at them. In late January or early February, John and DeAnn were at Mark's one evening, drinking wine and watching television, etc. Barbara was taking care of Cindy but was also drinking some wine. John lost track of time and fell asleep. When he woke up, no one was around. He went looking for DeAnn and found her downstairs hiding behind the couch, partially clothed. Mark was in the same room. John left, and they followed him to his home and told him it wasn't as it appeared. John blotted this out of his mind. John told DeAnn that he did not want her to see Mark anymore.

The relationship between the Dreschers and Mark continued. Cindy and Sarah Jane had bonded with Cindy and Sarah Jane thought of herself as her grandmother. She liked Barbara, who was young, attractive, and outgoing.

In February, Mark took a monthlong vacation in Africa. He talked to Jo Datz about bringing a female with him, but Jo Datz said that it was not a good idea, so he went with his brother instead.

Upon his return, he didn't call DeAnn. DeAnn finally called him and asked what was going on. He said to her that he needed to make a clean break. He was moving to Pleasant Plains, a small community outside of Springfield, and was buying a house there. Things were going okay for him. He continued to work and was promoted. However, he seemed to be distancing himself from his friends.

Sometime in the spring he decided to switch from the Jewish religion to a Christian church, where Barbara was a member. This upset Rabbi Datz. Mark asked him to bless his new house in Pleasant Plains, as it is the Jewish custom. Rabi Datz replied by asking, "Is there anyone Jewish living here?" Rabi Datz was upset that Mark had given up the Jewish religion. He refused.

In midsummer, Mark and Barbara decided to marry. She was a good nanny to Cindy. He told Ira and Sarah Jane that he planned on marrying Barbara, and they were happy for him. They took care of Cindy while Mark and Barbara took their honeymoon in Hawaii; they were overjoyed at the chance to spend time with Cindy.

Barbara adopted Cindy and had two more children by June 1998. She was pretty much a stay-at-home mom, having three young children (she subsequently had a fourth child). In1997 Mark's life revolved around work and raising the kids; he was active in church, teaching Sunday school. He read to the children at night and helped feed them and put them to bed. He had, at this time, pretty much made a new life for himself, moving to Pleasant Plains and attending a Christian Church, having severed his relationships with the Datzes and the temple. He still played golf with his boss, Mike Parker, who was one of his good friends.

His relationship with the Dreschers seemed to be changing, especially with Sarah Jane. Sarah Jane thought of herself as the grandmother of Cindy. Mark decided that Cindy should not refer to Sarah Jane as her grandmother. He said he had sought advice from a psychologist who had indicated that this would confuse Cindy. The other children had another grandmother, but Sarah Jane was not to be referred to as their grandmother. They exchanged letters; Sarah Jane became extremely upset. Cindy, she felt, was her grandchild, and she deserved to be called her grandmother. She was her first grandchild. She sent Mother's Day cards to Barbara, as a daughter-in-law. She couldn't imagine how calling her "grandmother" would be a problem. She felt that Donnah's greatest gift to her was naming the child after her mother and aunt.

Sarah Jane was devastated by Mark's attitude. They had welcomed him as a son in their family. They had counseled him and comforted him after Donnah's death, and now the relationship was terminated.

B. Charles Cox and Mark Winger

In October 1995, after returning from Ohio, Mark Winger called Detective Cox. He said he would like to get his .45 back. Cox agreed and set up an appointment at the police station. Cox greeted him at the door and showed him back into the office.

Cox said, "Mark, good to see you again. What's up?"

"I just wanted to get back my .45. It had been given to me by my father."

"I don't see any problem. I've got it here from the evidence room. All we need you to do is sign a release form for it."

Cox then asked how it was going, and Mark replied, "I'm trying to adjust. I really can't believe that this happened. It's a bad nightmare, and I hope I will wake up from it, but I know I won't. I really miss her." However, Cox noted that he said this without showing any emotion.

"I bet you do," Cox replied.

"I've gone back to work, and I got a nanny for Cindy."

"Did you go on through with the adoption?"

"Yes, she will be my child."

"Good for you."

Mark then asked, "How is this investigation going? Is there anything new?"

Cox thought it was a strange question. Mark knew the case was closed. No one had ever asked him that after the investigation was closed if anything was new.

"Mark, the case has been closed. Why do you ask?"

"Just curious whether or not you've got any more on Roger Harrington or anything else has turned up."

Cox answered, "No." They chatted some more. They talked about the weather and how Cindy is doing, and Mark then left.

In the summer of 1996 Mark again called up Cox and wanted to come in and talk to him. He set up an appointment. They greeted each other in Cox's office. Mark sat down.

"What can I do for you?" inquired Cox.

"Nothing really. I just came in wanting to talk to you. I wanted to tell you what is going on in my life."

Cox replied, "How is it going?"

"I am getting by. I've got a new nanny called Barbara. She is fun and she is a good nanny, taking care of Cindy. She seems to really love her. I think I may be falling for her myself."

"That's great. You've got to put this behind you."

"I know, and Barbara has been a real help because she is so upbeat. Cindy seems to be adjusting real well."

Cox said, "I'm glad to hear it."

"She is Christian, and I started going to her church, and I find that's helpful. I am converting."

Cox replies, "I can't help you there."

Then Mark asked, "Is there anything going on in the case? Any news?"

"Mark, this is the second time you've asked that. I told you the case was closed. There is nothing new."

Mark said, "Well, I just keep waking up at nighttime thinking of this, sort of like a nightmare."

"Well, the case is closed. You should put it out of your mind."

"Thanks, I'll try to."

With that Mark left.

Cox, puzzled over this visit after Mark Winger left, went to Williamson. "I've never had anyone come in and ask about closed cases that they were involved in. He keeps asking if anything is new. I wonder if there is something that he is worried about. He just wants to pump me for information, and he knows the case is closed. Do you think we missed something?"

Williamson replied, "There are loose ends, the note, the coffee mug, and the cigarettes. We never checked the telephone calls. I know we have nothing to go on with. It was either Mark or Harrington who killed Donnah. Harrington had a psycho history. Everyone said the Wingers had such a good marriage and no criminal history. It really seemed that Harrington did it, but there are loose ends."

Cox replied, "This gives me an uneasy feeling, when a guy comes in and asks me if there is anything new on a closed case. It gives me a bad feeling. I just wonder if there is something that we don't know or if there is something that we missed. Let's go talk to the boss about this. I think maybe we should take a second look at it. See if there is anything we missed. My gut tells me there is something that worries him."

Williamson said, "I am with you. Not checking the telephone records has always bothered me."

They went to the chief of the major case unit. They requested that the case be reopened. "Why?"

"We have a gut feeling that we missed something. Maybe we closed it too soon."

"Got any new evidence?"

"No, can't get it until it's reopened."

"Well, we don't reopen closed cases on gut feelings. We got other work to do."

C. The Harringtons

The Harringtons refused to believe that their child was a murderer. They couldn't believe that Roger would have bludgeoned someone to death. They were working folks and were not college educated, but they knew their son. They had grown up in Springfield and spent all their lives on the north side of town. That's where the factories were at one time. They remember Roger bounding up the steps with a big smile on his face when he would come home. He always seemed to be happy but irresponsible. They loved him. They buried him as a murderer, but they refused to believe he committed a murder.

The impact on their lives was significant. The Harringtons felt isolated from the community. Mrs. Harrington would only go out of the house to shop when she thought she wouldn't meet any of her friends or neighbors. She thought her friends and neighbors saw her as the mother of a murderer. Mr. Harrington quit his job. They became prisoners in their own home. They lost interest in everything that they had been doing. If they went out of the house it would be early in the morning or late in the evening. Their neighbors started worrying about them.

D. The Browns

Cash Brown was the natural father of Donnah. He had remarried. He never really did care for Mark, who he thought was rude, self-centered, and arrogant. Down deep he really didn't approve of the marriage, but because of his love for Donnah he hid his feelings.

Donnah's death came as a complete shock to him, made him think of his life and priorities. He had worked hard and regretted now that he did not spend more time with his children. His daughters, Donnah's sisters, complained that he worked too hard, and after Donnah's death they told him that they needed their dad. He sold his business in Connecticut and moved to Florida so that he could spend more time with his wife and his daughters. His wife watched him grieve. He would stay up at night and wouldn't be able to sleep. He was emotionally wounded. She would get up sometimes and see him sitting in a chair in the early morning hours just looking outside. It seemed a part of him had died. He could not sleep for many nights. It did change his life. He spent more time with his family and regretted not having done so in the past.

CHAPTER 13

DeAnn Schultz

Donnah Winger's death affected DeAnn Schultz more than anyone else, but it did not seem to do so immediately. She was very upset and was crying during the funeral and the burial. Her husband was there to comfort her. The stress of her marriage and her job all seemed to be put on the back burner.

DeAnn and John spent a great deal of time after Donnah's death at Mark Winger's home. This helped her to cope with Donnah's loss. They played games, watched videos, and sometimes DeAnn would go over without John.

In February of 1996, Mark planned a trip to Africa; he and his brother went for about a month. Upon their return in March, Mark did not call DeAnn. She wondered how he was doing. Finally, DeAnn called Mark and he told her that he didn't want to see her anymore; she reminded him too much of Donnah. He had to make a clean break. He sold his current house and moved fifteen miles outside of Springfield.

The stress on DeAnn was overwhelming. Her best friend had been killed. Her husband was supportive, but they didn't have the emotional bond. Her job and family were stressing her more and more. John was working long hours, and DeAnn was tired of all the paperwork she had to do for her job. The more she complained, the more distant John became. There was no intimacy in the marriage, either emotionally or physically. At one time they were over at the Datzes' while Mark and Barbara were there. She drank rather heavily and started to flirt with Mark.

Her headaches had returned. John suggested she see a psychiatrist, and she did so. Something was bothering her, more than just her job and family. No one seemed to know what it was. She switched psychiatrists and went to Dr. John Lauer, a psychiatrist who had extensive experience in treating seriously depressed patients. He started treating her in 1997. He tried every antidepressant known to man. She refused to use certain antidepressants because she said they would make her gain weight. DeAnn appeared to be scared. She was afraid of losing her friends. She was afraid of losing her family. She was afraid of Mark Winger. She was obsessed with Donnah's death, and every time she would hear about Mark or Donnah, she would have anxiety attacks. She was worried that something was going to happen to her. She had to quit her job. She felt she was a burden on her family; she wanted to end it all.

In January 1998, John saw Barbara with Mark at a shopping center with two small children. John said, "It was Mark Winger and Barbara. They had Cindy and another child with them. Did you know they had gotten married?" She did not want to talk about it. She seemed to get more upset.

That evening, she was found unconscious on the floor of the house. An ambulance was called. She was taken to the hospital. She wanted to die; this was her first suicide attempt. She was disappointed that she did not succeed. She was treated in the psychiatric unit. She became worried that Mark might have had something to do with Donnah's death. She had frequent anxiety attacks, and she was always short of breath when she heard about the murder; she felt something might happen to her. She had insomnia, and her migraines were getting worse and more frequent. She wanted to move out of Springfield, but her husband wanted to stay. Her husband was supportive and knew she was going through a rough time. Dr. Lauer wanted to treat her as an inpatient, but she declined. She promised to call him if she felt suicidal again.

She started outpatient therapy but didn't seem to get much better. In March 1998 she called Dr. Lauer. "Dr. Lauer, this is DeAnn. I can't handle it anymore. I can't handle it."

She had her five-year-old son with her. Dr. Lauer got a friend to take care of the child and took her to the hospital. She was continually thinking about suicide. It made more sense for her to die than to continue living. She felt she was a burden on her family. "I will hurt my son more if I continue living." She felt hopeless. Dr. Lauer gave her a series of ECT treatments.

On March 29, 1998, in the evening, while her son and husband were watching a movie on TV, she left the family room and went to her bedroom. She had another overdose. John found her on the floor and took her to the hospital. She could not seem to get over the death of Donnah. Every time she saw or heard anything about Mark Winger, she became short of breath and had anxiety attacks.

She was admitted into the psychiatric unit. She again talked about the death of her best friend. She was discharged with therapy and put in a bridges program.

After discharge, DeAnn got better. However, her headaches started to return, returning with greater severity. On July 1, 1998, she had a severe headache and overdosed because she wanted to sleep. Her daughter called the police, and DeAnn was transported to the emergency room.

Dr. Lauer told her, "DeAnn, I've tried everything I know to do. We have tried every drug and antidepressant that's on the market. We tried ECT, we tried talk therapy . . . what more can I do?'"

DeAnn replied, "I don't know. I just feel like a zombie sometimes."

Dr. Lauer continued, "You have something bothering you, and I haven't been able to find out what it is. You seem obsessed about the death of your close friend. Is there something that you need to tell me?"

DeAnn said, "No."

Dr. Lauer continued, "I can't help you if you don't level with me. The mind does not work that way. I have an obligation to treat you and help get you well. You have an obligation to me. I can only treat you as long as I feel you are cooperative with me. Psychiatry is a two-way street. You need my help, but I also need yours."

"I'm afraid I will lose my husband. I will lose my children, my friends—I can't do that. I will lose everything."

. The conversations are fictional as communications between a doctor and patient are confidential; they are used to dramatize the events.

Dr. Lauer replied, "You'll lose them if you don't tell me. You've had four suicide attempts, and those are real. You would have died unless your family found you. The next time they may not find you in time."

Sobbing, DeAnn replied, "I'll think about it and I'll call you."

"Promise," Dr. Lauer replied.

DeAnn left Dr. Lauer's office. She was more distraught than when she came in; a week or so later she called him up and said that she would like to talk to him.

She came into his office and sat down in the chair. It's a darkened office. He looks at her and says, "Well?"

There was silence.

DeAnn began, "I had an affair with Mark Winger before his wife was killed. I feel guilty. He told me he loved me. I can't live with myself. I have this horrible guilt. Maybe my affair with him had something to do with her death."

"Have you told anyone?"

"No."

"Did you tell the police about the affair?"

"No."

"DeAnn, this guilt is serious. You can't bury this. You'll not get better until you get this out."

"I can't help but think that because of my affair, Donnah was killed. If I tell anyone about it I'll lose my husband, my friends, my children."

"Well, you can't keep this inside. This is destroying you. Tell your husband. If you keep this inside you'll destroy yourself."

Around November of 1998 she went to the hospital because she was having a severe migraine attack. While there, her husband, John, wandered into the emergency waiting room and saw Mark. He hadn't seen him for a long time. He came back to DeAnn and said, "DeAnn, do you know who is here?"

"No. Who?"

"Mark."

DeAnn then froze.

After a few minutes she left with John and went home. She wanted to talk to Mark. She called him on the telephone.

"Mark, this is DeAnn. John saw you at the hospital. I need to talk to you."

"I wanted to talk to you too. You know I've always really cared for you, and I miss you. How are you doing? I miss you. You know things aren't going too well with me and Barbara."

DeAnn replied, "No, Mark. I want to talk to you about Donnah's death. My guilt has been destroying me. How have you lived with yourself?"

"I found Jesus and he has forgiven me."

"Did you have anything to do with Donnah's death?"

"What are you talking about? This guy Roger Harrington bludgeoned her. I don't know what you are talking about."

"I want to know if you had anything to do with causing her death."

"Of course not."

"I want to meet with you. I want to talk to you face-to-face. I told the psychiatrist about our affair, and he said I have to get it out."

"What do you mean you told the psychiatrist?"

"I told him we were having an affair."

"You're kidding! He could tell the police and we could get arrested."

"Mark, I don't know, but you put me through misery. You broke off our relationship when you got back from Africa, and since then you haven't even talked to me or called me. You know I tried to commit suicide four times."

Mark said, "What?"

"I've been hospitalized for depression and suicide attempts."

"Maybe we ought to get together and talk about this."

DeAnn said, "I want to do that. I want to talk to you about Donnah's death."

"I have a lawsuit against Bart Transportation. I can't meet with you in town."

"What do you mean?"

"I filed a lawsuit against Bart, and this could be worth millions for Cindy. But if it came out we were having an affair it would destroy Cindy's chance of recovery."

"I don't know anything about that. You say that you have a lawsuit?"

"Yes. I think they are about ready to settle. I can't meet with you in town because people might see us together and guess what's going on. I could meet with you up in Wisconsin next weekend because I'm going to go up there on business."

"No, I want to meet with you in town. I wouldn't want to go out of town to meet with you."

DeAnn did not go to meet with him. She was scared of meeting with him, alone out of town.

DeAnn decided to tell John, and in December of 1998 she said, "John, this is hard for me to talk about. I have to make a confession to you." She is barely able to speak; she is shaking.

John replied, "I know something is going on. You haven't been the same since Donnah died. You can't work, your migraines are worse, you have multiple suicide attempts. I just don't know what's going on, and whatever it is we have to get it behind us."

"I know. I have been obsessed with my own feelings. I have been very self-centered. I keep thinking that Mark might have killed her. I might have been one of the causes of Donnah's death."

"What in the world are you talking about?"

"Mark Winger and I were having an affair before Donnah's death."

"You're kidding."

"No."

"How could you? She was your best friend!"

"Please, please, don't make me feel more guilty than I already feel. We weren't getting along, we didn't have any emotional attachment, we lacked intimacy. I'm not blaming you. Our marriage wasn't working. Mark saw this and said all the right things to me. I was vulnerable."

"That son of a bitch! He has always been manipulative. He has always been out for himself. How could he do this to Donnah? How could you do this to me?"

"Please, it was a mistake. I can't handle my guilt anymore. I don't know what to do. Mark might have been involved in the death of Donnah."

"Have you told the police?"

"No, Mark threatened me that if I told the police it would look like I had something to do with the murder. I am afraid of him."

John replied, "Well, we'll get you a lawyer. You can't keep this inside."

John called a friend who referred him to Jeff Page, a former assistant state's attorney. Jeff talked to DeAnn and told her that he would try to get her immunity, that he would talk to John Schmidt, the state's attorney.

PART III

Persistence

If we are facing the right direction, all we have to do is keep walking.

~Buddhist Prophet Quote

CHAPTER 14

Behind the Scenes

Detectives Cox and Williamson were not happy campers. They wanted to reopen the case. They had their suspicions. Williamson wondered about the note found on the seat of Harrington's car. Cox was concerned after Winger came to see him two times, allegedly just to chat but really pumping him for information in this closed case. This had never happened to him before. It did not sit right. They asked to reopen the case, but the administration had told them to forget it. "We don't reopen old cases on gut feelings," they were told. "We got other work to do."

Cox attended a course on crime scene reconstruction and blood spatter analysis in Oklahoma, put on by Tom Bevel. He talked to Bevel during a break and described the crime scene. Bevel expressed concern that Winger's statement did not correspond to the physical evidence. Cox went back and asked again to reopen the case. He again was told to forget it.

Shortly thereafter, there had been a change in administration. A new police chief, Harris, had been brought on from the outside. He changed the command structure, and William Pittman was put in charge of the major case division.

Williamson and Cox raised again their concerns. They pointed out that the note in Harrington's car stated a time and address. They pointed out that Bevel thought the scene was inconsistent with Winger's statement. They noted the two visits with Cox, pumping him for information. They got the green light to take the full file to Bevel. They went to the evidence room, and they were told that the records had been checked out to Mike Metnick for the civil suit. They panicked but were able to obtain the file from Metnick. Cox took the records to Bevel in Oklahoma for a limited review.

It was also about this time that DeAnn Schultz learned of the lawsuit against Bart. She called Bart's attorneys and, unknown to Mark Winger or Mike Metnick, met with them and gave a transcribed and sworn statement. Bart's attorneys had also received a preliminary report from Bevel. These were filed in the court in the clerk's office with the case file.

After talking to the police DeAnn called John Nolan, one of the attorneys representing Bart Transportation in the civil suit. Nolan asked, "Who is this?"

"I can't tell you, but I am calling about the Winger suit against Bart Transportation."

"Tell me your name?"

"No. The case is going to be reopened. Don't settle."

This got Nolan's attention.

"Why?"

"The case is going to be reopened. I can't tell you more."

The caller hangs up.

Nolan was puzzled. They are on the verge of making an offer.

DeAnn had called from her home. The law firm had caller ID. Nolan called her back.

"You just called and told us not to settle. I need to know why."

"How did you get my number?"

"Caller ID. I need to talk to you."

After threatening to subpoena her, DeAnn agreed to come in.

"I had an affair with Mark Winger before Donnah died. I told the police that and the case is going to be reopened."

Nolan convinced her to give a sworn statement describing the affair. It was sixty pages long and told of the affair beginning in June of 1995 and ending in February of 1996.

This transcript was filed with a preliminary report by Thomas Breen with the clerk of the circuit court in the suit.

CHAPTER 15

The Reinvestigation—February 1999

After talking to her husband and to Page, DeAnn had a difficult decision to make. She knew she would be a pariah in the community if her affair became public but knew she couldn't live with herself if she did not. She knew she had no choice.

In the first meeting with Jeff Page in February 1999, she agreed to let it all come out. Page said he would talk to John Schmidt, the state's attorney. He wouldn't use her name, but he would make a proffer of what she would say and see if John Schmidt would grant her immunity. She wanted to keep her statements confidential. Page told her that if they did reopen the case she would be called as a witness. Everyone in the community would know of her affair. He wanted her to know that up front. She still agreed.

Jeff Page called John Schmidt.

"John, this is Jeff Page. I want to talk to you about the Winger case. Do you remember that case?"

Schmidt replied, "You bet. That was a case that was closed when the van driver was shot by the husband while he was pummeling his wife to death. I remember it well. The police recently started looking at it again. We might have the wrong guy. What have you got?"

"Well, I got a witness. I would like to make a proffer to you to see if you would grant her immunity."

"She? It's a woman? Why immunity? Is she guilty? Was she involved?"

"No, not from my information, but she is not willing to come forward, unless she can get immunity," Page replied.

"If she is not guilty, she does not need immunity."

"Bottom line—no immunity, no name, no witness."

"Tell me what she can say. I have to know what she will say first."

"She was having an affair with Mark Winger at the time of Donnah's death. She is concerned that Mark Winger might have been involved in Donnah's death."

"Keep going," Schmidt said.

"She had the affair with him from July 1995 to February 1996. It started two months before Donnah was killed."

"Do the police know about this?"

"No, she never told anyone."

"Why is she coming forward now?"

"She is racked by guilt. She has tried to commit suicide four times. Her psychiatrist said she had to let it out."

"So she had an affair . . . helps but not worth immunity. Is that it?"

Page replied, "She said that Winger made a number of statements to her before Donnah died, such as, 'It would be better if Donnah died,' while they were having this affair. They were talking about getting married, and he didn't want to divorce. He told her all she would have to do is find the body. He would be out of town. She said that she refused to go along."

Schmidt replied, "I'm getting interested."

"In talking with her, there is a lot more that she can add . . . what about immunity?" Page asked.

"Again, why would she need immunity if she only had an affair?"

"She won't come forward unless she is granted immunity, simple as that. She said she is not involved in the murder."

"How about use immunity on certain conditions?"

"What are those?"

"One, that she be absolutely truthful and not omit anything. Two, she not be involved in the murder. Three, if I find she has not been absolutely truthful or that she was involved in the murder, I would revoke the immunity, and I will be the sole judge of whether she has been truthful. I want her to understand that."

"I would expect nothing else. Do we have a deal?"

"Let me have someone run the file, see if this will change the reinvestigation. I can't see how it would not."

"I will talk to her. She wants this to be kept as confidential as possible until you agree whether to go forward with it."

"Agreed."

After this phone conversation, Schmidt pulled the file from 1995 and walked into Steve Weinhoeft's office. He asked Steve, a younger member of the State's Attorney's Office, to review the file. "We may have some new evidence coming in. Apparently Winger was having an affair at the time Donnah was killed that no one knew about. I want you to take a look at this file and see what you think of it."

Weinhoeft agreed, but since he was swamped in several other matters and this was a closed case, he didn't get around to looking at it for a couple of weeks. It was, after all, a closed case.

When he started looking through the file he thought, *Oh shit, we might have missed the boat.* There were a number of things that didn't ring true. What stuck out to him was the note saying, "2305 W-View Driver, 4:30." What was the explanation for the note? He became suspicious. Did the police blow the investigation? He noted that Winger was said to have a solid marriage.

He went back to Schmidt's office and told him he thought there were loose ends, and Winger might have gotten Harrington to come to the home so he could kill him. Schmidt told him about the proffer. Schmidt and Weinhoeft both agreed that the case should be reopened. He called Page, and Page gave him DeAnn Schultz's name. Schmidt referred DeAnn Schultz to Cox and Williamson to get her statement and for further investigation. He told Weinhoeft to keep on top of the case.

Schmidt called Cox and talked to him and Williamson. "We have a new witness in the Winger case."

"You mean we missed one?"

"Nope, she did not tell anyone until now. It is DeAnn Schultz. Does that ring a bell?"

Cox said, "Yep, she was one of Donnah's best friends. We talked to her. So what is it she has to add?"

"We have a proffer. She was having an affair with Winger at the time of the murder, and Winger made some incriminating statements to her."

Both Cox and Williamson said, "Oh shit. We suspected something was going on, but we didn't know what. Everyone said that the marriage was rock solid, but it looks like it wasn't. We could not find motive."

Schmidt said, "I want you to give this a fresh look, reopen the investigation, and take it from there. Steve Weinhoeft is to be the liaison with our office."

Cox and Williamson were relieved. They had gotten permission to talk to Bevel about the case, but they needed to reopen the whole investigation. This did it for them. Pittman was informed and told them to go for it. Cox and Williamson said, "We'll get ahold of DeAnn Schultz and get her statement."

Cox said to Williamson, "I talked to DeAnn originally. She didn't say anything about the affair. What has caused her to come forward now?"

"Don't know. I am sure we will find out. She sure adds a new dimension to this case. So much for a really good marriage—Donnah's parents, friends, and neighbors, all wrong."

Cox answered, "Yeah."

Cox and Williamson then set up an appointment to take a statement from DeAnn Schultz at Jeff Page's office on March 4, 1999. She told them the affair started on July 22, 1995, and ended in February 1996. "He said the right things to me, the things I needed to hear." She first met him out of town; she paid for the motel for the first night in Mount Vernon. They continued the affair in Springfield when he returned from Chattanooga. The affair was continuing on August 29, the day of Donnah's death, and continued until February of 1996.

When DeAnn heard about Donnah's murder, she was shocked. "My first thought was that Mark had done it." When asked why, she said, "There were statements Mark had made to me before she died." She recalled that Mark told her, "You know, we could be together if Donnah just died or something happened to her. All you would have to do is find the body, and I would be out of town."

"I said, 'Are you talking about murder? There is no such thing as a perfect murder.' This was right after he got back from his first training session in Chattanooga."

DeAnn continued, "Sometime later he again said that if Donnah just died, we could be together." He also told her several times that he had to get Roger (the driver) into the house. This was after he heard about the ride.

DeAnn continued, "He had called me on August 29 and asked me if I would love him no matter what. I told him yes."

Cox and Williamson were puzzled; they had interviewed her on August 29, and she had not told them of the affair; she had not told them of these statements. Now this is coming out some four years later. It sounded fishy to them.

They needed to corroborate what DeAnn Schultz had told them. They subpoenaed the motel records and found that DeAnn had paid for the first night in Mount Vernon on July 22, and Mark had paid for the second on August 19. They subpoenaed the telephone calls and found that there were 845 minutes of telephone calls between DeAnn Schultz and Mark Winger. They interviewed John Schultz; Tricia Ray and Shane Ray (roommates of Roger Harrington); Amy Jaffee, a friend; the daughter of DeAnn; Candace Boulton, a co-worker; Parker, his boss; and Tom Bevel, the expert on blood spatter.

They interviewed the first nanny. She told them on one occasion John Schultz had called looking for DeAnn. She went outside and looked in the driveway, and DeAnn's car was there. She came back and told John her car was there. She then went and knocked on Mark's bedroom door, and DeAnn came out a little bit later. "I told her that her husband was on the phone and wanted to talk to her." Cox and Williamson reinterviewed the neighbors, but again no one knew that there were any problems with the marriage.

They then talked to Terry Edwards, the former wife of Roger Harrington. She described several incidents where Roger had threatened her. They reinterviewed Susan Collins on January 11, 2000—she was in jail at that time.

They also reinterviewed Jo Datz, Donnah's best friend, thinking if anyone knew anything was going on with the marriage she would. On December 6, 1999, Cox asked her, "And what about this marriage?"

Jo Datz replied, "Donnah was a very open person. She spoke openly about her marriage, and everything seemed perfect. However, about two months before her death, DeAnn Schultz, a good friend, became obsessive, suffocating her relationship with Donnah." Jo Datz went on to say, "It appeared she was trying to move in on Mark and Donnah's life."

She further noted that at the baby shower on August 26, 1995, "DeAnn was glaring at Donnah. After Donnah's death, Mark had told me he missed having a physical relationship and needed a woman's touch." This made her uneasy. She thought that he was making a pass at her.

Mark told Jo Datz he was going to go to Africa in February and taking a female from the office with him; Jo Datz talked him out of that. He went there with his brother for a month in February or March. He bought a large diamond ring for his new nanny. He showed it to her.

Over the years following Donnah's death, she said, "Mark seemed to distance himself from everyone that was Donnah's friend. He also quit the Jewish religion, saying he was becoming a Christian because it was a lot easier. 'I am racked with guilt.' He refused to tell my husband whether or not he was baptized." The relationship between the Datzes and Mark Winger ended on that note.

Cox also interviewed a number of Mark Winger's friends about what he told them about the death of Donnah. There were inconsistencies in his stories, some of which were discounted; however, some seemed significant.

Cox, Williamson, and Graham kept in close contact with Weinhoeft. They received a report from Tom Bevel, noting that Winger's given statements were inconsistent with the physical evidence. They had the blood tested on the clothes but did not do any DNA testing. Bevel's reports were turned over to Weinhoeft. The police were pushing for an indictment.

Belz and Weinhoeft took the case to the Grand Jury on August 23, 2001. This was almost 6 years to the day that Donnah died. It is a simplified proceeding where the prosecution puts on its evidence; and the evidence can be hearsay.

The Grand Jury met in secret. There were only two witnesses, Williamson and Graham. Belz examined Williamson and Weinhoeft examined Graham. They testified as to the note, the statements that Winger made to DeAnn Schultz, the affair, the inconsistencies of the crime scene evidence, and they produced Bevel's report. No one was there to cross examine.

A grand juror asked why the case was not pursued in 1995. Graham replied, "I was not the original officer. He told a believable story. DeAnn Schulz had not come forward yet."

After an hour of testimony, the Grand Jury issued indictments of first degree murder against Mark Winger for the murder of Donnah Winger and Roger Harrington.

Officers went to Steve Weinhoeft; he had a bench warrant issued. On August 23, 2001, Graham and Williamson, in an unmarked police car, and followed by a marked police car with two officers in it, went to Winger's office. They entered the reception room and asked for Mark Winger. He didn't appear. They got more demanding and he appeared. They told him he was under arrest for the murder of Donnah Winger and Roger Harrington. They told him to get down on the floor. He initially refused. They started moving towards him and he got down on the floor. They handcuffed him, read him his rights, belted him in the police car and transported him to jail. He called Thomas Breen from jail.

He was arraigned on August 27, 2001. Thomas Breen was there. Bond was set for ten million dollars. Winger was remanded to the Sheriff. Winger would remain in jail until the conclusion of the trial in June of 2002. A motion for reduction of bond was made. The court denied it.

John Schmidt knew this case was going to take many hours of preparation. The previous investigation had been closed in 1995; there was a lack of evidence. He was not the State's Attorney in 1995. He sure didn't want to miss the boat this time. He took charge of the overall responsibility and assigned John Belz and Steve Weinhoeft to work it up. They had multiple meetings with the police officers, DeAnn Schultz and the other witnesses. They reviewed the prior records. They obtained the deposition of Mark Winger in the civil case against Bart Transportation and the statements of DeAnn Schultz.

They needed to show that Roger Harrington was not dangerous and that he did not bludgeon Donnah. Schmidt hired Dr. Joe Bohlen, a psychiatrist in Springfield, to examine Roger Harrington's records. He went over the statements of Susan Collins. They realized the case was not without its weaknesses; Roger Harrington's conduct in the van, his psychiatric history, his talk of death, his police records and Mark Winger's lack of a criminal record, the initial investigation and not finding him involved in the murder. It was going to be anything but a sure thing.

Steve Weinhoeft was the point man. He lived, slept, and dreamed about it. He thought that the note setting up the meeting with Roger Harrington and the affair with DeAnn tipped the case in their favor. He knew Winger had a competent attorney on the other side. They knew it would be a battle of experts, psychiatrists; specifically Crime Reconstructionist verses Crime Reconstructionist. DeAnn Schultz was not without her problems; deep depression, four suicidal attempts, and coming forward only after she had been dumped. He coordinated the police investigation with the State's Attorney's Office. They had their work cut out for them.

Telephone Records

Susan Collins

COUNTRY SUITES BY CARLSON
7051 McCUTCHEON ROAD
CHATTANOOGA, TN 37421
423-899-2300

WINGER, MARK
US NUCLEAR REGULATORY COMMISSI
2305 WESTVIEW DR
SPRINGFIELD, IL 62704

ACCOUNT: 112785
ROOM: 108
ARRIVE: 8/13/95
DEPART: 8/26/95

DATE	DESCRIPTION	COMMENT	CHARGES	PAYMENTS
8/13/95	LD 12175446464	17:10 01.27 108	3.04	
8/13/95	LD 12177877721	19:24 00.54 108	2.53	
8/13/95	LD 12175850567	20:25 01.06 108	3.04	
8/13/95	ROOM CHARGE	108	58.00	
8/13/95	ROOM SALES TAX	108	4.50	
8/13/95	ROOM TAX	108	2.32	
8/14/95	LD 12175446464	16:28 01.20 108	3.62	
8/14/95	LD 12175446464	16:42 01.19 108	3.62	
8/14/95	LD 12175446464	17:00 08.09 108	13.84	
8/14/95	LD 12175446464	17:36 39.31 108	53.22	
8/14/95	LD 12177877721	19:58 05.57 108	5.09	
8/14/95	ROOM CHARGE	108	58.00	
8/14/95	ROOM SALES TAX	108	4.50	
8/14/95	ROOM TAX	108	2.32	
5/95	LD 12175446464	11:59 04.59 108	6.02	
8/15/95	LD 12175850567	18:27 26.53 108	46.56	
8/15/95	ROOM CHARGE	108	58.00	
8/15/95	ROOM SALES TAX	108	4.50	
8/15/95	ROOM TAX	108	2.32	
8/16/95	LD 13059630120	16:42 01.04 108	3.62	
8/16/95	LD 13059630120	17:16 24.11 108	14.82	
8/16/95	LD 12175850567	18:00 12.52 108	39.39	
8/16/95	LD 12175551212	21:35 01.09 108	1.00	
8/16/95	LD 16185551212	21:37 00.51 108	1.00	
8/16/95	LD 16182427200	21:38 03.23 108	4.38	
8/16/95	LD 12175850567	22:12 58.54 108	32.22	
8/16/95	ROOM CHARGE	108	58.00	
8/16/95	ROOM SALES TAX	108	4.50	
8/16/95	ROOM TAX	108	2.32	
8/17/95	LD 12175446464	07:20 01.32 108	2.82	
8/17/95	LD 13059630120	17:38 22.02 108	13.79	
8/17/95	LD 12175850567	18:01 42.44 108	24.03	
8/17/95	LD 12175446464	20:39 01.38 108	3.04	
8/17/95	ROOM CHARGE	108	58.00	
8/17/95	ROOM SALES TAX	108	4.50	
8/17/95	ROOM TAX	108	2.32	

SUB TOTAL 604.79

Susan Collins

COUNTRY SUITES BY CARLSON
7051 McCUTCHEON ROAD
CHATTANOOGA, TN 37421
423-899-2300

WINGER, MARK
US NUCLEAR REGULATORY COMMISSI
2305 WESTVIEW DR
SPRINGFIELD, IL 62704

ACCOUNT: 112785
ROOM: 108
ARRIVE: 8/13/95
DEPART: 8/26/95

DATE	DESCRIPTION	COMMENT	CHARGES	PAYMENTS
8/18/95	LD 16155551212	16:57 00.50 108	1.00	
8/18/95	LD 12175446464	17:26 40.18 108	23.01	
8/18/95	LD 13059630120	18:12 14.35 108	9.70	
8/18/95	ROOM CHARGE	108	58.00	
8/18/95	ROOM SALES TAX	108	4.50	
8/18/95	ROOM TAX	108	2.32	
8/19/95	ROOM CHARGE	108	58.00	
8/19/95	ROOM SALES TAX	108	4.50	
8/19/95	ROOM TAX	108	2.32	
8/20/95	LD 13059630120	18:40 08.00 108	6.62	
8/20/95	LD 12175446464	18:48 01.40 108	3.04	
8/20/95	ROOM CHARGE	108	58.00	
8/20/95	ROOM SALES TAX	108	4.50	
8/20/95	ROOM TAX	108	2.32	
8/21/95	LD 12175446464	17:24 04.31 108	4.58	
8/21/95	LD 13059630120	17:35 11.25 108	8.16	
8/21/95	LD 12175850567	19:55 47.17	26.59	
8/21/95	ROOM CHARGE	108	58.00	
8/21/95	ROOM SALES TAX	108	4.50	
8/21/95	ROOM TAX	108	2.32	
8/22/95	LD 12175446464	12:01 01.37 108	3.62	
8/22/95	LD 13059630120	18:04 04.37 108	4.58	
8//95	LD 12175850567	18:18 12.34 108	8.67	
8//95	LD 16155551212	20:08 00.53 108	1.00	
8//95	LD 12175850567	21:32 13.11 108	9.18	
8/22/95	ROOM CHARGE	108	58.00	
8/22/95	ROOM SALES TAX	108	4.50	
8/22/95	ROOM TAX	108	2.32	
8/23/95	LD 13059630120	16:31 01.09 108	3.62	
8/23/95	LD 12177877721	16:32 19.43 108	18.02	
8/23/95	LD 12175446464	16:53 01.05 108	3.62	
8/23/95	LD 12175850567	16:55 27.01 108	24.42	
8/23/95	ROOM CHARGE	108	58.00	
8/23/95	ROOM SALES TAX	108	4.50	
8/23/95	ROOM TAX	108	2.32	
8/24/95	LD 12177936452	18:10 01.57 108	3.04	

==============

SUB TOTAL　　　　1,156.18

Susan Collins

COUNTRY SUITES BY CARLSON
7051 McCUTCHEON ROAD
CHATTANOOGA, TN 37421
423-899-2300

WINGER, MARK
US NUCLEAR REGULATORY COMMISSI
2305 WESTVIEW DR
SPRINGFIELD, IL 62704

ACCOUNT: 112785
ROOM: 108
ARRIVE: 8/13/95
DEPART: 8/26/95

DATE	DESCRIPTION	COMMENT	CHARGES	PAYMENTS
???5	LD 12177877721	18:12 24.58 108	14.82	
???5	ROOM CHAREG	108	58.00	
???5	ROOM SALES TAX	108	4.50	
???5	ROOM TAX	108	2.32	
???5	ROOM CHARGE	108	58.00	
???95	ROOM SALES TAX	108	4.50	
???95	ROOM TAX	108	2.32	
???95	AMEX PAYMENT	378775142791004		1,300.64

BALANCE DUE: 0.00

CHAPTER 16

Thursday, December 2, 1999

In Pleasant Plains, December 2, 1999, started as a normal day for Mark and Barbara Winger and their four young children. The newest child was only a few months old. They had gotten up, changed the diapers, and were getting breakfast. Barbara, as she normally does, went to the front door to pick up the newspaper. Mark helped with the children and was getting ready to go to work.

Barbara went outside and got the newspaper. She came back to the kitchen with the paper and opened it. She turned pale and shouted, "Mark! Look at the paper."

The headline on the front page was, "Suit alleges murder plot." Underneath the headline was, "Forensics expert links evidence to cover-up." To the right was a 1994 picture of Mark and Donnah Winger. To the right of that there was another small headline saying, "There was more than one woman in husband's life."

Mark grabbed the newspaper. He started turning red; he was angry. He said, "I never should have filed that wrongful death case. Those sons of bitches are trying to make me out to be a murderer."

Bart's defense attorneys had taken a transcribed statement from DeAnn Schultz without the knowledge of Mark Winger or his attorney. They had obtained an undisclosed report by a forensics expert who examined the crime scene photos. They filed the statements in the clerk's office. Someone called the newspaper and said, "You better take a look at this file." Sarah Antonacci, the reporter who covered the original murder in 1995, went through the court file. There was a report of the forensic expert blaming Mark for the murder. This was a sworn statement of an unknown lady (her name was blacked out); she said she was having an affair with Mark before and after Donnah's murder. She said that Mark had told her that it would be better if Donnah died when she was talking about divorcing her husband and marrying Mark.

Barbara asked, "Mark, who is this woman?"

"It's DeAnn Schultz. You remember her? We were over at the Datzes' in 1996, and she got drunk and started making a pass at me. You remember that, don't you?"

Barbara answered, "I sure do. What is she trying to do? Ruin our lives?"

"She is vindictive and trying to get even with me. She thought I was in love with her and became obsessive. I had an affair with her, but I broke it off after Donnah's death. She became very possessive. She then started drinking heavily. Her marriage had never been really good. She tried to commit suicide three or four times. She blames me."

"Why now?" Barbara asked.

"I saw her in 1998, somewhere around October or November at the hospital. She told me all the problems that she had with her depression and her suicide attempts. She lost her job and was seeing a psychiatrist. She has had all sorts of problems ever since the murder. She tried to call me a couple of times, and I told her to leave me alone. She blamed me for all of her problems."

"Why is she doing this to us?"

"I guess seeing her at the hospital, finding out that I had remarried and had children. Her life had fallen apart. I had got mine back together. She asked about me and how I could go on. I told her that I had found peace through Jesus and was forgiven for the affair. She got angry because I was able to go on with my life and she could not."

Barbara asked, "Did you see that part where the police said they are reinvestigating the case?"

"That's news to me. I was told the case was closed by Detective Cox."

"I'm scared."

"Me too," Mark said.

He was upset and was perspiring, even in December. Barbara, shaking, went to finish breakfast. The kids were wondering what was going on.

"I wonder if the Datzes or Donnah's parents are behind this. They haven't been speaking to me since I changed my religion. You know, we also had that argument with Sarah Jane over what Cindy should call her. I can't believe that they would be behind this."

Mark called in sick.

The reporters called Sara Jane and Ira Drescher to get their reaction on December 3, 1999. "At this point we are just devastated . . . it is extremely upsetting. All we know is that Mark and Donnah had a wonderful marriage. They loved each other dearly, and they cared for each other a lot."

Mark's phone started ringing at home. He didn't answer. He called Mike Metnick and asked him if he had seen the headlines.

Mike responded, "The newspapers have already called me. You should have told me about this affair. That is bad news. What is this about DeAnn's statement?"

"I have no idea."

"Mark, you should get yourself another lawyer. I would not be able to handle it, and you should have told me about your affair. Call the public defender."

Mark says, "Yeah, I'll call my dad."

Mike replied, "If I were you I would contact the public defender."

Mark waited and then called his dad after he is more composed. His dad asked him to send the news articles to him, which he does. He gets back to him.

"Mark, you're in deep trouble."

"I know."

"Why the hell were you having this affair?"

Mark replied, "It's a long story. I'll tell you about it but not on the phone. The public defender recommends a Chicago attorney, Thomas Breen. Please call him"

"Okay. I'll get back to you."

"Yeah, thanks. You know I don't have the money for a criminal lawyer, so if you could help me out. Thomas Breen has been recommended and is top-notch."

"You've got four kids now."

"That's right."

After four or five days, Mark's dad called back.

"Mark, I've talked to Tom Breen. He is a very competent criminal lawyer out of Chicago. We have got to meet with him."

Mark went to Chicago to meet with Thomas Breen and his associate. His father was there. Mark brought his deposition and the newspaper articles; he also brought the autopsy report.

Thomas Breen asked Mark's father to sit out in the waiting room because he didn't want to compromise the attorney-client privilege.

Mark admitted to the affair. He said, "She was having trouble with her marriage. We were very good friends. She was thinking of moving to Minnesota, and Donnah asked me to talk her out of it. She didn't want DeAnn Schultz to move. I was in Chattanooga, taking some courses for my work, and it was a two-week course, and Donnah wanted me to talk to her because DeAnn was thinking of moving in the next week. I called her and told her I was in Chattanooga and I could meet her halfway in Mount Vernon. We agreed to meet on the Saturday when I got a break at this course.'"

Mark continued, "She was very unhappy with her marriage. We had dinner together and drank some wine, probably too much. She did not feel she should drive, so she got a room and I stayed with her. I guess I was a little drunk too. We had sex that night. I was under a lot of tension at home too, with a new child. Donnah was so focused on Cindy I got depressed and I needed someone to talk to. I knew I shouldn't have continued this, but I just couldn't stop. After Donnah died, I needed someone to hold on to. We both sort of needed each other.

"I finally realized that this was going to go nowhere, and I broke it off after my trip to Africa. My brother went with me and we talked. He helped me get my head on straight. He advised me to have a clean break."

"How did she react?"

"At first I thought she took it well, but then she became quite bitter. Sometime around November 1998, I saw John at Doctor's Hospital when I was taking a child in for flu shots. Actually, I didn't see DeAnn, but I knew she was there, and she knew I was there. She called me and wanted to meet. I told her I couldn't do that and then told her of the civil suit. She told me she had tried to commit suicide three or four times, that she had lost her job, and was extremely depressed. She kept blaming me for this. She sounded bitter. I told her I married Barbara, and we had three children and adopted Cindy. She asked me how I could put it behind me. I told her I found Jesus. She was angry."

"Did you know anything about her statement to Bart's attorneys?"

"No."

"Well, I want to get some things straight with you before I agree to help."

---

* All of these conversations are fictional. Because of attorney-client privilege, Breen was unable to talk to me.

"Okay."

Breen told Winger that the state had a forensics expert. He said that there would likely be an indictment, and Mark would be charged with the murders. It would probably take a year or more to prepare a case once an indictment was issued. They would need to hire experts, and it would be very expensive.

"You have given your deposition and that will be very damaging. You've given a statement to the police. No more statements, not to anyone—your dad, your brother, your friends—do you understand?"

"Yes."

"We may or may not want you to testify at the trial. You have the right not to testify. We'll have to play that by ear as the trial goes along. My inclination now is that you've given enough statements."

Breen was hired.

Newspaper
Articles
December 2, 1999

THE STATE

ournal Register

THE OLDEST NEWSPAPER IN ILLINOIS

THURSDAY
DECEMBER 2, 1999

Suit alleges murder plot

Forensics expert links evidence to cover-up

By SARAH ANTONACCI and JEFFERSON ROBBINS
STAFF WRITERS
© The State Journal-Register

On Aug. 29, 1995, Springfield nuclear engineer Mark Winger became a victim — first witnessing his wife's violent death and then firing two fatal shots at her alleged killer.

More than four years later, court documents in a civil lawsuit point toward Winger as something more: a husband who allegedly cheated on his wife, hunted he could

See LAWSUIT on page 6

There was more than one woman in husband's life

By JEFFERSON ROBBINS
STAFF WRITER

When he investigated the murder of Donnah Winger, Springfield police detective Charles Cox seemed moved by husband Mark Winger's grief.

"It was very apparent that he and his wife were very much in love and that this should have never happened," Cox wrote in his formal report on the case.

But court records on Donnah Winger's 1995 death by bludgeoning

indicate an eight-year marriage that wasn't what it seemed.

This sketch of the Wingers' relationship is drawn from a deposition given by Mark Winger and a sworn statement from an unnamed woman who claimed an affair with him during his marriage, in the months leading up to Donnah's murder. Both documents were filed by defense attorneys in

See AFFAIR on page 6

A 1994 photograph of Mark and Donnah Winger.

FIGHTING ABOUT TRADE

U.S. suffers black eye over 'circus'

LAWSUIT

From page 1

arrange her death and perhaps even used a delusional man as the patsy in a double-murder scheme.

Winger was never arrested or charged with wrongdoing in the death of his wife, Donnah, 31, who was beaten with a hammer at their home in the 2300 block of Westview Drive.

She was allegedly attacked by Roger Harrington, 27, a driver for a Missouri shuttle-bus company who had driven Donnah Winger home to Springfield after a flight into St. Louis, and had apparently become obsessed with her. Mark Winger then shot Harrington in the head with a pistol.

After the dust settled from the criminal probe, with Winger cleared by police and prosecutors, he filed a wrongful-death lawsuit against Bootheel Area Rapid Transportation, the bus company that hired Harrington. In documents placed on file Wednesday in that case, attorneys for BART point to a sworn statement and a forensics analysis that cast Winger in the role of a calculating killer.

Winger's attorney Wednesday denied the allegations.

"A civil lawsuit never would have been filed had we not, based on the investigation that the city of Springfield Police Department did, believed that Mark Winger is absolutely and totally innocent and had nothing to do with the death of his wife or Mr. Harrington," said lawyer Michael Metnick.

★ ★ ★

On Aug. 23, 1995, Harrington drove Donnah Winger and her adopted infant daughter home to Springfield after her flight into Lambert Airport. During the drive, Harrington reportedly described "wild sex and drug parties" at his rural Sangamon County home and drove recklessly at speeds up to 85 mph, according to police. The van dropped her off at her house.

Mark Winger was in Tennessee on business until Aug. 26. When Donnah called Mark the day before he got home, he advised her to write down her account of the incident — a note police found pinned to the refrigerator the day of Donnah's murder.

A female neighbor staying with Donnah allegedly received a disturbing phone call from a man speaking in a monotone voice. She asked police to make periodic checks on the house.

Mark Winger called BART Transportation from Tennessee, asking to file a complaint against the driver, then called again after returning to Springfield Aug. 26. A second disturbing phone call allegedly came that day.

On Aug. 26, BART's owner called Harrington and suspended him from driving.

Harrington asked the owner to give Mark Winger his home number, and Winger called Harrington Aug. 29, telling him he would not press charges if Harrington would leave the family alone. According to Winger's statements to police, Harrington spoke strangely, as if answering questions from a third party on the telephone line.

That day, Mark came home about 3:40 p.m. with Donnah arriving soon after. Mark said he saw a hammer left out on the kitchen table by Donnah — a reminder to hang up a wall-mounted coat rack she'd bought him.

He said he went to the basement to exercise on a treadmill, then heard a bumping upstairs.

File/The State Journal-Register
Barbara Rondileman carries 3-month-old Bailey from the crime scene. The Wingers had adopted her in June 1995.

Fearing the worst, he grabbed his .45-caliber pistol as he came up and found Harrington standing over a prone Donnah in the front room, beating her in the head with the hammer.

Winger fired two shots, striking Harrington in the head. Both Harrington and Donnah Winger died at Memorial Medical Center about 3:40 p.m.

Harrington's death was dubbed a justifiable homicide by a Sangamon County coroner's jury, and the lead investigator, Springfield police detective Charles Cox, said there was no sign of foul play beyond Harrington's apparent murderous psychosis.

"There is nothing to indicate anything other than what the husband had described," Cox told the coroner's jury in September 1995.

★ ★ ★

Mark Winger filed his wrongful-death suit against BART in December 1995, charging the company should not have hired Harrington as a driver. The case has dragged through motions and counter-motions up to the present day.

Springfield police sought added forensic analysis in the case earlier this year, and lawyers with the Hinshaw and Culbertson law office of Springfield gathered depositions and statements as attorneys for BART.

Many of the allegations made against Winger in the civil lawsuit are based on a report compiled by forensics expert Tom Bevel of Oklahoma, who believes that the deaths of Donnah Winger and Harrington were "a staged, domestic, homicide by the husband" and that Harrington's murder "was used to explain Donnah's death."

Bevel, who has 27 years law-enforcement experience and has written a textbook about bloodstain-pattern analysis, said in his report that the evidence is not consistent with the story Mark Winger told police.

"It is my opinion that Mark Winger hired Harrington to the scene," Bevel wrote.

After Harrington placed his coffee mug, cigarettes and lighter on the table, Mark Winger held

the gun on Harrington and ordered Harrington to his knees close to the note (the one Donnah had written about Harrington's alleged behavior on the bus trip) on the refrigerator. Harrington was shot once in the top of the head. After Harrington fell to the floor, he was shot in the forehead.

Bevel believes Donnah heard the shots and came into the living room, where she was attacked with the hammer by her husband. He said he thinks Mark began to assault his wife before she ever saw Harrington on the floor, accounting for the distance between their bodies.

The blood spatters and trails on the wall and ceiling and on Mark's clothes prove that, Bevel says, noting also that none of Donnah's blood was found on Harrington's clothing.

Bevel, who is now working for Hinshaw and Culbertson, was originally asked earlier this year by the Springfield Police Department to look into the case.

"There's always been some kind of ... just some unanswered questions," said Cmdr. Bill Pittman, head of the department's investigation division. "The detectives on the case have never been satisfied on the way it was concluded in the beginning and have continually researched the evidence and reviewed statements from witnesses."

In January of this year, he said, Springfield police asked Bevel to look at some of the evidence.

"That's about all I can say," Pittman said. "I don't believe anybody was capable at that level of doing the stuff we thought needed to be done. I knew we didn't have the expertise locally and we had to find the experts to do it. There was some advice we needed."

In 1995, Pittman said, there simply was not enough evidence to continue the investigation. He said the evidence police had collected pointed to a "justifiable homicide" and that police worked the case for three days before presenting it to the state's attorney's office. It was the state's attorney's office that determined the case was complete.

Pittman would not say if police now consider Mark Winger a suspect in either or both of the deaths. But the case is active once again.

"We don't know if there will be charges in this case," he said. "We're actively investigating the case and reviewing the evidence and statements, and we've been continually working with the state's attorney's office on the case."

★ ★ ★

Aside from forensic studies, defense attorney John Nolan took a sworn statement from a woman friend of the Wingers who claims she began an affair with Mark Winger in the months before the killings. In her statement, she claimed Winger wanted to leave his wife and paraphrased him as saying, "It would be easier if Donnah died."

Metnick said if the woman knew of Mark Winger's culpability, she should have told police at the time.

"The statement is dated Nov. 9, 1999," he said. "If Mark Winger would have made these statements, why didn't she go forward to the police on Aug. 29, 1995, or Sept. 1 1995? This is four years later. Are we to say that this woman has just been quiet for four years? I really would question that, and she's not even making the statement to the police, apparently. She's making it to an attorney."

In her statement, the woman said Mark Winger warned her she could go to jail if she told police he might have had a role in the deaths.

Sarah Antonacci can be reached at 788-1529 or santonacci@sj-r.com. Jefferson Robbins can be reached at 788-1524 or robbins@sj-r.com.

WINGER

From page 1

coming from upstairs. He went upstairs, grabbed his gun, saw Harrington beating Donnah with a hammer and shot Harrington, killing him.

Though no criminal charges were filed, civil lawsuits have ensued.

Mark Winger sued BART in 1995, charging that the company should never have hired Harrington and should be held responsible for his actions. A motion filed by BART's attorneys Wednesday asks that Winger be held in contempt of court and forced to submit to a deposition before a Sangamon County judge.

Winger also sued Roger Harrington's estate, and on Wednesday, Harrington's family filed a mirror lawsuit against Winger, who has since remarried and now lives in Pleasant Plains.

On Thursday, the Harrington family's attorney, Randall Wolter, held a press conference, though he said new Illinois Supreme Court rules limit what attorneys can say about their cases. He did say the Harrington family hopes to resolve several issues by seeking legal redress.

"As you can imagine, this has been a nightmare since the first reports came out about it four years ago," Wolter said.

At the time the story unfolded, Harrington was painted as psychotic. At a coroner's inquest, Springfield police detective Charlie Cox testified he was told Harrington heard the voice of someone called "Dahm" who told him to murder and commit other crimes.

"The [Harringtons] are not aware of any mental problems," Wolter said. "He was always nonviolent. They are very straight-forward and down-to-earth people, and no matter what the outcome, this was a horrible event."

He also said the Harringtons are entitled to some sort of financial compensation, though they are more concerned with finding out what really happened.

"I'm sure this is something the Harringtons think about every day," Wolter said. "It's been such a nightmare they will stop looking at the Harringtons and their son as if they are some strange people. I can't tell you if they'd take monetary damages, and if they did, what they'd do with it."

In the lawsuit, the Harringtons are seeking at least $105,000. Wolter said he has not checked into what, if any, of Winger's assets they'd have access to.

According to a deposition Mark Winger gave in 1997 in the BART case, he received about $150,000 in a life insurance claim he made on Donnah's death. He was the sole beneficiary.

The insurance policy was held through USAA of San Antonio, a company that primarily serves members of the U.S. military and their families. Mark Winger is a graduate of Virginia Military Institute who served two years in the U.S. Army.

At the time of her death, Winger testified, Donnah also held about 300 shares of New York Times stock. She left no will.

Cmdr. Bill Pittman of the Springfield Police Department's investigations division said Thursday police had nothing new to say about the case except that they are continuing a criminal investigation that was resurrected earlier this year.

Pittman said Wednesday that in 1995, there simply was not enough evidence to continue the probe. He said the evidence police had collected then pointed to Harrington's death as a "justifiable homicide."

Sarah Antonacci can be reached at 788-1529 or santonacci@sj-r.com. Jefferson Robbins can be reached at 788-1524 or robbins@sj-r.com.

Ted Schurter/The State Journal-Register
Attorney Randall Wolter represents Roger Harrington's family.

CHAPTER 17

The Grand Jury

Belz and Weinhoeft took the case to the grand jury on August 23, 2001. This was almost six years to the day that Donnah died. It is a simplified proceeding where the prosecution puts on its evidence, and the evidence can be hearsay.

The grand jury met in secret. There were only two witnesses, Williamson and Graham. Belz examined Williamson, and Weinhoeft examined Graham. They testified as to the note, the statements that Winger made to DeAnn Schultz, the affair, and the inconsistencies of the crime scene evidence, and they produced Bevel's report. No one was there to cross-examine.

A juror asked why the case was not pursued in 1995. Graham replied, "I was not the original officer. He told a believable story. DeAnn Schulz had not come forward yet."

After an hour of testimony, the grand jury issued indictments of first-degree murder against Mark Winger for the murder of Donnah Winger and Roger Harrington.

Immediately following, the officers went to Steve Weinhoeft; he had a bench warrant issued. Graham and Williamson jumped in an unmarked police car and, followed by a marked police car with two officers in it, went to Winger's office. They entered the reception room and asked for Mark

Winger. He didn't appear. They got more demanding and he appeared. They told him he was under arrest for the murder of Donnah Winger and Roger Harrington. They told him to get down on the floor. He initially refused. They started moving toward him, and he got down on the floor. They handcuffed him, read him his rights, belted him in the police car, and transported him to jail. He called Thomas Breen from jail.

He was arraigned on August 27, 2001. Thomas Breen was there. Bond was set for ten million dollars. Winger was remanded to the sheriff. Winger would remain in jail until the conclusion of the trial in June of 2002. A motion for reduction of bond was made. The court denied it.

John Schmidt knew this case was going to take many hours of preparation. The previous investigation had been closed in 1995; there was a lack of evidence. He was not the state's attorney in 1995. He sure didn't want to miss the boat this time. He took charge of the overall responsibility and assigned John Belz and Steve Weinhoeft to work it up. They had multiple meetings with the police officers, DeAnn Schultz, and the other witnesses. They reviewed the prior records. They obtained the deposition of Mark Winger in the civil case against Bart Transportation and the statements of DeAnn Schultz.

They needed to show that Roger Harrington was not dangerous and that he did not bludgeon Donnah. Schmidt hired Dr. Joe Bohlen, a psychiatrist in Springfield, to examine Roger Harrington's records. Schmidt went over the statements of Susan Collins. He realized the case was not without its weaknesses—Roger Harrington's conduct in the van, his psychiatric history, his talk of death, his police records and Mark Winger's lack of a criminal record, the initial investigation, and not finding him involved in the murder. It was going to be anything but a sure thing.

Steve Weinhoeft was the point man. He lived, slept, and dreamed about it. He thought that the note setting up the meeting with Roger Harrington and the affair with DeAnn tipped the case in their favor. He knew Winger had a competent attorney on the other side. They knew it would be a battle of experts—specifically blood expert versus blood expert—and psychiatrists. DeAnn Schultz was not without her problems—deep depression, four suicidal attempts, and coming forward only after she had been dumped. He coordinated the police investigation with the State's Attorney's Office. They had their work cut out for them.

CHAPTER 18

March 2002—Final Preparation

Several months before the trial, John Schmidt pulled together those he asked to assist on the case—First Assistant John Belz, who had worked as a public defender and then as a first assistant state's attorney, and Steve Weinhoeft, an assistant who had played a major part in putting the case together.

Schmidt would head the team; he had been a prosecutor for twenty years and was elected to successive terms as state's attorney. He had tried many major felony cases, including murder cases. Schmidt called Weinhoeft and Belz to his office to plan their strategy and to talk about the strengths and the weaknesses of the case. Weinhoeft said, "We should start with Winger calling Harrington to come over to his house. If we can show that he got him to come to the house, we can show a setup. If we can show he set it up, we can show a murder."

Schmidt agreed. "That has been my thinking also. If we can prove that Winger lured Harrington to the house to kill him, we have premeditated murder."

The first witnesses would be Duffy, Collins, and Ray. The last two were at the trailer when Winger called Harrington on the twenty-ninth.

Schmidt asked, "Did they actually see him write the note?"

Belz answered, "No, they did not. They were there when he got the phone call, and then he left at 3:20 p.m. saying he was going to Winger's home."

"What kind of witness is Collins?"

Weinhoeft responded, "We could have done better. She is in jail on a charge of possession and has a prior conviction of deceptive practices. She has felony convictions. She has smoked marijuana and has used cocaine. She is not an ideal witness."

"Do we need her?"

"Sure do. She can testify to the phone call and to Harrington leaving to meet Winger. She is critical."

Schmidt replied, "We have to take the witnesses as we find them. What about DeAnn Schultz?"

Weinhoeft said, "I have spent a lot of time working with her. She is also not an ideal witness because of her affair with a best friend's husband both before and after the murder. Winger dumped her for the nanny. After that, she fell apart, attempted suicide multiple times, had serious depression and an ECT after the murder. When she got dumped, she started going downhill and was drinking. She lost her job and has been divorced."

"How is she now?"

Weinhoeft replied, "She stopped drinking and has a job as a playground supervisor at a grade school. She is still fragile."

Schmidt asked, "Do you think she can hold up on cross?"

"Don't know. She is credible. Her doctor told her that unless she came forward she would never get well, and she has. She seems to be getting better. Some of the cops think she was more involved than she says."

Schmidt then added, "Got rid of her guilt and the truth has made her whole."

Weinhoeft responded, "Not whole but much better. That seems to be the case. She still has this feeling of guilt. She thinks that she might be one of the causes of Donnah's death, the affair and all that. She was afraid to come forward before. She thought her whole life would be over, lose her friends, family, etc. She was scared of Winger. The doctor persuaded her to come forward. It took courage to come forward."

"What about waiting three and a half years to come forward?"

"She fell apart and tried to commit suicide four times. The doctor said that's it—he wasn't going to treat her anymore unless she leveled with him."

"Did she ever say that she knew who did it?"

"Never said he did it. That gives her some credibility. But there is also the problem that she went to Bart to try to sabotage any settlement with Winger. That makes her look vindictive. She gave them a sworn statement."

Schmidt continued, "Harrington is a real weird kid. I have had a psychiatrist that has looked at his records. He doesn't think he's dangerous but says a lot of strange things and has had some bizarre behavior."

Belz asked, "What about threatening to kill people and torture people, etc.?"

"That's a problem. He has said these types of things, but he was saying them to try to impress his therapist. He never did any of these things. He was not homicidal—he was schizotypal."

"What about the criminal record with his ex-wife and sister's boyfriend?"

"The psychiatrist will testify that the only time he got violent was when it was with a person that he was close to. Again we don't have an ideal witness here, but we've got to take them as we find them. Everyone that Roger lived with says he was a nice kid with a lot of problems. Breen's going to have fun."

Schmidt asked, "Are there any good witnesses in this case?"

Belz and Weinhoeft replied, "The cops should hold up. Cox will say that they closed the case too soon. Williamson always had his doubts about

Winger's story, but all the witnesses said it was a strong marriage. No one knew about DeAnn Schultz at the time. She puts a whole new light on the case."

Schmidt asked, "Where is the motive?"

"Passion, the hots for DeAnn, he wanted his own children, money. We don't have to prove motive. It would sure help if we could. He wanted a divorce but didn't want to pay alimony. Who knows?" they replied.

Weinhoeft had been the point man in the investigation. He spent days with Cox, Williamson, and Graham. He spent hours with DeAnn Schultz. He went over the voluminous files of the 1995 investigation.

Schmidt told Weinhoeft, "Spend the rest of your time prepping DeAnn, then Bevel. Learn everything you can about the blood spatter. You take Bevel, and then you cross their expert. Think Bevel will hold up?"

"He should. He has a lot of experience in testifying," Weinhoeft replied.

"John and I will do the crime scene and the other witnesses. I will handle the psychiatrist. I will open. John, you close. I will do the rebuttal, okay?"

Both responded, "Got you."

How could they convince the jury that Mark Winger, an intelligent person, a major in physics, a veteran, and a man with no prior history of violence, could possibly do such a crime? He was arrogant and smart. What was his motive? Was DeAnn vindictive? Mark with four small children was apparently a good dad.

The meeting ended; they felt they had a good case but not a sure thing. There was not going to be a plea; Winger claimed he was innocent.

"Let's go to work," Schmidt said.

PART IV

The Trial

Murder may pass unpunished for a time, but tardy justice
will overtake the crime.

~Dryden, "The Cock and the Fox"

CHAPTER 19

Picking the Jury

At 9:00 a.m., Monday, May 13, 2002, almost seven years after the murder of Donnah Winger and the death of Roger Harrington, the trial began. It was held at the Sangamon County Building, a seven-story brick building containing three floors of courtrooms, the Sangamon County Jail, and other county offices.

Judge Leo Zappa's courtroom is on the sixth floor; it is the only secure courtroom. Prospective jurors had been summoned; seventy to eighty jurors were present. Also present was the state, led by John Schmidt; the defendant's attorneys, led by Thomas Breen; numerous deputy sheriffs, and the defendant. The families of Mark Winger were sitting in the first row behind the defense; the families of Roger Harrington and Donnah Winger were sitting behind the prosecution. The courtroom was crowded with press and spectators.

As Judge Zappa entered the courtroom, the bailiff called for everyone to rise. Zappa took his seat on the bench and welcomed the jurors and thanked them for coming in to perform their civic duty. The attorneys eyed the prospective jurors, trying to get a feel for them. Did they seem to be looking forward to this, or did they seem to be dreading it? First impressions could be important.

Judge Zappa read an agreed statement of the case—that the case involved a double murder, and he gave the names of the parties and the witnesses. He asked if anyone in the jury pool knew any of these parties or the witnesses. Several raised their hands, and they were excused.

The attorneys were pouring over the jury questionnaires as the judge told prospective jurors, "This case could last two to three weeks. Is there anything that would prevent you from sitting on the jury for two to three weeks?" Several of the jurors raised their hands again—several young mothers, several elderly with medical problems, people who had committed to vacations. They also were excused. He then asked if there were any physical impairments that would prevent any jurors from hearing the case. He asked if they or members of their families worked for law enforcement; those that said yes were also excused.

Judge Zappa continued, "This is a high-profile case. Those that are selected will be ordered not to listen to the TV or read the papers pertaining to the case." The judge then read the charges against Mark Winger.

The jurors were called by number, randomly selected in panels of four. As they came forward, the attorneys again closely watched them. Did they seem open? Did they seem that they would take their duties seriously? Did they seem anxious to serve or too anxious? How did they look? Were they casually dressed or buttoned up and carefully dressed, etc.? What was their body language?

The judge initially questioned the panels and said, "The case involves double murders. Sometimes the testimony and exhibits may be graphic." He asked them if they knew about the case or had formed any judgments about the facts of the case. He asked them if there was anything in their background that would prevent them from being objective, fair, and a conscientious juror. As usual every juror thought that he or she could be fair.

Zappa turned to John Schmidt; Schmidt questioned the jurors, one at a time. Did they have any criminal record? Had they served on a jury before and was it civil or criminal? What clubs or groups did they belong to? Would they listen to the testimony? What books do they read or what TV programs do they watch? Many more questions were asked to determine the jurors' underlying characters. Schmidt wanted to get an educated jury, one who could analyze the facts of the case. "If the evidence shows that Mark Winger was guilty beyond a reasonable doubt, would you convict him? Even if he had remarried and had four young children, would you base your decision on the facts and not sympathy, etc.?" After the panel of four jurors was accepted by the state, Breen then had his chance to question them. Breen wanted a male jury, but the prosecution wanted a female jury.

Breen asked, "Would they be more likely to convict if they learned that the defendant had an affair at the time of the murder?" A juror raised her hand and asked to speak to the judge in private. The judge directed the bailiff to bring the juror to his office, and the attorneys went into the chambers with the judge. Judge Zappa asked what the issue was. She said that her former husband had an affair. She said, "I may have a hard time with this."

Judge Zappa excused her, saying, "I appreciate your candor."

The jury and attorneys returned. Mr. Breen resumed questioning. He asked each juror, "You understand that in a criminal case, the state has to prove its evidence beyond a reasonable doubt?"

Each juror nodded their heads yes.

"Do you understand that beyond a reasonable doubt means more than you think the defendant is guilty?"

"You understand that the defendant does not have to prove anything, that the burden is upon the state to prove guilt beyond a reasonable doubt. The defendant is by law presumed innocent through all of the trial?" Some looked as if this was legal mumbo jumbo, but the jurors again nodded their heads in agreement.

"There will be several police officers testifying. Because they are police officers would you give any more weight to their testimony than you would to someone who is not a police officer?"

He continued, "Would you listen to evidence and not form a decision until you had heard from the defense? The state puts its evidence, and the defendant is at a disadvantage. You hear what the state is saying, but you don't have a chance to hear the defendant's until they rest. Could you hold off making a decision until the defendant puts on his case?"

Each juror said yes.

"The verdict has to be unanimous. If you do not believe that the state has proven its case beyond a reasonable doubt, would you vote to acquit even if all the other jurors believe him guilty?"

Each juror said yes.

Many more questions were asked, and finally a jury of four men, eight women, and four alternates were selected.

The judge swore in the jurors, saying, "Stay away from the media. Do not read newspapers or watch TV or listen to the radio as it pertains to this case. The evidence that is presented in this case is in this courtroom. It is not on TV, and it is not in the newspapers. I want to have a commitment from each of you that you will not listen to TV or read the newspapers about the case while this case is ongoing. If you want to read the newspapers, have someone cut out the articles on the case before you read it. Do not discuss the case with anyone. Each day of trial, I will ask you if you have done so."

The jury selection had taken two days. After the jurors left the courtroom, Mark Winger was handcuffed and led back to the Sangamon County Jail.

CHAPTER 20

Opening Statements

On May 20, 2002, the case was finally called for trial. The jury had reassembled. The courtroom was packed again with the families of Mark Winger, sitting behind him, and the families of Donnah Winger, sitting behind the state's attorney's table. Winger was seated at the defense table, dressed in slacks and an open shirt. The jury was sworn in by the bailiff.

"Ladies and gentleman, I asked you last week, when you were selected, not to read, watch TV, or talk about the case with anyone. Has anyone done so?"

No one responded.

"Good."

Zappa repeated, "If you want to watch TV or read the newspapers, ask someone to videotape the TV or clip out the newspaper articles. Stay away from the news stories of this trial."

"During the course of the trial you can take notes. Put your name on the outside of the envelope in which your notes are contained. They will be collected from you when you leave the jury room. Use your memory and notes. Do not talk to anyone about the trial or the testimony until the trial is over. The only evidence you are to base your decision on is that produced in this courtroom. Do you all understand what I am saying?"

The jurors nodded that they understood.

"Okay. Now that we got that out of the way, Mr. Schmidt, are you ready?"

Schmidt answered, "Yes, sir."

Schmidt was a big man with a booming voice. He walks to the jury box, about five to ten feet from it. He opens with his central theme, using no notes.

"Opening statements are used to show what we intend to prove, and we will prove that on August 29, 1995, the defendant, Mark Winger, beat his wife to death with a hammer and shot Roger Harrington twice in the head in his home at 4305 Westview Drive. He called 911 and said that 'an intruder has beaten his wife and I shot him. I don't know who this intruder is.' The police responded as did the paramedics and the firemen. What they saw were two bodies in the dining room area—that of Roger Harrington with two bullets in his head, lying face up, and that of Donnah Winger, who had been bludgeoned and was lying on her stomach six to eight feet away. They were still alive at the scene. They both are pronounced dead a half hour later after being transported to Memorial Medical Center.

"This is a brutal, premeditated, and vicious crime," Schmidt said. "There are three pools of blood on the floor. Blood spatter is on the south wall, the ceiling, and on the carpeting. The police interviewed Mark Winger. He said he did not know who the male was—he lied. He had told Roger that he wanted to meet him at his home. He invited him over to his house to shoot him. And he did. He then bludgeoned his wife and tried to blame Roger for it. He lied to the police, and the evidence will show that he set up these murders.

"Harrington received a call the day before the murder from Bart Transportation, his employer, after Winger complained about the ride his wife had had from St. Louis. Harrington was told that until he got the complaint resolved, 'You will not be working anymore.'

"On the morning of the murder, August 29, at 9:07 a.m., Mark Winger called Roger Harrington. He told him he wanted to meet with him. Roger Harrington made a note of this call. Roger wanted his job back and went to Winger's home."

Schmidt then described Harrington. "He was schizotypal but not dangerous. He was odd and he spoke inappropriately. But the evidence will be that he was not a psychotic killer. He was not a raging lunatic. He was lured to 4305 Westview by the defendant. He had a perfect patsy and lured Roger to his home so he could blame Roger for the death of his wife.

"Winger told Cox he shot Roger Harrington twice, two times, one shot following the other—he lied. The second shot was when Harrington was on his back. It went straight through his forehead into the floor. After the first shot he called 911. Harrington was groaning. Winger hung up and shot him again. He wanted to make sure he was dead. Dead men tell us no tales.

"So why didn't we arrest him in 1995? We had no evidence that Mark Winger wanted his wife dead. The evidence at that time was that he was a good husband and had a loving marriage. They were just adopting a child. There was not enough evidence at that time.

"After the case was closed, Winger had asked Cox twice if there was anything new on this closed case. Cox never had anyone do that before. Cox became suspicious. Well, what evidence was there to reopen it? Williamson wanted to check the telephone records but was not given the authority to do so. They had their suspicions. The head of the major crimes division said that we don't open cases on suspicions. The case remained closed."

"Then there was a change of administration in late 1998, and the detectives Cox and Williamson were allowed to take a second look at it. Cox took a course on blood spatter by Tom Bevel. The spatter was inconsistent with Winger's statement. About the same time, DeAnn Schultz came forward and told of her affair with Winger. She was thinking of leaving her husband. Donnah told Mark. Mark, knowing that she was vulnerable, called DeAnn and wanted to meet with her. On July 22, 1995, the affair began. There was intensity and passion. They had sex together in motels, in the cars, etc. They spoke on the telephone numerous times when Mark was out of town. They met twice in Mount Vernon, and they met numerous times in Springfield. They talked about divorcing their various spouses. Winger said that it would be a lot easier if Donnah died. He wanted out of the marriage but did not want to divorce. He said that all DeAnn would have to do was find the body. He said this several times. He continued to talk about Donnah dying. Then a perfect opportunity came along. Donnah had a ride with Roger Harrington on August 23, 1995. He talked of spirits, of killing people, that this spirit told him what to do, etc. Mark told Donnah to write it down. Then he told DeAnn that he had to get Roger into the house. Winger jumped on the opportunity. On August 29, 1995, Roger Harrington came to the house, and then Donnah and Roger Harrington were both killed, Mark telling the police that Roger was hammering his wife to death and he shot Harrington. That was a lie. Roger had never been violent towards third persons.

"This affair lasted until February of the next year, Mark broke it off. DeAnn had not told anyone about this affair or their conversations. Winger told her that it would look like she was involved. He scared her. In late 1998 she told her doctor of her affair after three suicide attempts. She then told her husband. He told her she needed an attorney. She went to an attorney who contacted us. She is testifying under a grant of immunity. She will testify as to her affair and to a number of incriminating statements that were made by Mark Winger.

"Mark Winger said he shot Harrington twice in rapid succession. The evidence will show that statement was a lie. On the 911 call he said that the baby is crying and then hung up. You will not hear the baby crying on the 911 tape. Lauralee Smith, who lived next door, will tell you that she was unloading her kids from the car at the time, and she only heard one shot. As Winger told DeAnn, dead men can't tell tales. He made sure of that. Winger said Harrington rolled over off of Donnah. That was a lie. Harrington was in the kitchen when he was shot.

"A trial is somewhat like painting a picture or a puzzle. One part comes in, and then another, and then finally the whole picture is there. In this case you will hear from Tom Bevel, who will testify that the murders could not have happened as Winger said. The blood on the wall was inconsistent with how the defendant described the crime scene. He said Harrington was swinging east to west. The blood spatter shows the swinging north to south. You will hear from Dr. Bohlen, who will testify that Harrington was not dangerous. We submit that when you have heard all of the evidence, it is compelling, and you will find that Mark Winger killed his wife and blamed it on Roger Harrington, a perfect patsy. We will prove it beyond a reasonable doubt. We are going to ask you to find the defendant guilty of two vicious murders."

With that, Schmidt looked the jurors in the eye and sat down.

The court then said, "Mr. Breen, do you wish to make your opening statements now or wait until the state puts on its case?"

"Thank you, Your Honor. We will make our opening statements now."

Breen and Pugh had decided to not reserve their opening. Usually opening statements were reserved for when it was questioned whether the state could make a prima facie case. If the defendant's attorneys thought they could, they would go ahead. They did not want the jury to hear the state's opening without knowing that there were questions about what happened.

"Mr. Pugh and I represent Mark Winger, who is the gentleman sitting between us in the open shirt. What we and the prosecution say in our opening statements and what we say in our closing arguments are not facts, but they are arguments and just that. The evidence is what is gathered from the witnesses. If what Mr. Schmidt said or what I say is not supported by the evidence, you should disregard it.

"I want to emphasize what the judge instructed you with regard to the news media. The newspaper and the news media frequently are inaccurate and misstate the facts. It is important that you do not look at the TV or review the newspapers. The only evidence you should go by is that of the witnesses on the witness stand and what is produced in this courtroom.

"You are to keep an open mind until you have heard all of the evidence. The defendant carries with him a presumption of innocence through the whole trial."

Breen then pauses and then, looking at the jury, continued. "On August 29, 1995, Roger Harrington and only Roger Harrington beat Donnah Winger to death with a hammer. It is absolutely uncontradicted that Mark Winger did kill Roger Harrington by shooting him. That shooting is entirely justifiable."

"On August 29, detectives investigated the case at great length. They talked to Mark Winger on the twenty-ninth and then on the thirtieth. They took photographs of the crime scene, spoke to witnesses, investigated the marriage of Donnah and Mark, and talked to the people about the fact that they were just adopting a little baby. They talked to the neighbors, friends, and the parents.

"They talked to Mark's office and learned that Donnah brought the baby into the office on the twenty-ninth, the day of the murder. Mark and

Donnah went to lunch together. Donnah was happy. She had taken the baby to his office before they had lunch. They talked to the witnesses, they looked at the photographs, they looked at the crime scene, they ran the case by Dr. Hindman, the pathologist, and they all concluded that the evidence was perfectly consistent with what Mark had said.

"So years later, we are now faced with this murder charge of Donnah Winger and Roger Harrington? It is because of a civil lawsuit. That is what happened. I'll get to that later.

"I need to talk about Winger getting involved with DeAnn Schultz. I can't justify that—it happened. That doesn't mean that Mark committed the murder. DeAnn Schultz had a lot of problems from 1991 on. She globed onto Mark Winger and Donnah Winger. DeAnn's marriage was in shambles, it was a wreck. She and her husband 'lacked intimacy.' DeAnn was going to move from Springfield. She called an old boyfriend and told Donnah about wanting to move. Donnah told Mark and asked him to talk to her. She needed intimacy. She came onto Mark.

"I can't justify what Mark did, this affair. But that does not mean he was a murderer. He had no record of violence, was stable, had a job, a good education, and good friends. After Donnah's death, Mark needed someone. He was depressed and lonely.

"Mark finally got his head on right after his trip to Africa with his brother. He said this affair is wrong. He broke off the affair with DeAnn, her life fell apart. She could not handle his rejection. He told her she needed to find someone else. She began to drink, lost her job, had psychiatric problems, and attempted suicide four times. She learned that Mark had been able to get his life together, had remarried, and had children with his new wife.

"Her life had fallen apart. His had not. She could not handle that, so now, four years later, she calls the attorney for Bart. She told them, 'Don't settle.' She gave a secret statement to them and the police after she learned that Mark had remarried and had three new children. She now says she remembers conversations from four years ago. Her credibility will be a big issue.

"Now let's talk about Roger Harrington, the man who killed Donnah. She came back from Florida into St. Louis. She took a limo ride back home. The limo driver was Roger Harrington. The conversation during the ride may have started innocently but turned weird and, by the end of the conversation, had Donnah Winger frightened and scared. She told Mark about it, and he became upset.

"She wrote a note. 'We entered into the van, he introduced himself as Roger. He told me he was anorexic. As we went to Springfield he was going over 75 mph. If he wanted to pass other cars he would drive up very closely behind them and honk until they moved over. I noticed his hands shaking and tapping on the steering wheel. It was as if he was agitated. He started talking about the spirit Dahm. He reveals himself as a dragon. Dahm makes him do some bad things like setting car bombs and killing people. When that happens he confides in a psychiatrist. That makes Dahm mad. Dahm makes him do things to his body, appears to him when he is driving, takes him out of his body and makes him fly about the treetops. Then he comes back into his body and sometimes doesn't know where he is. He told me about nude parties at home and that he likes older women. The party is once a month. He gets drunk. He said he smokes marijuana with the people he lives with— all of this at the time he was driving fast and beating the steering.'

"Donnah's note said, 'I felt as if my life and the life of my daughter were in the hands of a nut.'

"Then Mark called Bart and complained. Roger's job was at stake."

Breen continued, "Roger Harrington had a violent past. He beat his wife, put a gun to her head, and told her he was going to kill her. Once he said he was going to kill her and himself. He handcuffed her. There were several protective orders in 1990 and 1991 that were filed by his ex-wife in this very court.

"He got mad at his sister's boyfriend, broke in his home, and cut his furniture with a knife. He left the knife in the wall. Another time he was beating up his wife, and Detective Cox had to forcibly drag him off his wife.

"He told his psychiatrist and social worker how he enjoyed torturing children and that murder was his destiny.

"That's the Roger Harrington who was driving Donnah and ended up beating Donnah to death. Psychiatrists who treated Roger Harrington for a long period of time committed him to mental institutions. You will hear how he told a psychiatrist that Dahm wanted him to cause pain to people. You will hear how he drew pictures of large people hurting little people. You will hear that he said murder was his destiny.

"You will hear that Mark Winger was working out on his treadmill downstairs and heard the baby crying or a noise. He hears his wife scream and runs upstairs. He grabs his .45. He sees Roger Harrington beating his wife with a hammer and shoots him.

"The evidence is also going to show some four months after the murder that Mark Winger filed a lawsuit against Bart Transportation and Roger Harrington's estate. The lawsuit was defended by an insurance company for Bart. They hired Thomas Bevel to defend the case.

"Besides adopting Cindy, Mark had three children of his own after he got remarried in September 1996. DeAnn saw him at Doctor's Hospital in November 1998. She called him. He told her about the lawsuit against Bart. There will probably be a large settlement offer, he said. He told her about his remarriage and that he was happy with his new life and his children. He was happy again. DeAnn was still miserable. She blamed him for her misery. She was angry. He has gotten his life together. She has not. She wanted to get even. She went to the police. She called up the lawyers representing Bart and told them not to settle. She then got immunity.

"The 911 tape, it shows the reality of what Mark Winger was going through, and he will have to relive it. Harrington was told to straighten the matter out with Mark. He learned that Mark got off work at 4:30 p.m. Roger showed up unexpectedly. The fact of the matter is that on August 29, 1995, Mark Winger had no appointment with Roger Harrington. Mr. Harrington wasn't expected to be there at 4:30 p.m. or any other time. Mr. Harrington ended up being a stalker. On August 29, 1995, Roger Harrington ended up in their dining room with Donnah and Mark in the basement. He wanted to get his job back, but something set Harrington off and he killed her. The state has to prove its case beyond a reasonable doubt. Once you have heard all the evidence, you will have no doubt that Mark Winger is not guilty.

"Thank you for listening." Mr. Breen then sits down.

Judge Zappa says, "Thank you, Mr. Breen. Is the state ready for its first witness?"

"Yes, sir."

Chapter 21

The Prosecution

A. May 21, 2002

1. Ray Duffy

Schmidt, Belz, and Weinhoeft agreed that they should start with Winger setting up the meeting with Harrington on the August 29, 1995. The trial lawyer's adage is to start strong and finish strong; your weakness is in the middle. In order to convict they had to prove that Winger set up the meeting.

Belz called, as their first witness, Ray Duffy, the owner of Bart Transportation. Bart transported passengers from Springfield to various airports in the area, including St. Louis. The van driver was a minimum-wage job. Bart did not check past employment; all they wanted to know was that he had a valid driver's license.

When Harrington was interviewed, Bart learned that he had been arrested for assault, battery, and breaking and entering; but the charges were dismissed. They did not know of his psychiatric history. They hired him in March 1995.

Duffy testified, "On August 25, 1995, in the late afternoon, Mr. Winger called me about the ride his wife had from St. Louis. It was a Friday."

"What did he say?"

"He complained that Roger drove erratically and fast, that he had inappropriate conversations with his wife. He talked about hearing voices, about smoking marijuana, about killing people, about planting a car bomb, and having nude parties. He said he lived with an older woman. Mr. Winger was angry. He wanted to know Roger's last name and telephone number."

"I said I would investigate the complaint, but I couldn't give him Roger's last name or telephone number until I talked with him."

"What happened next?"

"I instructed dispatch not to use Roger until we could get to the bottom of this. I was unable to get a hold Roger until Monday."

"What happened then?"

"On Monday, Mr. Winger called again. He wanted to talk to Roger. I got hold of Roger Monday afternoon. I told him that Mr. Winger wanted to talk to him. I told him of the complaint from Mr. Winger. We had a serious problem. I told him what Mr. Winger had said. He remembered the ride. She sat on the front seat with a baby in a bassinette carrier. He laughed when I asked if he had a psychiatrist. He said he didn't have any psychiatrist. He told this ride he was living in the country with an older woman, and they would go around with no clothes on when they wanted to. He was just making conversation with her. He denied telling the ride he heard voices that told him to kill people or plant car bombs. I told him, 'Mr. Winger wants to talk to you,' and he said, 'Okay, give him my number.' I told Roger he would not get any more rides until this was straightened out. I called Mr. Winger on Monday and gave him Roger's number."

"Did you have any more conversations with Roger Harrington after Monday afternoon?"

"No."

"What occurred after that?"

"On Wednesday, Detective Cox called me. I had heard there was a murder in Springfield and that Roger was implicated. I told him of our conversations with both Roger and Mr. Winger. I did not hear from him again."

"On December 29, 1995, was your company sued by Mark Winger for the death of Donnah Winger?"

"Yes, a civil suit had been filed against Roger's estate and Bart Transportation for damages."

"In March or April of 1999, did you receive a telephone call from DeAnn Schultz about this suit?

"Yes, but I did not know it was her. I found that out later. She also called our lawyers, and they were able to trace the call."

"What did she tell you?"

"She said the murder case was going to be reopened and that we should not settle the case."

The state had no more questions.

"Mr. Breen, your cross," the judge said. Breen wanted set up his story so that Winger was concerned about her wife's safety.

"Mr. Duffy, you had a number of conversations with Mr. Winger, did you not?"

"Yes."

"The first was on Friday when Mark Winger was out of town, is that not correct?"

"Yes."

"He told you he didn't want you to talk to Roger until he got back in town because he was concerned about Roger's going after his wife, is that not correct?"

"Yes."

"He told you that Roger drove from seventy-five to eighty miles per hour, he heard voices, saying different things, in one case to kill a person and another to set a car bomb, that he was living with an older woman. They had parties, and people went around naked, is that not correct? He had a spirit Dahm who told him to do their thing."

"That's what Mr. Winger told me. Roger denied saying these things but admitted telling her that he lived in the country with an older woman."

"Roger Harrington also denied smoking marijuana, did he not?"

"Yes."

"When you talked to Mark Winger on Monday, the twenty-eight, he told you he got off work at 3:30 p.m.?"

"Yes."

"You called Roger, did you not, and told him, 'We have a serious problem. You will not get any more rides until this matter is cleared up with Mark Winger?"

"Yes, I did."

"That was on August 28 you told him that?"

"Yes."

"The murders occurred on the next day?"

"Yes."

"In March 1999, did you receive the phone call from DeAnn Schultz?"

"Yes, I did. She told me that the case on Donnah Winger was going to be reopened, that we should not settle the case."

"And what did you do after that?"

"I called my insurance company."

"Subsequently, what happened to the lawsuit?"

"On February 17, 2000, it was dismissed."

Breen continued questioning Duffy.

"In your conversation, Roger denied having a psychiatrist, denied hearing voices, and he denied having the spirit Dahm, did he not?"

"He did deny that."

"Subsequently, you have learned that he had been hospitalized involuntarily several times and that he had talked about killing people or go down the river with weapons of mass destruction, did he not?"

"Yes."

"And that he had a spirit called Dahm that had a hold over his life and that told him to kill or hurt people, did he not?"

"Yes, but he never told us that when we hired him."

"Mark never asked for Harrington's number, did he?"

"My notes said, 'Either give him my office number or give me his number, and I will call him.'"

"Harrington knew that his job was on the line because of the complaints of Mrs. Winger."

"Yes."

"He knew where Donnah Winger lived?"

"Yes."

On recross, Belz asked, "Did Bart Transportation or you have any complaints other than this one about Roger Harrington?"

"No. People in the office thought he was very mild mannered and easy to work with. No one had any complaints about him. He was prompt, on schedule, and courteous."

The witness was excused.

2. Susan Collins

To prove that Winger called Harrington, Weinhoeft called Susan Collins, who rented space in her trailer to Roger Harrington.

Collins, at the time of trial, lived in Axle, Texas; she was forty-four years old and had been married fourteen years.

"Have you ever lived in Springfield?" Weinhoeft asked.

"Yes, until about five years ago. I lived at 728 S. Dial Road in Dawson, Illinois, with Roger Harrington, my daughter, my son-in-law, and my grandson."

"When did Roger move in?"

"First part of August 1995. I rented a room to him and provided board for $200 a week. My daughter moved in a week or so later."

"Mrs. Collins, I need to get this out of the way. You were convicted of deceptive practices, a felony offense, in 1994, is that not correct?"

"Yes."

"You also have been convicted of possession of a controlled substance in Houston, Texas, last year, is that correct?"

"Yes."

"You learned this morning that you are wanted, a bad check case out of Mason County."

"I just learned that."

"Have any promises been made to you regarding those cases?"

"No, sir."

"How long had you known Roger Harrington?"

"Close to three years. He was pretty much my best friend. I saw him every day, and we would swim and clean pools."

"Did you ever have a romantic relationship with Roger Harrington?"

"No, sir."

"Tell us about Roger."

"He was real shy. The kind of person you could open up to, talk to, never judges you."

"Did you ever see Roger smoke marijuana?"

"He smoked marijuana a couple times a day. Marijuana didn't affect him. It just mellowed him out. I smoked marijuana with him."

"As to the spirit of Dahm that we hear about, can you tell about that?"

"It was his guardian angel. It was like someone watching over him. I had that in common with him because I have a guardian angel."

"Did he ever talk to you about a ride on August 23?"

"He came in that night, and it was late, and he had the strangest fare from St. Louis. A lady didn't want to pay the extra $20 for a baby seat."

"What happened?"

"A couple days later his boss called and told him he was laid off until he got this straightened out with Mr. Winger and his wife."

"How did he react to this?"

"He was confused. He just wanted to work things out. He didn't show any anger. He was anxious to get back to work."

"What happened?"

"On Tuesday morning I received a telephone call. It was a male and he asked for Roger. I hand Roger the phone, and he went into the dining area."

"Did you hear the conversation?"

"I only heard portions of it."

"Did you have caller ID?"

"Yes, the caller was from the state of Illinois."

"Go ahead."

"Roger asked for a pen and paper. I gave him a bank deposit slip from Farmer's State Bank, and he wrote on it." She then identifies a bank slip with the name "Mark Winger" and "4:30 p.m." with an address of 2305 W-view. "I saw Roger write on the note."

"Did you spend the rest of the day with Roger?"

"Until about 3:20 p.m. when he left. He said he was going to start work again the next day. That evening I got a frantic call from my daughter. 'Mother, I heard it on the scanner, there had been a shooting.' After that I got a call about a half hour later from the police and went to Memorial Hospital."

"And?"

"The police asked if I could identify Roger's body. I was hysterical, but I did. I talked to the detectives for maybe forty-five minutes to an hour. They drove me to the house, and I showed them Roger's room."

After the noon recess, Breen started his cross-examination. It was extensive. He wanted to discredit Collins. He wanted to show to the jury that she said the note was written on the afternoon of the twenty-ninth after a call from someone at Bart's office, not in the morning after the call from the state of Illinois.

"When were you first convicted for drugs, Mrs. Collins?"

"I don't remember, probably 1997 or 1998 or maybe 1999. I am not so positive."

"How many convictions were there?"

"Two, I think."

"The convictions were what?"

"Paraphernalia and possession of a controlled substance."

"What kind?"

"Objection!"

Judge Zappa said, "Sustained. Only the conviction and what it was for may be used to impeach."

Breen continued, "When was the last time you used drugs?"

"I probably smoked pot about six months ago."

"Have you had a drug problem?"

"That was after Roger was killed."

"What kind of drugs?"

"That's confidential."

Breen said, "Judge, direct her to answer."

Judge Zappa replied, "You have to answer, Mrs. Collins."

"Cocaine. I went through a couple of treatment centers for evaluations. I have been clean over two years."

"Were you convicted of possession of marijuana six months ago?"

"Right."

"When you smoked marijuana with Roger Harrington once or twice a day, where was that?"

"Usually out on the deck."

"This is 2002. Do you have any problem remembering back to August of 1995?"

"I remember pretty good. Yeah, we smoked in the morning."

"The police spoke to you twice, once at the hospital and afterwards in the trailer, did they not?"

"Yes."

"Did the police take a statement from you on the twenty-ninth?"

"Yes."

"On the statement you told the police that it was on Monday, the twenty-eighth, that he received a call from work and asked for a bank statement."

"No, absolutely not. That happened on the day the ID box showed the number coming up. That's when I handed him the deposit slip."

"Then the police report is an error?"

No response.

"Did you not tell the police that yesterday (August 28), Roger had explained to you the problem after he had come back to the kitchen from talking to someone from his work, and at that time he had written on the back of the deposit slip the name and address?"

"I don't recall."

"Let me show you your statement." He hands her the statement.

"Yes, that is what it says."

"That was your statement to the police."

"Yes."

"So he told you he was going to Mark Winger's house and had to be there by 4:30 p.m., is that what you're saying?"

"Yes."

Breen, showing her the statement, asked, "That wasn't in any statement you made to the police in August 1995, was it?"

"No, sir. But it was in my 2000 statement."

"Where did you make your 2000 statement?"

"The county jail."

"You were in custody?"

"Yes, sir."

"Are you in custody now?"

"Yes, sir, on a five-year-old warrant."

"Were there other calls on the caller ID?"

"Yes."

Breen handed her the note and asked her if that was the bank slip she was talking about; the writing was partially in pencil and part in ink.

"Yes."

"Are you saying he wrote all this at the same time?"

"Yes, as far as I know."

"He wrote the name 'Mark Winger' in pencil and then put down the pencil and picked up a pen and wrote down the rest of the information all at the same time, is that correct?"

"That's very possible."

"I am not asking if that is possible. I am asking did he?"

"I don't know."

"So he could have written it with a pencil first and then a pen second at different times?"

"I have a coffee can with a bunch of pens and stuff in it. If he grabbed one, wrote down the name, put it back, he could have grabbed a pen to finish writing."

"Or he could have written that information down on two different occasions on August 29, isn't that true?"

No answer.

"What you're telling us is that you didn't see him write this down, did you?"

"No, sir."

"You also told the police that Roger got a call in the afternoon on the twenty-ninth from his office."

"Yes, that is my statement."

"So you told the police something different on August 29, 1995, than what you are testifying to today?"

"I guess so."

"Did you smoke pot that day?"

"Probably. We got up early and smoked a little and went to play Nintendo."

"Did you know he was talking about Dahm telling him to kill people and hurting people and put others in pain?"

"That's a false statement."

"Do you mean he lied to his psychiatrist?"

"I don't know anything about what he ever said to them."

Breen, looking disgusted, said, "I have no further questions."

Mr. Weinhoeft then redirects.

"Do you remember giving a statement to the police on January 11, 2000?"

"Yes."

"In that statement in 2000 you said, 'Roger told me that was Mark Winger, the strange fare's husband, and he is going to meet with him at 4:30 p.m. that day to get it taken care of so he can get back to work.' Did you tell the police that?"

"Yes, sir."

On recross Breen asked, "In 1995, 1996, 1997, 1998, and 1999, did you tell any of the police officers that?"

"No."

"When you're in jail in the year 2000, the police talked to you, and they told you that the case has been reopened, and they had a theory of how Roger got to Mark Winger's house, did they not?"

"Yes, sir."

"Mrs. Collins, in your August 29, 1995, statement to the police, you talk about the bank slip."

"Yes."

"She stated at that time Roger had written a name and address on the back of one of her deposit slips. That's what the statement says."

"Right."

"This statement also says that note was written on August 28, 1995, the day before the murder."

"That's what it says."

"Yes, that's what it says."

Breen had her giving conflicting statements about when the note was written and that her last statement was written when she was in jail. The damning statement was made when she was in custody some five years after the murder and after the police had explained their theory to her. Breen and Pugh felt pretty good about creating "reasonable doubt." He had no further questions for her.

B. May 22, 2002

On the second day of trial the prosecution set the crime scene. These witnesses were perfunctory, reciting when they got to the scene, what they saw, and the condition of the victims.

1. Officers Jones and Filburn

Officer Jones and Filburn were the first to arrive at the crime scene; they entered with guns drawn and saw Mark Winger leaning over the body of his wife and saw a male on his back, five to six feet from her, facing the same direction. Donnah's body first had been lying on her stomach; she was turned over so she could be treated when the paramedics entered. The paramedics and firemen tried frantically to stabilize the victims; they did CPR and put IVs in. The victims were still breathing, gasping, breathing shallow. After trying to stabilize them the paramedics said, "We got to get them to the hospital." They placed them on the gurneys, but the male went into cardiac arrest. One said, "We are losing him," and started CPR as they sped off to the hospital.

The testimony was cut and dry. Exhibits and photographs were identified as well as the clothing of the victims. There was no controversy regarding their testimony.

2. Norval Morton

Norval Morton, the crime scene technician, arrived at the scene and found blood on the walls and the carpet. He drew pictures of the location of the blood on the floor and on the walls; he videotaped the scene of the crime. He took pictures of the blood on the floor after the carpet had been removed. A bullet was stuck in the floor in the middle of the pool of blood.

He continued, "On the south wall of the dining room there was blood spatter going up and down, the staining continued and there were some blood spots on the ceiling. You could see the blood running down. There was tissue on the south wall about three feet from the floor, and blood was also found on the back wall.

"I took photographs of Mr. Winger's hands. The right hand had much more blood on it than the left hand. Both hands were relatively clean. His handprints were recovered from the hammer, but it was hard to obtain because of the many prints on it. I also recovered shells, which were located in the dining room. There was a telephone on the floor in the dining room. This was a wall-mounted phone in the kitchen area."

Pictures and drawings of the scene were admitted without objection. There were no questions on cross-examination.

3. Officer Charles Cox

John Schmidt then called Charles Cox, the lead detective in 1995. He was vulnerable because in 1995 he concluded Winger had justifiably shot and killed Roger Harrington. The case had been closed. Schmidt knew that he had to face up to this issue and meet it head-on.

Cox got the call about 4:30 p.m. and arrived at the house at maybe 4:45 to 5:00 p.m. with Detective Williamson. The area had been cordoned off; two ambulances, fire trucks, and police cars were at the house. In the dining area he saw two bodies surrounded by firemen, paramedics, and police. They were working on the victims. He first observed the scene, described what he saw, and then went into the bedroom to interview Winger.

"Winger was very distraught. He told me that he shot and killed Harrington as he was bludgeoning his wife with a hammer. He described how he was downstairs working out, heard a noise, came up, and saw Donnah being bludgeoned, and he shot and killed Roger."

"What else did the defendant say?"

"He called 911. He then hung up because he thought the baby had fallen off the bed. He also described the ride with Roger Harrington and said that

DeAnn Schultz had stayed over while he was out of town because Donnah was upset and frightened because of the ride."

Schmidt asked, "Did Winger have DeAnn Schultz's phone number?"

"He said he didn't have it, but he did have John Schultz's work number."

"When giving the statement, how did he act?"

"He would be calm for a while and then become very emotional. He had to pause several times. He asked several times how his wife was and then would become very emotional again, crying and rocking back and forth. I saw no tears. He had blood on his hands. He was a good actor."

"Objection."

Judge Zappa said, "Strike the last statement. The jury is to disregard it."

Cox then identified a floor plan, how Mark Winger came up the stairs, and where he went. He pointed that out to the jury. "Mark said he came up the stairs, turned through the bathroom and into the bedroom where the baby was. He heard something in the dining area and got his gun. He went into the hallway and saw his wife being beaten. That's when he shot Harrington. He said Harrington rolled off his wife and started to get up, and he shot him the second time."

Schmidt led Cox through Winger's statement to him in August of 1995 and their investigation of the marriage—that DeAnn had not come forward yet.

Schmidt had no further questions.

Breen brought up that the original investigation did not find Winger culpable.

"What was Winger's emotional state?"

"He was very emotional, and he would forget something and then add something. This was consistent with someone trying to relate a dramatic event. The conversation would break down because Mark was distraught and upset. At times he would cry, and we would stop questioning him until he could compose himself."

"You didn't record the statement or videotape it, did you?"

"No."

"You had the equipment present in the room, didn't you?"

"Yes."

"You didn't ask Mark to sign the statement or any statement, did you?"

"No."

"You just typed up the notes that you took?"

"Yes."

"He never read them over to determine if they were accurate?"

"No."

Breen then asked if other officers were involved in the investigation.

Cox said, "There were crime scene technicians, there were other police officers who were interviewing the neighbors, and officers that went to Roger Harrington's home."

"After the investigation, what did you do?"

"On August 30, we all conferred together, the technicians, Sergeant Murphy, Detective Young, Detective Williamson, and the lieutenant was there. In all major cases, that is known as a roundtable, where everyone that's involved in the investigation gets together to talk about what leads there are and what information each had."

"What was the result of the roundtable discussion?"

"We thought that Winger's story held up."

Breen then asked about the telephone calls that had been made to Winger's home on Friday and Saturday, asking for Donnah.

"These were the calls from a male who had hung up as soon as he was informed that Donnah was not present?"

"Yes, he asked for Donnah or Mark Winger."

Cox was asked if they tried to locate who made these calls, and he said not in 1995. They tried to do that in 1999, but the records did not go back to 1995.

Breen asked, "When you interviewed the defendant, he appeared to be crying and rocking back and forth?"

"Yes."

"You said he was cradling his wife when the police first came in?"

"Yes."

"You saw the location of the bodies and of Roger Harrington?"

"Yes."

"You went over and took out Harrington's wallet to get his ID and took time to observe the scene?"

"Yes."

"You did not note any inconsistencies in your report about the locations of the bodies?"

"That's correct."

"In fact, you thought nothing that Mark told you was inconsistent with what you saw at the scene?"

"Yes."

"Did you state in the coroner's inquest in 1995 that Mark Winger's statement was consistent with the crime scene?"

"Yes."

"You conferred with the pathologist, Dr. Hindman?"

"Yes."

"He told you that the forensic findings were consistent with Donnah Winger having been struck from behind?"

"Yes."

"After you had identified the male as Roger Harrington, then Mark told you about the ride?"

"Correct."

"Winger had a caller ID box installed after these suspicious calls?"

"Yes, it was installed because Donnah was concerned about these unidentified calls."

"Did you ever order any mud sheets on the Winger telephone?"

"Not as part of the initial investigation. We tried to in 1999, but it was too late."

"So the police were not able to verify those hang-up calls on the Friday and the Saturday?"

"That's correct."

Breen then focused on Harrington. "Roger Harrington had told Donnah that Dahm made him kill people, stab people, and place car bombs?"

"That's correct."

"Winger requested DeAnn to call the police because he was concerned about safety?"

"That is correct."

"Winger said Harrington told Donnah that he had parties in the country where they would run around naked, smoke marijuana?"

"Yes."

"You had seen the blood on the walls?"

"Yes."

"You knew about the note?"

"Yes."

"And you found what Mark Winger said credible?"

"Yes."

"No further questions."

Schmidt got up quickly from his chair.

"You have changed your mind?"

"Yes."

"When did you start having your suspicions?"

"In late 1995 and 1996."

"What caused you to have these suspicions?"

"Mark Winger came to the police station, the first time to get his .45 back. He kept pumping me if there was anything new in the case. I told him it was closed."

"Did he come in a second time?"

"In 1996 he came in to tell me that he was getting married and again asked me if there was anything new in the case. He kept asking if anything was new. I had never had anyone ask about a closed-file murder case. It did not feel right. I became suspicious. I wondered if we had missed something."

"What did you do?"

"I talked to Doug Williamson. He never felt comfortable with the case. He thought there was too many loose ends, particularly the note."

"What did you do then?"

"We went to the administration and were told, 'We don't open closed cases on gut feelings or suspicions.'"

"Did you know about DeAnn Schultz at that time?"

"No. She had been questioned along with friends and neighbors. Everyone said it was a solid marriage, and they were good people."

"In hindsight was the position of the bodies consistent with Winger's statement?"

"No. If Harrington rolled off of Donnah, he would not be six feet from Donnah."

"No further questions."

4. Doug Williamson

Schmidt followed up with Williamson. Williamson had not testified at the coroner's inquest, but he had testified at the grand jury. The defense didn't have much for cross-examination.

Williamson had fourteen years in the police department. He was assigned to the detective bureau in 1991, four years before the Winger murder, in the major crimes unit that dealt with murders, rapes, and robberies; but he was a junior member of the department. The department consisted of a sergeant in charge and four detectives.

"You reviewed the crime scene."

"Yes."

"What did you see?"

"It was a chaotic scene—firemen, paramedics, and police, all trying to stabilize the two individuals. There was a hammer in the middle of the floor, covered with blood from the back to the top. There was blood spatter and brain material on several walls. There were pools of blood on the floor."

"Did you go into the master bedroom?"

"Yes. Mark Winger was there being interrogated by Detective Young and then Cox. He asked for a Diet Coke."

"Did you get him one?"

"I went into the kitchen and got him one out of the refrigerator. I saw on the refrigerator door a handwritten note describing the van trip from St. Louis. I gave it to an evidence tech to preserve it." He identified Donnah's notes of the ride.

"What did you do next?"

"I went outside and inspected Roger Harrington's car. I saw a note saying, 'Mark Winger 2305 W-view, 4:30 p.m.' I also gave that to the evidence tech." He again identified that note.

"At some point in time was the defendant asked to demonstrate what he did and saw?"

"Yes, he showed Young, Cox, and myself the route he took from the basement to the master bedroom and then out to the hall and where he saw Donnah being beaten. His wife was in a fetal position, on her hands and knees, being struck in the back of her head."

Williamson got down off the witness stand, knelt down on his right knee, and swung his right hand up and down to demonstrate what Winger had demonstrated to them.

"Winger then shot him. He said Harrington rolled off his wife. He continued running up to Harrington and fired a second shot in the head."

"After your investigation what happened?"

"There was a meeting of all the officers who were investigating the case, to talk it over and see what conclusions we could draw. We discussed that Winger had no criminal record and that Harrington did. Harrington had a psychiatric record and Winger did not. Harrington had a record of violence and Winger did not. We talked about his marriage. We were told they had a good marriage. There were no police records on Winger, but there were on Harrington."

"Was any conclusion reached?"

"Yes, it appeared that Mark Winger was telling the truth, that he was emotionally upset. However, there were some loose ends, such as the note. I asked to subpoena some telephone records. I was told no. We had only two suspects, Winger and Harrington. Although there were some loose ends, nothing pointed to Winger. The case was basically closed at that time."

"Was the case reopened in January 1999?"

"Yes. In January or February of 1999 I was asked by a Sergeant Dowes to subpoena the telephone records. We had been concerned about those for some time. Dowes told Cox and myself that we could go ahead and also get a blood expert to review the blood spatter on some of the clothing and do that but nothing more. It was opened on a limited basis."

"What did you do next?"

"I subpoenaed the telephone and motel records, Winger's telephone, and the records from Mount Vernon. Cox took some of the materials to Thomas Bevel for review. Shortly after that, DeAnn Schultz came forward. That blew the case wide open."

John Schmidt handed him a stack of records for telephone calls and asked, "Are these the records that you subpoenaed?"

"Yes, they show over eight hundred dollars of telephone calls during July and August, 1995, between DeAnn Schultz and Mark Winger. The motel records from Mount Vernon showed that DeAnn paid for July 22, and Mark Winger paid for August 19, 1995."

Schmidt then said to Breen, "Your witness."

Breen asked, "You testified that you went into the room where the bodies were and observed the scene?"

"Yes."

"You saw where the bodies were?"

"Yes."

"You heard Winger's description and saw his demonstration of what happened?"

"Yes."

"You didn't see any inconsistencies with what he said and what he demonstrated had happened and with what you had observed?"

"That's correct."

Switching his questioning, Breen asks, "When you were outside did you talk to the neighbors?"

"Other officers canvassed the neighborhood."

"None of them said that there was any problem with the marriage?"

"That's correct."

"You didn't even make out your own police report as to what you observed and saw, did you?"

"No, I did not."

"You didn't take any notes while Mark Winger was being interviewed?"

"No."

"You knew that there had been a premises check ordered for his house because of concerns about the van driver?"

"Yes, I did."

"That would have been a Thursday evening, August 24?"

"Correct."

"You never asked Mark Winger for the records of his telephone calls in 1995, did you?"

"No."

"You could have done so without a subpoena?"

"Yes, but they would not show incoming calls."

"Now the incoming calls to the house were of some importance to you as well as the outgoing calls. Correct?"

"Yes."

"Mark told you that he had strange telephone calls in the house?"

"Yes, he did."

"Were you curious to find out who those strange calls were from?"

"Yes."

"Yet you did not check with the telephone company?"

"That's correct."

"Mark said he got the caller ID after these hang-up calls?"

"Yes."

"That shows he was concerned?"

"I guess so."

"You didn't make any notes that his reenactment didn't fit your observations of the scene?"

"No, I did not."

"Wasn't this case reopened because DeAnn Schultz came forward about her affair?"

"Absolutely not."

"What caused it to reopen in February 1999?"

"We had a change in command staff, and the new command staff, including Sergeant Dowes, gave us permission for a limited reopening to do some testing."

"Mark Winger had, several years prior to that, filed a civil lawsuit against BART Transportation."

"I found that out later."

"You began to work with John Nolan, Bart's attorney, who was defending Bart, on the case then?"

"Yes, I did."

"And you provided them information, and they provided you information?"

"Yes."

"Weren't you taking an active role to help defend Bart Transportation?"

"No."

"In mid-February or March of 1999, DeAnn Schultz gave you a statement?"

"Yes."

"And you are saying just coincidentally in January and February you had gotten permission to reopen the case?"

"That's absolutely correct."

"DeAnn Schultz had nothing to do with it?"

"That's correct."

"Mark Winger on August 30, 1995, told you about the mug and the cigarettes on the table in the dining room, did he not?"

"Yes."

"It was only a result of Mark Winger saying that, that you obtained these items. They were already in the trash when you collected them."

"That is correct."

"He did not try to hide that from you?"

"No."

"That not what a guilty man would do?"

"Objection!"

"Sustained."

"Now after DeAnn came forward, you interviewed her, in March of 1999?"

"That is correct."

"You interviewed her for two and a half hours and quit after that because she was tired?"

"Correct."

"You wrote up that interview?"

"Yes."

"I'll show you this exhibit. Is that your interview?"

"Yes."

"She signed it. It is only a half page for a two-and-a-half-hour interview. So there were things you discussed that you did not want to put in. It's not complete."

"Objection!"

"Sustained."

"At least you did not write down everything she told you, right?"

"Yes."

"This is standard police practice? Only putting in the statement what will help you and not anything that hurts?"

"Absolutely not!"

"You omitted much of what she told you."

"I only put in what was relevant."

"You did not include anything in this interview that might have been exculpating."

"Objection!"

"Sustained."

"Reading this statement only takes five minutes at most. What did she say during the remaining two hours?"

"I don't recall."

"How long did you and Charlie Cox observe the scene of the crime?"

"At least ten minutes."

"You and he knew the position of the bodies before the case was closed in 1995?"

"Yes."

"You didn't take any notes while Mark Winger was talking, did you?"

"No, sir."

"You didn't make any diagrams?"

"No, sir."

"When Mark demonstrated what he saw to you and Cox, neither of you noted any discrepancies with his story and the crime scene?"

"That's right."

"It was mid-February or March of 1999 that DeAnn Schultz came forward, was it not?"

"Yes."

"You interviewed her on March 8, 1999."

"Yes."

"The first written report you received from Tom Bevel was in October 1999, is that not correct? Over six months after she came forward?"

"Yes."

"You say she had nothing to do with reopening the case?"

"That's what I said."

"No further questions."

5. Ralph Harrington

Ralph Harrington was the father of Roger. Schmidt needed to call him to identify Roger's watch and ring, but he did not want to open the door for examination on Roger's odd behavior.

"Was Roger right-handed?"

"Yes."

"After his death were you given his watch and ring by the coroner?"

"Yes."

"What did you do with them?"

"We put them in a drawer in his room."

He then identifies Roger's ring and watch.

"Are they in the same condition as when you received them seven to eight years ago?"

"Yes."

"Did he wear both on his right hand?"

"You don't see any blood on either, do you?"

"No."

On cross, Breen asked, "You received them from the coroner's office?"

"Yes."

"You don't know if the coroner had the watch and ring cleaned before they returned them?"

"No, I don't."

6. Lauralee Smith

Lauralee Smith lived next door to the Wingers with her husband and two daughters. They weren't really close friends, but they were neighbors, and they talked about different things while they were in the yard. On August 29, 1995, she got off work around 3:30 p.m. She went to pick up her children at her mom's house. She stayed for about forty minutes and then came home. Her mom lived in Jerome, which is a very short distance from 4305

Westview. When she got home around 4:30 p.m. she saw a car parked out from the wrong way. Mark's truck was in the driveway.

Schmidt asked her, "Did you observe anything unusual about the Winger residence itself?"

Mrs. Smith answered, "The front door was open, and the storm door was shut. I thought it was odd because it was August and air-conditioning time . . ."

"What did you do?"

"I pulled into the driveway and started unloading my kids. They were four and nine years old."

"What was the first thing you did after you parked your vehicle?"

"I put the top up."

"How long does that take?"

"About a minute."

"And how long did it take to get your children out?"

"That takes forever, getting my stuff out of the front of the car first, then lifting the seats, pulling open the door. The seat is heavy. My daughter can't lift it. Then getting all of our paraphernalia, her bag, her toys, and everything out that she took to Grandma's. Then I went around to the other side for the other one. They couldn't open the doors themselves. It all took about three minutes or more."

"What did you hear about 4:30 p.m.?"

"I heard a gunshot. One gunshot, after I had just unloaded the kids."

"Are you certain?"

"Yes."

"Do you have any experience with guns?"

"I fired a gun once. I also lived next to Mather Gun Club."

"After that one gunshot what did you hear?"

"Nothing. I then went into the house."

"Why didn't you call the police?"

"There was no other noise. I blanked it out as soon as I walked into the house."

"No further questions."

On cross, Breen attacked her recollection. Winger said he fired two shots in quick succession.

"When were you contacted by the police?"

"August 7, 2001."

"And that was the first time the police officers ever interviewed you as to the events that occurred back on August 29, 1995?"

"Yes."

"That was the first time you told police that you have only heard one shot?"

"Yes."

"That was six years ago?"

"Yes."

"And that was after they told you their theory that the second shot was fired when Winger hung up the phone on the 911 call?"

"I don't recall."

"They suggested that theory to you, didn't they?"

"I said I don't recall."

"You recall only one shot six years ago, but you cannot recall something a year ago?"

"I guess so."

"No further questions."

7. Candice Boulton

Candice Boulton was a co-worker of Mark Winger's in the Nuclear Safety Agency. She knew both Donnah and Mark and had visited their home on several occasions. She was very bright and had multiple degrees from colleges and universities. She attended the course in Tennessee with Mark and then drove back on Saturday together.

On the drive back, they talked about the course and what they had learned. They stopped for donuts and coffee, and Mark paid for them. He was going to put them on his expense account. About halfway into the trip Mark mentioned to Candice the ride that Donnah had with Roger Harrington. He told her what Donnah had told him. He then asked what would happen if Donnah died, if he would he be able to keep Cindy. Candice replied that she knew many single dads who had custody of their children. She did not think that it would be an issue. She thought that was a strange question for Mark to be asking her.

When they got to Springfield, Mark asked Candice if she could take the car back on Monday to the car pool. He was going to work on Monday and she had the day off. She agreed and took the car back late Monday. She looked through the car to make sure they had not left anything in it, and she found some change. She thought that it must be Mark's because he had paid for the coffee and donuts. Upon returning home after work on Tuesday, she called him around 4:00 p.m. The telephone rang and rang, but no one answered. She did not think any more about it, but that evening she got a call from the police. They found her phone number on his voice mail. They told her Donnah had been murdered.

On cross-examination Breen asked her about working with Mark Winger. She testified that he was very businesslike and no-nonsense. He was bright and got along with his co-workers. She had never heard him get mad or angry with the people who worked under him when they made a mistake.

She thought that Mark and Donnah had a good marriage, and she never heard Mark making any remarks indicating that they were not getting along.

C. May 23, 2002

1. DeAnn Schultz

DeAnn Schultz was called on May 23, 2002. She was not without her problems. Although an attractive lady with long dark hair, she was very high-strung and narcissistic. In 1995, her marriage had fallen apart. She was under stress with her teenage daughter and a young adopted child. Her husband had been working long hours in a new job. She was employed as a psychiatric home health nurse, a demanding and lonely occupation. She lost her job in 1997 and had been recently reemployed.

She was divorced from her husband in 2001. She was now working again as a nurse for Lincoln Correctional Center, where she had to triage patients and would administer medications; her life seemed to be coming back together.

On the day before she was supposed to testify, Steve Weinhoeft called her aside and said, "You're up tomorrow."

"I'm nervous."

He told her to review the statements that she had given to the police and to John Noll. "Just stick to the truth, and you will be okay. But most importantly get a good night's sleep."

The next morning she was alert and fresh. Weinhoeft told her, "Look to the jury when you are answering. Don't look at me."

She said, "Okay."

Weinhoeft started by asking her about her marriage.

"My husband and I were experiencing marital difficulties, and there were a lot of intimacy problems. Basically I wasn't happy in my marriage. It just seemed to cause other problems. I confided this to Donnah. Donnah was a good listener. In July 1995, I talked to Donnah about getting back together with an old boyfriend."

"What happened after that?" Weinhoeft inquired.

"About one week later I received a call from Mark at my home. He was in Chattanooga, Tennessee. He asked me how I was doing. He told me that Donnah told him that I was unhappy in my marriage. He said he treasured my friendship. He said he liked me, that he was attracted to me and things like that. He gave me compliments. He told me how attractive I was, how smart I was, how much fun it was to be with me. It was nice to hear these things, these compliments."

"Go on."

"He talked about his own marriage, that he was unhappy. He felt neglected. He suggested that maybe we could meet the next weekend and talk about it. This was on a Wednesday. From the way he talked I know he was thinking of more than just talking. I said I would call him back later."

"Did you call him back?"

"I called him back the next day and agreed to meet with him. He suggested we meet at the Comfort Inn in Mount Vernon on Saturday. I told my husband that I just needed to get away for the weekend."

"We first met on July 22, 1995. We had dinner and wine. We had sex that night. He gave me confidence. The next day I went home to Springfield, and he went back to Chattanooga."

"And after that?"

"The next week we talked pretty often on the phone. The conversations were pretty much getting to know each other because we didn't talk on a personal level before. We talked about our families, typical things you talk about when you're getting to know one another. He said he didn't love his wife anymore."

"Did this relationship continue when he got back?"

"He got back about July 30. The relationship got more intense during this period. He kept telling me he loved me. We would tell each other how we loved each other. We saw each other during his lunch hour. We normally met in the parking lot of Jungle O Fun. In person it was more physical. The relationship was very intense. We saw each other almost daily."

"Did you talk about divorce?" Weinhoeft asked.

"We had conversations about getting divorced. I remember at Mark and Donnah's home, waiting by the tailgate of Mark's truck, I said I would divorce John. He said it would be easier if Donnah just died. He had been thinking about it for some time. All I would have to do was find the body. I told him that was crazy, what are you talking about."

"Did he repeat that again?"

"About the middle of next week he called me in the afternoon. It was in the kitchen of my home. He repeated, 'It would be easier if Donnah just died. I don't want Cindy to grow up in hot, humid Florida with Donnah's family.' I said I don't really want to hear anything more about it, about anyone dying. I would cease to be a vital person if anyone was hurt. I'm going to divorce John, and you have got to do what you have to do."

"Did he go out of town again?"

"The following week he returned to Chattanooga for two weeks to finish his training. He was there from August 13 to August 26. We would talk two to three times a day. We told each other that we loved each other."

"Did you meet again with him when he was on this second trip?" Weinhoeft asked.

"On August 19, 1995, we got together again in Mount Vernon."

"Where was Donnah Winger?"

"Donnah had taken Cindy to Florida to visit her parents on August 18. She came back on August 23. She called me when she got back and told me about the limo ride. Her comment was pretty casual and she said, 'Oh, by the way, DeAnn, I have a patient for you,' and described her trip."

DeAnn continued, "That evening I was over at Donnah's, and Mark called. It was a Thursday. He spoke to Donnah first, and then he asked to speak to me.

"I told him about the ride and that I thought that the driver was mentally ill. I said it sounded like the driver was schizophrenic and off his meds. He wanted me to call the police to tell them what had happened. He appeared to be concerned. I had called the police and was told the most they could do was a premises check. I stayed overnight at Donnah's on Thursday and Friday. On Friday evening Cindy was on the changing table when Donnah got a call. I picked the phone up and said, 'The Winger residence.' A male voice asked for Mr. or Mrs. Winger in a slow, halting voice. He did not identify himself. I told him Mrs. Winger was not available, and he just hung up."

"What happened on the twenty-sixth?"

"On the twenty-sixth we attended a baby shower for Joe Datz, a good friend of Donnah's. My daughter, who was fifteen, babysat Cindy. She got a similar call from a man who asked for the Wingers and hung up when told Donnah was gone. When Mark got home he asked about the van driver. I told him that he sounded very odd. He sounded like he needed help. Mark asked Donnah to write down what had happened on the ride."

"Please continue."

"That evening John and I went to the Wingers' to watch a movie and have a cookout. On Sunday, August 27, Mark and Donnah came over, and we had a cookout together. That was the last time I ever saw her alive."

"What happened on Monday, the twenty-eighth?"

"I had a conversation with Mark, and he told me he needed to get that guy into his house. Then on August 29, 1995, I received a call from Mark at work. It was early afternoon. He asked me if I would love him no matter what."

"Then what happened?"

"I went home after work—it was six o'clock or so. I received a call from a newsperson. She knew I was a good friend of Donnah Winger. She told me that Donnah had died. I rushed over to the house. There were police everywhere. I went to the Datzes' to be with Mark. I spent the night at Mike and Jo Datz's house. I slept on the couch in the living room."

"Did you have a conversation with Mark?"

"It was early in the morning; I was sleeping and he woke me up. We went into a little bay area where there was a little couch. He said that the case was high profile, to say nothing about having an affair. Mark seemed to be more concerned about the investigation than the death of his wife. He said he thought Officer Cox believed him. After everyone got up I went home."

"Did you go to the funeral?"

"The funeral was in Springfield, and the burial was in Florida. I went to both. Mark went to stay with his parents for about two to three weeks. On his return he brought a nanny with him. I continued to have the affair with Mark. It was mostly at lunchtime."

"Did you ever talk about marriage?"

"We had talked about getting married. He wanted to give me a wedding ring. Something that was symbolic."

"Did he talk about Donnah's death after he returned from Ohio?"

"In the weeks following he told me at one point that dead men don't talk. He said it didn't happen the way the paper said it did. He told me he didn't want me to know about what happened—ignorance is bliss. I was so emotionally involved I just put it out of my mind."

"Did your affair end?" Weinhoeft asked.

"Yes, in February 1996. It ended abruptly. It was after the original nanny was let go and he hired another nanny."

"What happened?"

"He had spent a month in Africa with his brother. When he got back, he didn't call so I called him and left messages. He wasn't returning my calls. When he did call back he said it was over. He said to me, 'You need to find somebody else,' that kind of thing. This was in March 1996."

"What was your mental state before Donnah's death?" Weinhoeft asked.

"Prior to August 1995 my mental condition was good, at least it wasn't bad. I was a little bit depressed, and I had chronic migraines, but I worked."

"And after Donnah's death?"

"My mental condition changed. I spiraled down, just downward. It was bad and it got much, much worse. I became very depressed. I cut back on my work. I could not take care of my children, and I started drinking. I was not able to maintain a job. I wanted to die. I did not have anyone to talk to. I was ashamed of my affair. I worried that might have had something to do with Donnah's death. I thought everyone would be better without me."

"What happened next?" Weinhoeft asked.

"On January 18, 1998, I took a bottle of pills because I wanted to die. I was scared. I didn't think anyone would understand. It seemed the easiest way out. I again attempted suicide on March 29, 1998. I tried it again in July. My doctor didn't know what to do with me. I received ECT treatments. I had lots of different medications. My depression consumed my life. It consumed the life of my family. My family was great."

"What happened in October of 1998?" Weinhoeft said.

"On October 23, 1998, I was at the hospital for a migraine, and Mark was there. My husband said he was there. I called him at work. I wanted him to know what I was going through. I wanted to meet with him to see if he would admit to me that he killed Donnah. I wanted him actually to say it.

"On our first conversations he sounded pleasant. He sounded pleased to hear from me and said he missed me, kind of like in the old times. I said I wanted to meet with him. I told him about the problems I was having—my depression, my suicide attempts, loss of job, etc. I cried. I told him what I was going through. I asked him how he could live with himself. He said, 'I have found Jesus and I am forgiven. I married Barbara and have three children. I got on with my life.'"

"What else did you discuss?"

"He said he had a lawsuit against Bart. He had to be real careful about meeting. They did not know about our affair. We couldn't meet face-to-face in Springfield because of that. He mentioned the possibility of getting millions for Cindy."

"Go on."

"I told him after my fourth suicide attempt that I told my psychiatrist, Dr. Lauer, about our affair. He wasn't happy because the psychiatrist could go to the police. 'Then our gooses would be cooked,' he said."

"What did Dr. Lauer tell you?"

"Dr. Lauer said he had tried everything. There were no more options, he said. I had to tell him what was bothering me. He was going to discharge me, so I told him of my fears. I didn't know what to do. I was afraid to tell anyone. That's why I tried to kill myself. I would lose my friends, my family. I was scared if they knew about my affair. I felt helpless."

"Did you tell your husband of the affair?"

"At Dr. Lauer's urging, I told John, my ex-husband, of my affair in January of 1999. He put me in contact with Jeff Page, my attorney. He talked to the state's attorney about what I knew. That's when I got immunity for my testimony. He put me in contact with the police."

Weinhoeft concluded his examination.

Breen had to destroy her credibility. He had her written statement to the police and her sworn testimony to the attorneys for Bart. He needed to show that her testimony was inconsistent, her memory is faulty, and that she was vindictive. If the jury believed her testimony Winger would be convicted. Her life had fallen apart and his had not. She wanted to get even.

"Ms. Schultz, you indicated, did you not, that you had a conversation with Mark on the morning of August 30 at Rabbi Datz's home?"

"Correct."

"And at that time he told you not to mention the affair to the police?"

"Yes."

"And other than that he told you to answer the questions from the police. Isn't that right?"

"Yes."

Breen pulled out the transcript of her statement that she made at John Nolan's office in November 1999. Breen asked her if she said after Donnah's death, "Mark told me to stay as far away from the police as possible, to answer their questions but not offer any information about the affair."

"Do you remember giving that answer?"

"Yes."

"As a matter of fact, you didn't want to talk to the police about the affair, did you not?"

"No."

"You also never mentioned these alleged conversations about Donnah dying to the police when they interviewed you in 1995?"

"No."

"Mark never told you not to mention them?"

"No."

"Did you not think that these conversations were relevant to the police investigation?"

"I don't know."

"Let's go back to the month of August 1995. Donnah gave you the details of the ride, didn't she?"

"Yes, she asked me to come over. I ended up staying overnight. We talked about the ride. She was concerned."

"You told Donnah that this driver needs help and he sounded schizophrenic, didn't you?"

"Sounded that way, yes."

"Tell us about the Friday telephone call."

"I answered the telephone between seven and eight and heard the voice of a man. The voice was low and halting, a monotone. It was an odd telephone call. He asked for Mr. or Mrs. Winger, and I responded that Mrs. Winger was not available. I asked for his name. He did not give it and hung up."

"Mark had asked you to call the police?"

"That's right."

"Do you remember calling the police on August 24 at 10:19 p.m.?"

"I remember calling the police."

"Do you remember telling the police that Donnah Winger was quite upset with a limousine driver, and the man had told Donnah about killing people? Do you remember telling the police that?"

"Yes."

"That she was frightened, he knew where she lived, and that her husband was out of town."

"Yes."

"The police said that they would do extra patrol?"

'Yes."

"Donnah was actually your best friend," Breen asked.

"Yes, we worked out together, socialized with our husbands, talked frequently on the telephone."

"You betrayed her by this affair?"

"Yes, I was so unhappy in my marriage. I really did not think it through."

"When in Springfield you had sex with Mark Winger many times?"

"Yes."

"Where?"

"In the car, in hotel rooms, and in our homes."

"And it was this time that Mark told you that he wanted to marry you and that he loved you?"

"Yes."

"He wanted to leave upbeat and happy Donnah and Cindy and marry you?"

"Yes."

"And you were already married and had two children, a teenage daughter and a little boy?"

"Yes."

"You didn't find it odd because he suddenly wanted to marry you?"

"No. I was surprised when he said he was unhappy with his marriage."

"And that's because you had heard nothing but great things about the marriage, isn't that right?"

"Yes."

Breen then questioned DeAnn as to the conversation Mark had talked of Donnah dying.

"He said he had been thinking about it for some time. Just kind of threw it out, and I said that was crazy."

"Talked about what? Killing his wife? Talked about how it would be easier if she would die?"

"Yes."

"You never told the police about these conversations about dying, either before or after Donnah's death until February of 1999?"

"No, I did not."

"Did you ever tell Donnah, your friend, the one you talked to confidentially? Did you ever tell her that Mark was unhappy with his marriage, and she might be in danger?"

"No, I didn't."

"It was only after you broke up you became suspicious that Mark might have something to do with Donnah being murdered?"

"I became suspicious. In the first week or so I wondered. I could not believe that Mark would kill Donnah."

"But you never told anyone for three and a half years?"

"I could not. I was afraid to. I would lose my husband and my friends. Mark said that it would look like I was involved. I was scared."

"You went to Donnah's memorial services in Springfield and the burial in Florida, did you not?"

"Yes. I drove down with my husband. I met the Datzes in Florida."

"You didn't mention suspicions to John, the Datzes, or the sisters, or the Dreschers?"

"No, I didn't."

Breen then cross-examined her on the statement that she had given to Williamson and Cox in February of 1999.

Breen asked, "Do you recall on January 14, 1999, telling Officer Williamson that Mark was a very religious man and that divorce would not be an option?"

"Yes."

"According to what you have said today, this religious man who was opposed to divorce apparently had no problem talking about murder, is that right?"

"Objection!"

"Sustained."

"Were you hurt when you broke up with Mark?"

DeAnn said, "Yes, I loved him. I was hurt. Mark said that he couldn't see me anymore."

"Did you ask him why?"

"He wanted a clean break."

"As a matter of fact, you kept this affair secret from your husband of eleven years until 1999. Isn't that correct?"

"Yes."

"You never told him about it?"

"No."

"Even though the affair ended in February of 1996?"

"I was afraid he would leave me."

"Well, DeAnn, I am having some trouble with this. In August, you thought he might have something to do with the death of your best friend, Donnah. He allegedly made these statements, you didn't go to the police, you didn't tell anyone about them, you didn't come forward when they were investigating it, isn't that correct?"

"Yes."

"And you continued to have your affair in September, October, November, December, January, and February, isn't that correct?"

"Yes, it is."

"And all this time you suspected that he had killed Donnah?"

"I never really sat down and started thinking about it."

"Now when the affair broke up, it was in February, was it not? After Mark got home from his trip to Africa?"

"No, it was more like March."

"He never called you, did he?"

"No."

"You had to call him?"

"That's correct."

"He told you at the time that this affair was over. You should find someone else. Is that not correct?"

"Yeah, that is right."

Switching topics again, Breen continued, "Mrs. Schultz, you were interviewed by the police in 1995? You did not tell them of your affair or of these alleged statements, did you?"

"No."

"You did not tell them about either the affair or the statements in 1995?"

"No."

"In 1996?"

"No."

"1997?"

"No."

"In 1998?"

"No."

"You talked to him in November of 1998 and told of your problems, right?"

"I told him what had happened to my life."

"He told you he had remarried and had three children by his wife?"

"Yes."

"He had gotten his life together. You hated him and blamed him for what happened to your life?"

"Objection!"

"Goes to motive, Judge."

"Overruled. Answer the question, please."

"I was overwhelmed by my guilt, of my affair—that it might have caused Donnah's death."

"You wanted to get even for what happened to your life?"

"No."

"That is why you went to the police?"

"No."

"That is why you called Bart and told them not to settle?"

"No."

"You hated him and wanted to get even with him for destroying your life?"

"Objection!"

"Sustained."

"You wanted to make him suffer as you had?"

"Objection!"

"Sustained."

"You were a woman scorned?"

"Objection!"

"Sustained."

"No further questions."

Breen turned his back on the witness and walked away. It had been damning testimony, but could she be believed?

2. Dr. Joseph Bohlen

Schmidt needed to show that Harrington, although eccentric and strange, was not violent or dangerous.

Schmidt had worked with Dr. Joseph Bohlen, a psychiatrist, on other forensic cases. Schmidt asked Weinhoeft to collect all of Harrington's medical records and have Bohlen review them. Harrington had serious problems. In order to make a diagnosis Bohlen reviewed Harrington's medical and criminal files. There was a danger in this—Harrington's long medical history gave credence to the defendant's theory, but it had to be done.

Dr. Bohlen summarized Harrington's long medical history. He did not find anything remarkable before Harrington turned eighteen. The first records of hospitalizations were on May 10, 1990. He was diagnosed as having an adjustment disorder with emotional features and a personality disorder that was not specified.

He also examined his criminal records. In 1990 he had a domestic dispute with his wife, where he pushed her down, kicked her legs and hit her in the chest. She had bruised ribs. In January 1991, he was upset with his former wife and pointed a gun at her. He said he was going to hurt her or himself. The police took him to the emergency room, and he was committed for a week. He was diagnosed as compulsive, rebellious, hostile, aloof, and lacking in relationships and intimacy. He had a personality disorder secondary to depression. In February 1991 he was hospitalized for abrasions on his wrist, an apparent suicide attempt. In April 1991 the police took him to the emergency room for bizarre behavior, and his toxicology screens were positive for marijuana. He left against medical advice. In April 1992 he was diagnosed as having a personality disorder; he was antisocial, schizotypal, and had passive-aggressive tendencies. In June 1993 he was treated because a delusional spirit, Dahm, had taken control of him and wanted him to perform mass destruction. He was smoking pot, and his psychiatrist thought he had a histrionic or dissociative behavior.

In July 1993 he was seen twice and assessed with behavioral issues at St. John's Hospital. Dahm was telling him to take a trip down the Mississippi and to cause destruction with a weapon. He was smoking pot and had tested positive for alcohol. He walked out of the emergency room and was admitted involuntarily to McFarland, a state-operated mental-health facility, and was diagnosed with psychoactive substance-induced organic mental syndrome, marijuana abuse, and personality disorder. He had delusional thoughts and visions of destruction. He talked about terrorizing and torturing children, his friends, and family members. He was discharged after five days.

In August 1993 he described homicidal fantasies; he wondered if he could get more thrills out of life with the death of someone else, that he must kill someone to feel the experience of their pain, but he had not chosen the victim. He would choose them on the basis of who deserved to die. The therapist, however, did not believe that he was a danger to himself or to others. A week later he came back to the therapist and talked about his own death and putting out a contract on himself, but that wouldn't work because he wanted to face the killer himself. Again the therapist did not think he was a threat.

On October 26, 1993, he was admitted to a drug treatment center for substance abuse. He was discharged from the program for refusing to eat and odd behavior. He was transferred to McFarland's as an involuntary patient for two weeks; he frightened other patients with his bizarre drawings. He was diagnosed as having a schizotypal personality disorder, living in a fantasy and psychedelic type of experience, but no aggression was noted. He had "overwhelming thoughts of death and destruction." He was having auditory hallucinations and thought disorder, a delusional disorder related to chronic drug and alcohol use. His prognosis was poor, and he continued to have death fantasies.

On December 31 he described a new suicide plan that involved handcuffs, ropes, sleeping pills, and a lot of marijuana. The counselor thought he just wanted to get her attention. In May 1994 he was hospitalized with chronic undifferentiated schizophrenia. The last contact was in January 1995, when the therapist made a diagnosis of paranoid schizophrenia, drug and alcohol history, and marijuana dependency on a daily basis.

Breen did not object to any of this testimony; the more screwed up Harrington was, the more likely it was that he committed the crime.

Dr. Bohlen turned to the DSM Statistical Manual IV, the bible of psychiatrists, listing certain characteristics that categorize various forms of personality disorders—paranoid, schizophrenic, neurotic, etc.

Schmidt asked, "Do you have an opinion based upon the records as to what his psychiatric diagnosis is?"

Dr. Bohlen answered, "My diagnosis is that he had a schizotypal personality disorder, chronic marijuana and alcohol abuse."

"And what is a schizotypal personality disorder?"

"It is a pervasive pattern of social and interpersonal deficits. In simple terms, these people are odd and eccentric. They have a difficult time fitting into relationships with other people and society. It includes unusual perceptional experience, including delusions."

"Can you give an example?"

"You bet! In his case it would be Dahm's spirit. He talked about being able to fly, and the sprit would direct him as what to do."

"What else?"

"Mr. Harrington liked to utilize morbid ideations to keep people at their distance. He reported in August 1994 that Dahm had ordered him to go into a state of nothingness for seven days. He believes that Dahm will give him pain unless he does what Dahm wishes. He said he has seen people die in front of him by knife, die with a gun to their head. He carried a jewel box in his pocket in which he claimed the spirit lived."

Schmidt then asked him, "In your opinion is Dahm a delusion?"

"He just used the figure of Dahm to get attention."

"Doctor, how many times was Roger Harrington seen at the Springfield Mental Health Center?"

"By his counselor, twenty-five times. He had two evaluations by psychiatrists there between August 10, 1990, and January 9, 1995."

"Is it not a responsibility they have is to evaluate him to determine whether he is a danger to himself or others?"

"Yes. Throughout this course of treatment he was never determined to be a danger to himself or others."

"Was he ever found as a danger to someone else?"

"No, he was not."

"In review of the records, have you ever found anything where he made a threat to another person?"

"Not in the medical records. As to the arrest records they seem to be related to his wife or ex-wife. He didn't want her to leave."

"As to the burglary and criminal trespass and damage to property, what happened there?"

"His sister had been beaten up and her nose broken by her boyfriend. Her three brothers went to the boyfriend's house and trashed it. It was retaliation."

"What about torturing children in the notes of August 13, 1993?"

"The therapist concluded he was preoccupied and concluded he was not a danger. 'Will continue weekly contact with Roger. Will continue to monitor for dangerousness.'"

"And what is your diagnosis after reviewing all of these matters?"

"He certainly had cannabis dependency. He has a schizotypal or odd and eccentric personality disorder. My conclusion, based on these records and statements of the people he worked with and lived with, was that he was not violent. He would not be capable of bludgeoning Mrs. Winger to death, and he was not dangerous."

"Can you explain your reasoning?"

He had never acted out on these fantasies. The only time he demonstrated any act of violence was in the family relationship, never towards a stranger."

"Thank you, Doctor," Schmidt said. "Your witness."

Pugh asked, "Directing your attention to July 24, 1993, Mr. Harrington was discussing a canoe trip down the Mississippi with a weapon of mass destruction. Isn't that right?"

"That's correct."

"Involuntary commitment papers were filed against him, is that not correct?"

"That's correct."

"Some of the doctors saw Mr. Harrington as a danger to himself or others?"

"To himself."

"They didn't tell Mr. Harrington to go home, isn't that correct?"

"That's correct."

"And Harrington reported at this time that the spirit of Dahm was encouraging him to do these things of a violent nature and gave him actual commands?"

"Yes."

"Mr. Harrington was not treated from January 1995 until his death, was he?"

"No, he wasn't."

"You stated there is nothing in the record that indicated that Mr. Harrington was having any psychiatric problems between that day and the date of the death of Donnah Winger?"

"That's correct."

"But you didn't include in that the statements that were written down by Donnah Winger, did you?"

"No."

"That indicated that he was still having delusions about murder and death, didn't it?"

"You can say that."

"And he was not being treated at that time even though his therapist recommended continuing therapy?"

"Correct."

"You also saw the statement of his former wife, who was interviewed by the Springfield police, in which she said that Roger had threatened to kill her several times and had barricaded himself in their home, threatening suicide? Do you recall reading that?"

"Yes."

"Do you recall that the police recovered a blowgun, a hunting knife, a shotgun, and shells from his home?"

"Yes."

"Do you recall that Mrs. Harrington received two separate orders of protection for acts of violence up against Mr. Harrington?"

"The act of violence was hitting her in the chest. I don't know how much one was provoked by the other."

"You were aware that he was involved in a residential burglary? Mr. Harrington and two others kicked in the door of Mr. Schuler's trailer door?"

"Yes."

"And Mr. Harrington and the two others used knives to cut up the furniture within the house?"

"That's what I understand."

"And the knives were left sticking out of the wall?"

"I don't recall that."

"Doctor, would you characterize those as acts of violence?"

"Yes. These are relationship disputes. He and his brothers retaliated. This was in the context of a marriage."

"The individual record you read on Mr. Harrington mentioned a drug-induced psychosis?"

"That's correct."

"Drugs such as cannabis, cocaine, LSD can produce psychosis as well?"

"I'm not sure about cannabis, but psycho stimulus like speed, cocaine, and hash and LSD can do that."

"Mr. Harrington used crack cocaine and LSD?"

"I read that in one record that he did it in the past."

"You are not saying that it was impossible that Mr. Harrington could have suffered from drug-induced psychosis at any time after January 9, 1995?"

"I have no evidence about what drugs he might have been taking."

"In reviewing the records did you find that there was a correlation between Mr. Harrington's marijuana use and the statements regarding Dahm?"

"Yes, those were the times he came for appointments at the mental health center."

"You diagnosed Mr. Harrington as having a schizotypal personality disorder?"

"Yes."

"Under stress this disorder can destabilize and the symptoms reemerge?"

"That is my opinion."

"Losing a job would be a stressful circumstance?"

"It typically is."

"So it's your opinion that using drugs can cause destabilization, and losing a job can also?"

"Yes."

"One of the subcategories of personality disorders is antisocial personality."

"Yes."

"Antisocial personality disorder is psychopath?"

"Yes."

"Isn't it correct that psychopaths have difficulty sustaining a long-term marital relationship and frequently use drugs or alcohol?"

"Yes."

"One of the symptoms of a sociopath is lack of concern regarding society's rules and expectations—breaking the law?"

"Yes."

"And Roger Harrington used and possesses unlawful drugs, which meant that he was breaking the law?"

"Yes."

"Another symptom is repeated violation of the rights of others?"

"Yes."

"Domestic battery and kicking in the door or a house and tearing up a house with a knife would constitute violation of the rights of others?"

"Yes."

"A third symptom of psychopathic behavior is unlawful behavior. Unlawful behavior was engaging in pot smoking and crack cocaine, kicking in doors, tearing up a home?"

"Yes."

"Another symptom is the lack of regard for the truth. Harrington was manipulative?"

"Yes."

"Manipulation is a form of deception, is that not true?"

"Yes."

"And the fifth point for psychopathy is neglect or abuse of children?"

"Yes."

"And he mentioned to those treating him that he expressed a desire to torture children or their parents and family?"

"Yes, I related to his odd and eccentric behavior, but there is no evidence that he acted on these statements."

"Another point for a psychopath is having an unsteady job or frequent job changes through quitting or being fired?"

"That's true."

"And in reviewing his work history you found that his longest job was six months?"

"I think that is right."

"A psychopath has an antisocial personality, has tendency toward physical aggression. Those acts of domestic battery and residential burglary were acts of physical aggression?"

"Yes, one to property and one to a person."

"Now, Doctor, how many of those points would you have to meet to be called a psychopath under DSM IV?"

"I believe it says five. Many have similar and many have different traits. There are some traits that overlap for antisocial behavior with schizotypal."

"So schizotypal personality disorder and antisocial personality disorder certainly have some of the same attributes, is that not correct?"

"Yes."

"Isn't it a fact that Mr. Harrington talked about homicide and suicide?"

"Yes. But the counselor did not find himself to be a risk to himself or others."

"At his treatment at the drug abuse center, he was being treated for crack cocaine abuse, as well as marijuana abuse?"

"Yes."

"And the notes show that he was thinking of death when he was admitted?"

"That's correct."

"He was in McFarland's for fourteen days, was he not?"

"Yes."

"While at McFarland he discussed torturing of children and his friends and family members, and that would be his way of gaining respect. Is that not true?"

"Yes."

"While at McFarland, didn't he tell the social worker that he sees a thrill in the death of someone, and he wants to kill someone to vicariously experience their pain?"

"Yes."

"He was a loose cannon waiting to go off?"

"Objection!"

"Sustained."

"Losing his job caused him to explode when he saw Donnah?"

"Objection!"

"Sustained."

"No further questions." Pugh turns and sits down.

Harrington met the criteria for a psychopath. Schmidt had to reconstruct his testimony and put it in perspective.

"Dr. Bohlen, you still remain of your opinion that Mr. Harrington was schizotypal and not a psychopath."

"Yes."

"Can you tell the jury why?"

"The therapist took notes of all these statements. Roger talked about suicide, talked about weapons of mass destruction, talked about killing, etc., but none of these were ever actually done. She saw him twenty-five times. His statements were bizarre. He was saying those things to get her attention. You have to look at this record as a whole."

"What was the therapist's assessment?"

"That he had a personality disorder and not dangerous. All the psychiatrists, social workers, and psychologists I deal with would say personality disorder and nothing more."

"You testified how Mr. Harrington spoke and his attention-getting or—seeking behavior?"

"As the social worker became more acquainted with him, there was more awareness that these were manipulative attention-seeking ways to keep involved in the therapy. I know the therapist. She is an attractive young lady. He wanted to get her attention."

"The statements to Donnah Winger about Dahm and out-of-the-body experiences, wild sex parties in the country, those were just attention-seeking statements."

"That's my opinion."

"As for the domestic battery, you see that differently from a violent behavior."

"It's between someone with whom another person has a relationship. It is difficult to tell who caused it."

"You testified that you didn't know about the marijuana in the urine test on the autopsy. Does that change your opinion?"

"No, it doesn't."

"Is your opinion, based within a reasonable degree of medical certainty, Roger Harrington was not a sociopath or a psychopath?"

"Yes, that's my conclusion"

"Can you tell us why?"

"First-year medical students start reading medical books and think, 'My gosh, I've got all the symptoms of this or that disease. I'm going to die, etc.' If you look really hard you can find evidence that would fit a lot of different mental health diseases. If you have seen enough antisocial disorders, they are in a class alone. These are people who are mean-spirited, and they don't care what you think. They are always going to get their way, and Mr. Harrington doesn't come close to that categorization."

"And how many psychopaths have you treated?"

"During the first five years before my practice really got up to speed, I moonlighted at Jacksonville Correctional Center, and that place is full of psychopaths. My opinion is that Mr. Harrington did not have an antisocial personality. He was not a psychopath."

"Thank you, Doctor."

Schmidt sat down.

Judge Zappa said, "Thank you, gentlemen. As it is late we will break for Memorial Day weekend. I will see you back next Tuesday. I want to remind the jurors not to discuss the case and not to read newspapers or watch TV on this case. With that, I will see you next Tuesday."

D. May 28, 2002

1. Thomas Bevel—Crime Scene Expert

On May 28, after the Memorial Day weekend, Judge Zappa welcomed the jury. "I hope you all had a good weekend. I trust you kept away from the newspapers and TV."

All of the jurors nodded to indicate that they had.

Judge Zappa looked at Schmidt. "Are you gentlemen ready to continue?"

Schmidt answered, "Yes."

Judge Zappa said, "You may continue, Mr. Weinhoeft."

Weinhoeft stood. "Our next witness is Thomas Bevel."

Thomas Bevel was an expert witness on crime scene evidence. The prosecution called him to show that Winger's statements were inconsistent with the crime scene. Bevel had examined the photos and clothing from the crime scene and the statements of the witnesses. He was one of four leading experts in crime scene analyses in the country. He had written those reports on his analyses. However, Bevel had not requested DNA testing of the blood to determine whose blood it was. He had written in his report that none of Harrington's blood was on Donnah's clothes, and none of Donnah's blood was on Harrington's clothes. The defense's experts requested DNA testing during the trial that proved Bevel's conclusions wrong. The prosecution had to live with this error during Bevel's testimony.

Weinhoeft spent an hour qualifying Bevel. This is dry stuff, and the jurors listened but didn't seem particularly interested, but it had to be done. Bevel spent twenty-seven years at the Oklahoma City Police Department; he investigated forensic evidence of crime scenes during all of that time. After retiring in 1996 as a captain, he started a consulting service, analyzing forensic evidence of crime scenes. His expertise was blood spatter patterns and analysis. His business was thriving. He taught courses in bloodstain analysis and crime scene reconstruction throughout the country. He testified to his various certifications and courses he took for those certifications.

After being qualified, Bevel said that blood spatter was like hitting a puddle, and the water spatters in a definite pattern. The higher the velocity of the strike, the smaller the drop. He then defined castoff as similar to having a paint brush that you would swing back and forth. It would cast off paint. The liquid would spatter in a certain pattern. When castoff occurs it shows the direction of the swing.

"There is a vast body of knowledge on the pattern analysis of blood, but as to tissue stains there is not much study and not much knowledge. There is not much knowledge of tissue staining versus bloodstaining. When the tissue is mixed with blood it tends to be heavier and therefore travels further."

Weinhoeft handed the crime scene photos to Bevel. They are blown up on a screen. "Mr. Bevel, would you please describe what these photographs represent?" The jurors started paying more attention.

Bevel responded, "These are photographs of the crime scene. The first photo is taken looking east from the kitchen to the hallway. It shows two bodies. The feet are both pointing west. The second shows two pools of blood around Mr. Harrington, one under his head. There are two independent events, one creating the smaller stain and the other the larger stain."

"What do the blood patterns on the photos show?"

"The smaller bloodstain is not connected to the larger stain, There is approximately two feet between the two. It is consistent with Mr. Harrington being on the left side of his face on the carpet, and at some point he was rolled over from the smaller bloodstain to the larger stain."

"Can you tell from the position of the bodies where Harrington would have been standing when shot the first time?"

"From the location where there is the first bloodstain, you would basically rotate him up towards his feet so that he would be standing near the kitchen refrigerator. Then he landed face down, creating the blood flow and the contact transfer to the carpet. He was then rolled over as he was moved from face down to face up and shot a second time in the forehead at close range."

"Was Winger's statement to Cox that he shot Harrington when he was leaning over Donnah inconsistent to the physical evidence?"

"Harrington was not shot as he was leaning over Donnah Winger. The physical positions of the bodies were not consistent with that description."

"I have put on an overhead depiction showing the positions of the bodies. Please describe for the jury."

"The first is a depiction of where the bodies were. The feet of both bodies are facing the kitchen or west as shown by the photograph. I have a depiction of where the bodies were as found and have contrasted that to what Winger said."

Actual position of the bodies

A male juror fainted—too much blood. Judge Zappa called a recess and paramedics were called. He was excused from jury duty. The other jurors were then asked by Judge Zappa if they were okay. They said yes. He was replaced with a female alternate.

"Do you have a depiction of where Winger said the bodies were?"

"Yes, this is a depiction of what he said to Detective Cox and in his deposition in the civil trial."

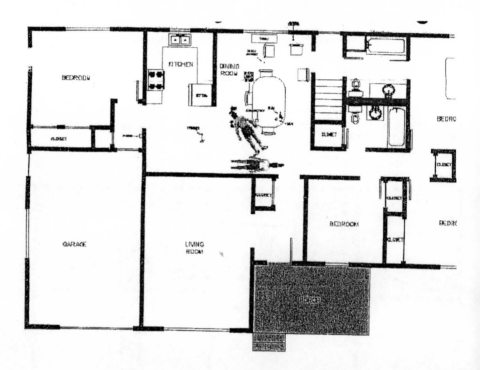

Position of the bodies according to Mark Winger

"The actual evidence in the first diagram is totally inconsistent with what Winger told Detective Cox. It could not have happened as he said. Winger said that Harrington rolled off of Donnah when he shot Harrington. The pictures of the crime scene show that Harrington was six feet from Donnah."

Weinhoeft continued, "Winger said he shot Harrington twice, once a grazing shot and the second shot in the forehead seconds apart. Please describe the path of the second shot."

"The bullet path from the second shot is traveling in a fairly close proximity to the first wound track that is filled with blood, and that will force the blood that is in the first wound track out. It is called back splatter. There was splatter present on Harrington's shirt. It could go in a 180-degree range in a cone shape. There is an illustration of that shot."

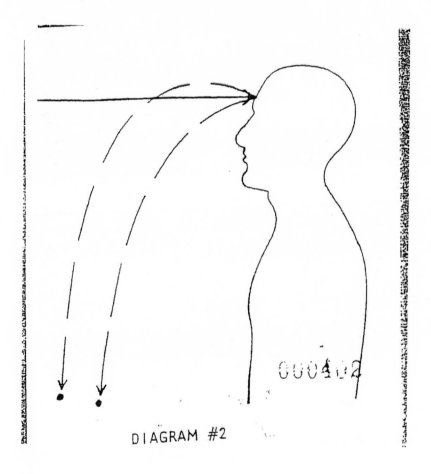

DIAGRAM #2

"What is the significance of that shot?"

"It was close range and after Harrington was rolled over."

"Did you examine the back of Mrs. Winger's shorts?"

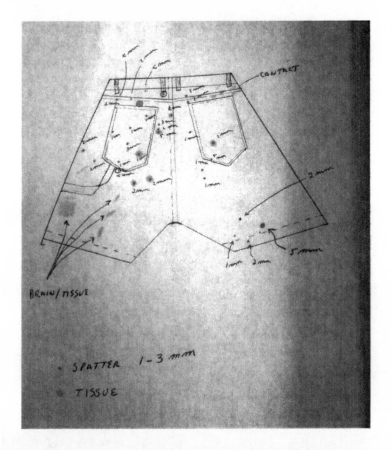

"I did. Mrs. Winger originally was face down. She was subsequently rolled over by the paramedics. There were no high-velocity-impact bloodstain patterns on the shorts consistent with someone being shot with someone leaning over her. Those bloodstains were Donnah Winger's, and they would be consistent with impact spatter when her head was struck."

"At the bottom of Donnah's shorts, is there a large yellowish-colored stain on the left side of her leg?"

"The majority of those stains are consistent with tissue. The stain at the left edge of the pocket was consistent with Harrington's blood. There are two possibilities of how those stains were created. One is from the projection from Mr. Harrington, going onto the carpet and subsequently rolling over. The other possibility is the projection from Harrington being shot the second time and going far enough to actually get on her shorts. The stain at the top edge of the pocket was consistent with Harrington."

"If the assailant was kneeling when administering the strikes to the victim on one knee, would you expect there to be blood splatter on the shoes and socks?"

"I would at least look for it on the shoes and socks. I find no evidence whatsoever of blood splatters on the wife's shoes."

Weinhoeft put on the overhead the photo of the south wall. "Looking at the south wall, can you tell the ladies and gentlemen of the jury the direction in which the hammer was being swung?"

"Yes, I can. The evidence, as shown in the photographs, would tell me that the killer was facing the south wall and swinging the hammer in a north-south direction."

"Please tell us why you concluded that."

"There is cast-off spatter on the south wall. If someone was swinging the hammer toward the south wall it would create roughly a ninety-degree pattern of elongated stains, and if there was sufficient force on the back swing it would produce castoff both back and forward motion. This pattern is consistent with castoff. The blood was going straight out, and that means you would have to be swinging in a north-south direction—inconsistent with the defendant's description of Harrington swinging from right to left."

"Where was Donnah Winger when she was receiving the blows?"

"She was next to the south wall."

"Is there any blood on the ceiling?"

"Yes, it also had a cast-off pattern. It would be from the forward swinging. You can see that on the fingers of the blood on the ceiling."

"What do you mean by fingers?"

"The bloodstains are not round but are elongated, showing the direction of the force."

"Was there any blood on the west wall?"

"There was. This was the result not of the swinging of the hammer. Blood spatter would not track that far. It was the result of Donnah Winger's shirt being thrown against the wall by the paramedics. In addition, if the blood was coming from the hammer, I would expect there to be blood on the ceiling near the west wall, and there was none. The evidence is that the shirt was thrown against the wall and the blood elongated by dripping from where it hit."

"Was there any evidence showing the position of the attacker facing the hallway as the defendant stated?"

"No."

Weinhoeft had seen the defendant's expert report and knew what he was to testify to. He therefore asked questions anticipating what the defense would be.

"In examining the front of Harrington's shorts, did you find any of Donnah's tissue on them?"

"Yes, and that would have been caused by the hammer strikes that were to the chest of Mr. Harrington. Winger told Detective Cox that after the 911 call he struck Harrington in the chest with the hammer because he was groaning. The hammer was blood soaked with Donnah's tissue and blood, and in my opinion that's how Donnah's tissue got on his shorts."

"So your conclusion is that Winger's statement was not consistent with the crime scene?"

"That's right."

"And the position of Harrington's body is not consistent with what Winger described?"

"Yes."

"Did you examine Winger's shirt?"

"Yes, I found contact smear when he took off his shirt and rolled it up. The blood had soaked through. I found spatter patterns on the outside consistent with Donnah Winger's blood. The inside of the shirt had spatter that was consistent with castoff."

"Was there castoff on the back left sleeve of Winger's shirt?"

"Yes, it was Donnah Winger's blood."

"Was there any brain tissue on Mark Winger's shirt?"

"On the right side of his shirt."

"So in your examination of the clothing, the defendant's blood was on Donnah's clothing, and Donnah's blood was on the defendant's clothing?"

"Yes."

"Is that consistent with Defendant Winger hitting Donnah on the head with a hammer?"

"Yes."

"That's all. Your witness."

Pugh began his cross by pointing out that there are no absolutes in the interpretation of bloodstains and that experts can and do disagree in their interpretations of the stains. Breen agreed.

Pugh then asked, "You never saw the crime scene or the south wall. You only looked at the photos?"

"That's correct."

"Therefore, you could only estimate the size of the stains from the photographs?"

"That is correct."

"The greatest amount of blood spatter was just west of the doorway?"

"Yes."

"And that is in close proximity to where Donnah Winger was found?"

"That is correct."

"So you would agree that most of the blows from the hammer were in the vicinity of the south wall?"

"I would agree."

"The majority of the bloodstains were found to the right of the door frame and traveling upwards?"

"That is correct."

"Isn't it true there are some stains on the lower portion of the wall to the west of the major stains seemed to be traveling downward?" True.

These are to the right of the light switch. They could be coming off the upward swing or also part of the parabolic arch going up and them coming down with gravity."

"As to the west wall, you observed tissue and blood about halfway down the west wall, isn't that correct?"

"Yes, tissue had some movement to the west and down."

"You also observed some blood down on the west wall?"

"Yes."

"You thought that they could have been caused by someone throwing the bloody shirt of Donnah Winger to the wall?"

"I recall that."

"Did anyone testify that the shirt was thrown against the west wall?"

"No, sir, but the shirt in the picture appears to have been thrown there. It wasn't wadded up."

"Now referring to Mark Winger's T-shirt, you identified some of the stains were diluted with sweat as if he had been working out?"

"Yes, it would be consistent with a man sweating."

"On Mark Winger you identified three stains you found to be significant for DNA testing?"

"Yes. Two stains were consistent with Donnah Winger's blood type."

"So there were only two stains on Mark Winger's T-shirt that reflects blood type consistent with Donnah Winger's?"

"Only two were tested. We could not test all of the stains."

"You had her clothing as of January 18, 2001, a year and a half ago, and did not request any DNA testing?"

"That's correct."

"You, at our request for DNA testing, recently identified eight stains to be DNA tested. Three of those were on Mr. Winger's T-shirt, and the remaining five were on Harrington's shorts and T-shirt?"

"That's correct."

"The opinion that you gave, before the DNA testing, as to Mrs. Winger's shorts and her shirt not having Harrington's blood on them was in error, right?"

"Yes, sir."

"There is nothing in your report of 2002 regarding Mrs. Winger's shorts, is there?"

"Not that I recall."

"When was the DNA testing first done?"

"At the beginning of this trial."

"So you originally based your opinion and conclusions of Mr. Winger's guilt on incomplete results?"

"I did not have the DNA results."

"Laber and Epstein, our experts, identified a cluster of stains on the back of Donnah Winger's shorts, which were Harrington's blood, did they not?"

"Yes, they did."

"You never saw anything of any significance prior to their reports, did you?"

"That would be accurate."

"Just below the left pocket, Harrington's blood was found on the back of Donnah Winger's shorts, is that correct?"

"That's correct."

"And you are aware that Mr. Winger told Detective Cox that the first shot he fired was when Roger Harrington was behind his wife and he shot him in the head."

"That's correct."

"This could have been back spatter."

"Yes."

"You testified the second shot of Mr. Harrington's head projected blood in a cone fashion across the room to Mrs. Winger. That is not referenced in any of your written reports, is it?"

"Only verbally to them and you after the DNA testing."

"That was only after your written opinions that there was none of Harrington's blood on Donnah and none of Donnah's blood on Harrington."

"Yes, that's correct.

"Your written report was wrong, was it not?"

"I still agree with that. My report only refers to blood."

"But you will agree that the blood and tissue on Roger Harrington's clothing matches Donnah Winger's DNA?"

"Yes, tissue mixed with blood."

"Now you are quibbling right—it says blood and tissue. That means blood was there?"

"My report says no blood. I was referring to blood alone."

"And there were two more stains of Donnah's on the fly of Roger Harrington's shorts, right?"

"Yes."

"You would agree that the tissue stains that start at the right side of Mr. Harrington's shorts, which makes its way down the midline to the left-hand side of the shorts, were Donnah's."

"Yes, sir."

"That could indicate that Harrington was leaning over Donnah?"

"Well, I guess so."

"Looking at the pictures of the crime scene, there were two blood pools near Mr. Harrington?"

"Yes."

"There is some blood dropping between the two stains, is there not?"

"Yes."

"You testified that the stains would be consistent with someone being rolled over."

"That's correct."

"Could that be consistent with a person trying to get up or moving their own head?"

"I wouldn't be able to say that's absolutely impossible."

"The rollover is not in any of your reports, is it?"

"No."

"Mr. Bevel, how many times have you testified before a jury?"

"Over a hundred."

"You were hired by Bart Transportation to defend the suit Mark Winger had brought against it, isn't that correct?"

"Yes, sir."

"And their intent in hiring you was to prove that Winger killed his wife and not Harrington."

"Objection!"

"Sustained."

"No further questions."

Steve Weinhoeft, on recross, asked, "Mr. Bevel, when you were asked about the rollover you said you couldn't exclude the possibility of Mr. Harrington moving himself to the second bloodstain based upon the carpet alone. Are there other factors which would indicate a rollover?"

"Yes, there are other factors. The blood was found along the forehead and also the distance between his head and the blood pool. It is consistent with the bullet trajectory found in the carpet. This makes the rollover the most probable resolution based upon the physical evidence."

Weinhoeft also asked if the recent DNA testing changed his opinion that Winger was the one who wielded the hammer or his reconstruction of the events of the murder. He said it did not. Again, he confirmed that there is a significant difference between the analyses of blood splatter and tissue splatters. Weinhoeft then asked if Bevel was retained by the Springfield Police Department before being hired by Bart. He answered, "Yes."

Pugh, not giving up, pointed out that there were seventeen or eighteen stains tested on Harrington's shirt, either of ABO or DNA and that five of them were Harrington's and five were Donnah's and the other undetermined. Bevel was asked if Dr. Hindman found blood on Harrington's right hand, and he answered, "Yes."

Judge Zappa said, "You may step down, Mr. Bevel."

"The state rests," Schmidt said.

"We have some motions," said Breen.

"Okay, the jury is excused while we hear these motions. We will reconvene on May 30 at 9:30 a.m."

Bevel's Exhibits

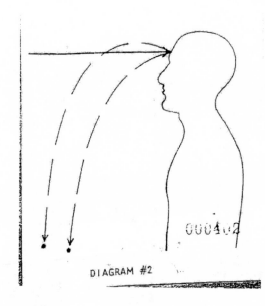

DIAGRAM #2

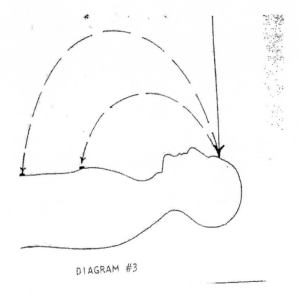

DIAGRAM #3

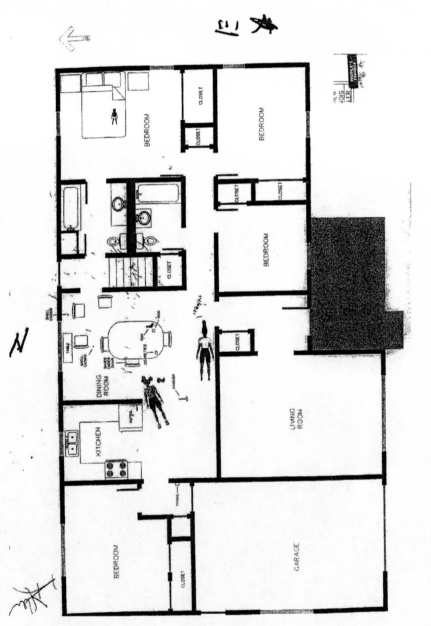

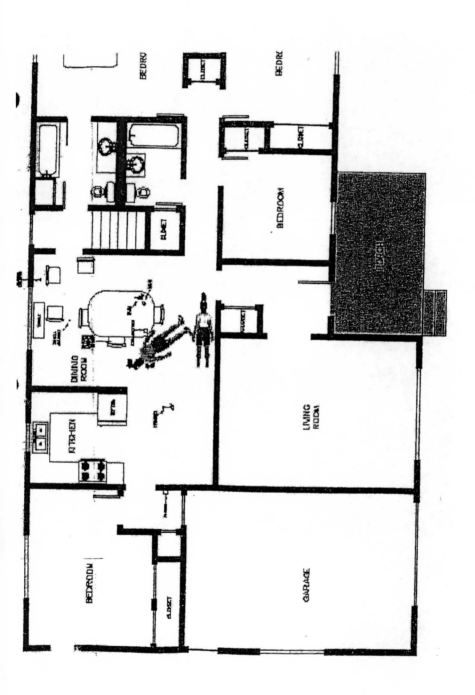

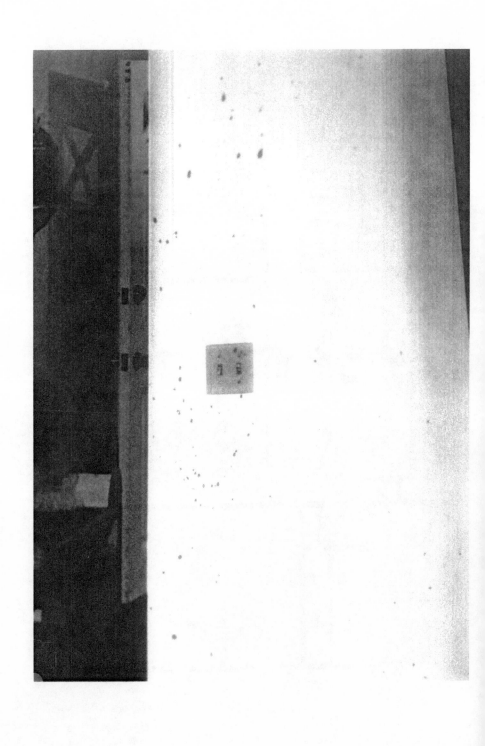

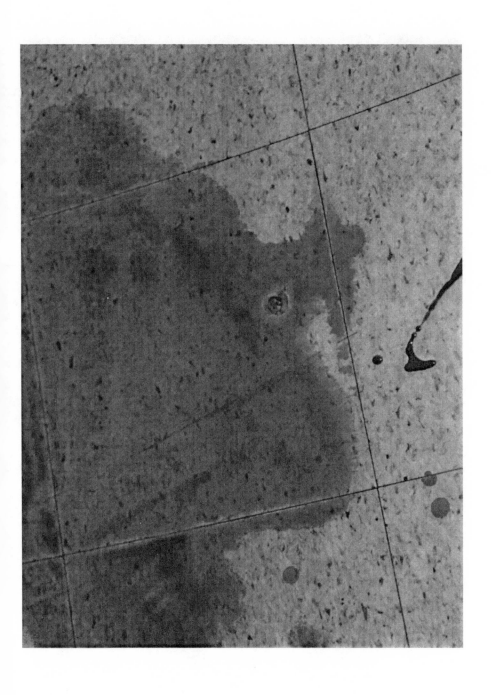

DONNA W.

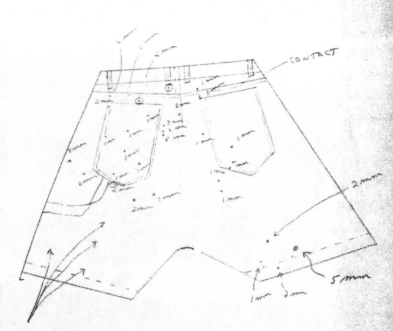

BRAIN/TISSUE

CONTACT

2 mm

5 mm

1 mm   2 mm

• SPATTER 1-3 mm

• TISSUE

HARRINGTON - T-SHIRT
BACK

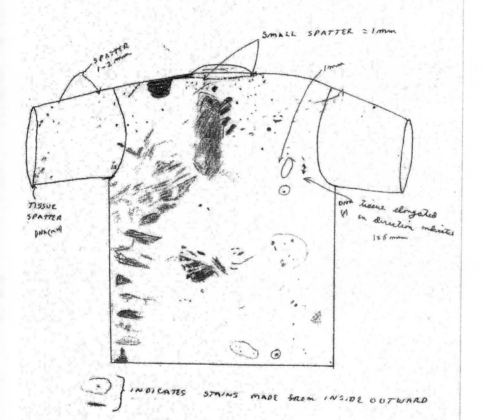

SMALL SPATTER ≈ 1mm

SPATTER 1-2 mm

1mm

TISSUE
SPATTER
DNA(M)

DNA tissue elongated
(A) in direction indicates
186 mm

} INDICATES STAINS MADE FROM INSIDE OUTWARD

PART V

The Defense

*Assume we have a box, and in that box are a cat and a mouse. We put the lid
on the box; we walk away. When we come back the mouse is gone. Is there any
reasonable doubt on what happened to that mouse? If when we come back,
we open the box and there's a big hole in the side of the box. Is there reasonable
doubt of what happened to that mouse? Well, let's turn to the holes
in the prosecution's case . . .*

~Litigation News, American Bar Association

CHAPTER 22

The Defense

A. May 29, 2002

Breen and Pugh decided not to call Mark Winger. He had not told anyone about the affair. He had given a deposition in the Bart case, a lengthy statement to Cox, and different descriptions of how the crime occurred to friends. He was just too vulnerable on cross-examination. He wanted to testify, but the conflicting statements and his arrogance persuaded his attorney not to put him on the stand.

To establish reasonable doubt they would rely upon their psychiatrist and crime scene expert and their prior cross-examination.

As the jury, parties, and their attorneys assembled in the courtroom on May 29, 2002, Judge Zappa said, "Mr. Breen, are you ready?"

Breen replied, "You bet."

1. James Cavanaugh

Breen's first witness was called James Cavanaugh, a psychiatrist with extensive experience with violent psychiatric patients. He was called to contradict Dr. Joseph Bohlen. His opinion was that Harrington was considered dangerous and not just harmless and weird.

Dr. Cavanaugh was from Chicago. He graduated from Williams College and obtained his medical degree from the University of Pennsylvania. He interned at Cook County Hospital in Chicago and was a professor of psychiatry at Rush Medical College. He was the director of the Section on Law and Psychiatry. He was the chief executive officer of the Isaac Ray Center and former president of the Illinois Psychiatric Society.

He had extensive experience in evaluating individuals who could be violent. He was one of the four psychiatrists evaluating John Hinckley, who attempted the assassination of President Reagan, when he raised the defense of insanity. He consulted with the FBI and Secret Service in evaluating detainees to determine their risk to the president or to the members of the cabinet. He advised the Secret Service about individuals who were making threats against political figures. He authored over fifty articles and contributed chapters on forensic psychiatry in at least eight to ten books.

As did Dr. Bohlen in evaluating Roger Harrington, Cavanaugh reviewed the available psychiatric records, the records from St. John's, from McFarland Mental Health Center, and the Central Illinois Mental Health Center. He reviewed the court records, Harrington's high school records, employment records, Dr. Bohlen's notes and report, the notes of Donnah Winger describing her trip with Roger Harrington, and the autopsy files and articles explaining the relationship between marijuana use and violent acts.

Breen asked, "After having reviewed these materials did you form an opinion as to the psychiatric condition or mental health of Roger Harrington?"

"I made a probable diagnosis. Roger Harrington could be dangerous." Cavanaugh continued, "I sure would have liked to have talked to Roger, but obviously that was not possible. Based upon the records I feel comfortable making a probable diagnosis. Actually four diagnoses are probable."

"And what are they?"

"Number one, he has a schizotypal personality disorder. Two, he has an antisocial personality disorder. Three, he has a delusional disorder. Four, he has a substance-induced psychotic disorder."

"What's a schizotypal personality?"

"A schizotypal personality is just shy of being schizophrenic. It is characterized by bizarre thinking, superficial relationships, and odd behavior. It is a marginal person that doesn't fit into the mainstream. Those types of people get involved with antisocial acts. Frequently you will find that they are involved in substance abuse. Under stress, they can become psychotic. They don't manifest these psychotic disorders on a day-to-day basis, but under certain stressors they can."

"What about an antisocial individual?" Breen asked.

"An antisocial individual is one that can be superficially charming, but underneath you find that they have engaged in various kinds of illegal behaviors. They can be very manipulative. They can break the law and generally are outside the mainstream. They have very low self-esteem. They don't keep jobs very long, and they have unstable interpersonal relationships."

"The third category was a delusional disorder?"

"It is a false belief system. Delusion is reality to the individual. It's like it is actually there. In Harrington's case, Dahm was a figure that influenced his life and would fly over his head. This figure sometimes punishes him and makes him become anorexic. It gives him hallucinations about killing people. This is a classic delusion."

"And what is a substance-induced psychotic disorder," Breen asked.

"That is an individual who has a full-blown psychosis. They are out of touch with reality, have hallucinations or delusions, hear voices, see things when they are under the influence of a substance. It could be marijuana, alcohol, PCP, cocaine, or heroin. Many people can use marijuana and not become psychotic, but the people who have underlying psychiatric difficulties are prone to show deterioration. He loses touch with reality and maybe hears voices and sees images."

"Did Roger Harrington need continuing psychiatric treatment?"

"He was a chronic psychiatric patient and needed ongoing treatment. His prognosis was guarded particularly with regard to substance abuse and the psychological deterioration and psychosis."

Cavanaugh continued, "There are gaps in the psychiatric records in this case. The last time he saw a therapist was in August 1994. The last telephone contact was in January 1995. There are no records of treatment for about a year before the murder."

"Could you form an opinion as to the psychiatric condition on August 23, 1995?"

"Yes, at the time frame of the trip he was speaking and acting bizarrely, talking of killing people, marijuana parties. He was driving fast, talked of Dahm, and was excitable. He seemed to be having a psychotic episode."

"Doctor, do you believe that Roger Harrington was potentially dangerous on August 29, 1995?"

"No doubt in my mind about that. He was receiving no treatment. He continued to use marijuana and had a history of being involved with other illicit drugs such as crack cocaine. He was fascinated with knives and guns. He had homicidal fantasies. He would commit suicide, kill people, and serve time for murder. He saw it as his destiny. He wondered if he could get more thrills in life out of the death of someone else or himself. He wants to kill someone and vicariously experience their pain. This was all in his record."

Breen continued, "As to a person who smokes marijuana, there is the testimony that that person is just mellow and not violent. What is your experience?"

"An individual who doesn't have any particular psychiatric or medical problems, he or she are quite commonly not going to have any unusual reactions other than feeling mellow, but we are not talking about that with Roger Harrington. This is not a normal, stable, put-together normal human being. This is the type of person, when you add marijuana, you can see a decomposition, which means they get symptomatic and can become psychotic. This is particularly true if there is a stressor—losing a job, etc. In coming to my conclusion, I also had an expert on drugs and human behavior, Dr. David Hartman, review the matter, and he agreed with that conclusion."

"Were there any records to support your conclusion?"

"On January 4, 1991, he was reported as having an explosive temper outburst in the emergency room. In July 1993 he had psychiatric hospitalizations for hearing voices and had suicidal ideation. He had delusions of Dahm. This spirit died in 1575 and came to Harrington at the age of sixteen. Harrington was involuntarily committed at this time. In November of 1993 he was diagnosed with a personality disorder and complaining of hearing voices. He said he likes to see people in pain. In March 1994 his urine was positive for amphetamines, speed, and marijuana. He refused treatment at various times and left the hospital AMA (against medical advice)."

"What else did you find in the records?"

"He was admitted to the Triangle Center, a drug treatment center, and was discharged because they couldn't handle him. Due to his preoccupation with death and other morbid topics he was dismissed from the agency. He also said that 'My hero is Dr. Kevorkian.' He said, 'I almost killed my wife.' When asked how it related to death, he said, 'I've seen people put a gun to their head. I've had a gun put to me twice, one by an enemy and one by a friend.' He had these morbid fantasies."

"Did you also review his employment record?"

"His longest period of employment was eight months. The average was three months. Harrington stated he had experienced LSD, PCP, cocaine, crack, and heroine. That shows an antisocial background."

"Was there a closing summary of the therapist?

"On April 4, 1995, it states he had problems of a spirit controlling his body. Auditory and visual hallucinations. Homicidal and suicidal thoughts. Was receiving weekly individual therapy. Psychiatric treatment was recommended but refused. Was diagnosed as chronic and undifferentiated schizophrenic. This was based upon the last contact in January 1995."

"Did you review Donnah Winger's note about her ride on August 23, 1995?"

"You bet. It is consistent with his psychiatric record. In my opinion, in reviewing these records he was potentially dangerous. He had an explosive personality. It could be triggered by losing his job. There was no question in my mind that he could be dangerous."

Breen had gotten what he wanted. He turned to Schmidt. "Your witness."

Bohlen's testimony was that Harrington was harmless and just trying to impress a young female therapist by his statements. There was a clear conflict of opinion.

Schmidt asked, "Doctor, you have no medical records at all of Harrington's mental status in August 1995?"

"No, but I do have information about him, Donnah's notes."

"You have information about his behavior and what people thought of him in 1995?"

"Yes."

"Are you familiar with the statements of his friends and employer that they found Roger to be mellow and a nice person and that he never mentioned Dahm to them?"

"They knew him only superficially."

"He never saw Roger commit any acts of violence?"

"That's correct."

"One statement was from a friend with whom he was living in August 1995?"

"He had only been living there for one month."

"For a full diagnosis of antisocial behavior, it would require history of conduct disorder before the age of fifteen, wouldn't it?"

"That is right, but more importantly it would include an opportunity to examine him and get the history."

"There is no history before fifteen having a conduct disorder?"

"No, there isn't."

"And therefore you can't make a full diagnosis of antisocial personality, can you?"

"I don't have a full diagnosis of anything. I testified from records, and what I believe the most probable diagnosis was antisocial personality, commonly called psychopath or sociopath."

"Yes. Sociopaths normally have numerous contacts with law enforcement?"

"They may but not necessarily."

"Can sociopathic people be charming?"

"Yes. But if you get below the surface you'll often find meanness and not adhering to society's rules."

"Roger Harrington's arrest records are related to domestic violence, is that not correct?"

"Yes, domestic relationships where he hit his wife several times and broke into a house and sliced up the furniture of his sister's boyfriend."

"When you talked about sociopathic persons, they talk about killing or torturing animals in their youth?"

"That can be one of the childhood precursors."

"As with Roger Harrington you don't have that information, do you?"

"No, I do not."

"You don't know anything about Roger Harrington before he turned fifteen, do you?"

"That's correct."

"Sociopathic personalities lack remorse?"

"That's classic."

"Didn't Mr. Duffy say that Harrington told him that he was sorry?"

"I believe he said that, but I make a distinction between wanting the job back and having remorse."

"Doctor, one of the things you look at is the person's past to determine the future?"

"That's called an analytic technique, yes."

"On August 30, 1993, at the Springfield Mental Health Center, he made the statement that he had homicidal fantasies wishing to kill someone vicariously and feel their pain. Do you remember that?"

"Yes."

"But the therapist didn't think he was a danger to himself or others, isn't that correct?"

"That's correct."

"The therapist could have committed him against his will, couldn't she?"

"She could have."

"The therapist was using her best judgment and did not think he was a danger to himself or others?"

"I am sure it would have been better for him than to have been committed. Retrospectively I question why he was not."

"Being fired from a job could be a stressor?"

"I said that."

"Do you know if Roger was fired from his job?"

"I know he was fired from the job before Bart, where he was described as argumentative and he missed many days of work within the first two to three weeks."

"Then he got a job with Bart?"

"Yes, that's correct."

"On July 25, 1993, Roger Harrington was admitted to McFarland because Dahm had told him to float down the Mississippi with a weapon of mass destruction, and Dahm was a delusion?"

"That's correct. He planned to do it on Monday. Since Monday had gone he was then discharged."

"On July 25 1993, it was a voluntary admission, was it not?"

"Well, they filled out a certificate, but they didn't proceed with it because he signed himself under the threat of being committed."

"So this was a voluntary admission, wasn't it?"

"Yes, under threat of being involuntarily admitted."

"And the psychiatric team said they did not believe him to be committable—a danger to himself or others?"

"That's correct, but he was diagnosed as a delusional disorder related to chronic drug use and also a schizotypal personality disorder. He was not seen as an immediate threat."

"Doctor, are you familiar that Harrington's tox screen in the path report came back negative for alcohol and for cocaine?"

"Yes, but did come back positive for cannabis in his urine."

"Doctor, you are familiar with personnel records from Bart Transportation?"

"Yes."

"They stated he was very cooperative and enthusiastic about his job. They never had a problem with him. He was patient, even tempered, a pleasant person, courteous, and a gentleman. Is that not what the company said? They also described him as clean-cut with good manners."

"Yes, it did."

"Did you consider this in your forensic diagnosis?"

"Yes, I did. It was his personnel report. Two people that superficially knew him said that he could be pleasant and very charming, etc. I see no way that could jib with the extensive, detailed, repetitive clinical information. It is clear that he is a chronic psychiatric patient. You could argue what the proper label is, but the bottom line is that he's crazy."

"There was a note from a detective who interviewed a Mrs. Sherburn, who knew Roger Harrington for two and a half years and lived with him for six months. Sherburn said he was different, but he was never violent towards her or around her. Did you read that report?"

"Yes. And in the eyes of a lover, many things happen."

"He never did any of the things he talked about, did he?"

"No, if you exclude Donnah and his ex-wife."

Breen had a few questions on redirect.

"As to the records before Mr. Harrington was fifteen, there were no records available to your knowledge."

"That's correct."

"That doesn't mean that there were not actually any records. It was just that no one could get them?"

"That's correct. As a juvenile they would be sealed. I do have some school records where he was an extraordinarily poor student, straight Ds and very low in class ranking. He had to repeat the tenth grade. I also have military records where he did not serve long. He got out on a medical discharge."

"How long have you been in forensic psychology?"

"For over twenty-five years."

"In your analysis did you rely upon your day-to-day experience?"

"As a clinician I am guided by my experience. You pay a lot of attention to the records, but in the final analysis you have to put it all together based on your experience and judgment."

"As to Roger Harrington's mental illnesses, do they get better over time?"

"Typically no. In Mr. Harrington's case his psychiatric problems would just start up and spontaneously remit. He needed to be in treatment, and one of the reasons is that he could lose impulse control. He needed it. The records are very clear about that. He wanted out of the hospital, and he knew if he didn't say he was going to go out to kill someone or himself they would let him out. This should not be equated to the fact that he is normal or he is not potentially dangerous. If the patient just states that he or she has a destiny to kill, that would not be sufficient for commitment. The threat has to be imminent."

On recross, Schmidt asked, "He never acted on his statements to kill others, to feel their pain, to torture others, etc.?"

"No."

"He never showed the underlying meanness of a sociopath to his friends?"

"No."

"In fact, that was just talk, right?"

"Right, unless you consider his action towards his family and ex-wife."

Schmidt said, "That's all I have."

Judge Zappa said to Breen, "Call your next witness."

2. Terri Edwards

Terri Edwards was Harrington's ex-wife. They had met in November of 1989 and were married on December 19, 1989. They remained married for a year until Terri filed for divorce in 1990.

Breen asked, "During the course of the marriage were there instances of violence in your home?"

"Yes, there were."

"When was the first incident?"

"Roger and I had not been married very long, about three weeks, and we had an argument about household chores. He pointed a shotgun at me in the kitchen and told me to say good-bye. I got out of the apartment and called the police. He was arrested."

"Were there other incidents of violence?"

"Several months later when we had moved into a trailer court, Roger and I were having a dispute, and things became really violent. He threw me down and got on top of me and was hitting me in the chest and cracked my ribs. The police came to the trailer court. I think it was Officer Cox, and Roger was arrested. I had to go to the hospital."

"There was another incident, wasn't there?"

"Yes, in the trailer, and I was trying to leave. He wasn't going to permit that to happen. He threatened to kill me, tried to handcuff me."

"Did you ever file for orders of protection against him because you were concerned about his violence?"

"Yes, I did."

"Could you tell when he was going to get violent?"

"It would happen when he became agitated."

"No further questions. Your cross."

Belz asked, "Have you ever seen Roger being violent to strangers?"

"No, I would characterize Roger as a bit of a wimp."

Breen then asked, "Did you think he was a wimp when he pointed a shotgun and told you to say good-bye?"

"No."

"When he beat you up and sent you to the hospital?"

"No."

"So he could be violent when he was agitated?"

"Yes."

"No further questions."

3. Tim Young

There were inconsistencies in the police reports on who made what calls to Harrington. Breen called Officer Tim Young. He had interviewed Susan Collins at Memorial Medical Center and at her residence. Collins had told him that Harrington received calls from work on August 28 and 29. If Harrington received a call on the twenty-ninth, it would strengthen his arguments that the note was written after the call from Bart on the twenty-ninth.

Breen asked, "Detective Young, did Mrs. Collins tell you that Roger had received a telephone call on Monday, the twenty-eighth, afternoon from work when they told him there was no more work for him until he straightened out the problem with Winger."

"Yes."

"Did Susan Collins tell you on Tuesday, August 29, the day of the murder, that in the afternoon Roger talked to someone from work, and they told him he was supposed to talk to this guy and to get things straightened out?"

"Yes, sir. The conversation was at the hospital."

"Did Susan Collins also say to you, Detective Young, that Roger had written a name and address on the back of one of her bank deposit slips that afternoon after that call on the twenty-ninth?"

"Yes, sir, she did. She told me that the name was that of the person who had made the complaint concerning one of his fares."

"At the house Mrs. Collins told you Roger had talked to someone from work for approximately ten minutes?"

"That's correct. Roger had walked out of the room on the portable phone and went to his bedroom to talk to that man from work."

"So she told you that there was a call from work on August 29, the day of the murder?"

"Yes."

"Susan Collins said that the call that Roger had received from work went on for a lot longer than the one from the husband?"

"That's correct."

"She wasn't able to hear the conversation, isn't that correct?"

"Yes, sir. Collins told me that after the call from work the husband wanted to meet him around four thirty."

"Detective, you also interviewed Susan's daughter, Tricia Ray?"

"Yes, sir."

"Ray told you that on August 29, in early afternoon, Roger had talked to someone from work?"

"Yes, that's correct."

Breen had established that there was a call from Harrington's place of work on the afternoon of the twenty-ninth. He could argue that the note was written after the call from his employer. He decided to leave it good enough alone and sit down.

Belz then asked on cross, "There were two different conversations with Mrs. Collins, were there not? One at the hospital and one at the trailer?"

"Yes, that's' correct."

"Did she not tell you when she was interviewed at the trailer after she had calmed down and said that the name and address were written on a bank slip at the time of the call from the husband?"

"Yes, she stated that the morning after he had received the call from a woman's husband that he wrote down on the back of the bank slip the name and address and time. She told me that when we were out at her trailer."

On redirect Breen asked if Tricia Ray was at the residence at the time of this interview.

Detective Young said, "Yes, she was."

"Tricia Ray did tell you, did she not, that Roger received a call from work in the afternoon, didn't she?"

"Yes, she did."

"Did Tricia Ray say she wasn't around for the call at 9:07 a.m. because she was in bed?"

"Yes, she said that."

"Detective Young, they had caller ID, did they not?"

"Yes, sir."

"Did you write down any of the other numbers other than the one from Mark Winger's office or the time at which these other calls were received?"

"No, sir, I did not. I do not recall any calls before or after 9:07 a.m., but there may have been. I didn't write them down."

"So there could have been a call after 9:07 a.m. on the twenty-ninth from Harrington's dispatcher or someone else from work?"

"I did not note any."

"No further questions."

One by one the defense proceeded to poke holes in the prosecution's case. First Harrington was said to be crazy and possibly a psychopath; now the note couldn't have been written after the call from Bart. Breen now needed to poke holes in the prosecution's crime scene expert's testimony. For that they called Terry Laber.

B. May 30, 2002

1. Terry Laber

Terry Laber had been employed by the state of Minnesota in its laboratory in St. Paul, Minnesota, from 1971 to 2000. This department has undercover agents, homicide agents, etc., in addition to laboratory scientists who process the forensic evidence that has been collected. Laber's job was to analyze evidence of crime scenes, in particular bloodstains, body fluid stains, and trace evidence, and then present these findings to the court. He was the supervisor of the serology unit from 1974 to 1998. In 1998 he was promoted to assistant laboratory director, supervising two units of the laboratory. After retirement he was rehired by the state as a project consultant to train police officers in bloodstain pattern analysis. There are only four to five blood spatter experts in the United States, and two of them were used in this trial.

In 1991 Laber began training in DNA analysis with an FBI task force formed to study DNA analysis. He was one of the original members of this task force. His qualification testimony went on for twenty-four pages of the transcript; it was impressive.

Laber had reviewed the photographs, the lab reports, the ABL testing, the report of Tom Bevel, the police reports, autopsy photos, the crime scene photos, etc. He needed DNA analysis. He requested it on the eve of the trial. On May 24, 2002, while the trial was ongoing a report was received with the DNA results of bloodstains on the clothing of Mark Winger, Donnah Winger, and Roger Harrington.

Pugh asked the court to recognize Laber as a DNA expert.

"Objection!" shouted Weinhoeft. "He qualified as a bloodstain expert but not a DNA expert," Weinhoeft said, rising from his chair. He wanted to keep this DNA testimony out.

"He is probably the foremost expert in the country. He has spent over ten years in this area," Pugh replied.

Judge Zappa responded, "Denied. Let's get on with it."

Pugh asked, "Take a look at the photographs of the south wall. What do you see?"

Bevel had said it was castoff. Laber disagreed.

"Impact stains. Impact stains project back to the impact site. There is a point of origin, and that is where the blood originated. When there is impact the blood can go off in a direction that would be fan shaped on the wall going in different directions. If you take a string and align it with the direction of the bloodstain the blood should come back to the area of impact."

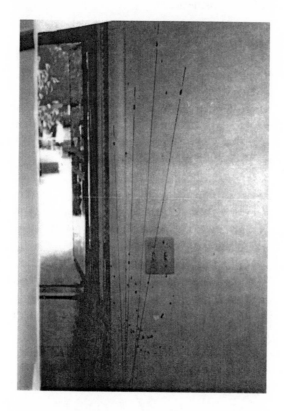

As to the south wall, he said, "All bloodstains converge at some point on the floor, indicating that they are coming from impact. These are also gravity stains going down, indicating impact. The stains don't have the characteristics of castoff. The angles and the details of the stains are all impact."

"Are there stains on the ceiling above the south wall?"

"At the center of the ceiling there are six different round stains. They are situated long on the edge of the wall, traveling in a line east and west. The ceiling is rough. When the blood hits a rough ceiling it shoots out spines, and you can determine the direction of those spines. There are other stains on the wall going up very near on the ceilings, which are impact stains traveling in an east-west direction along the edge of the ceiling. There are six individual stains on the ceiling, but they are in a line along the edge of the ceiling, going in an east to west direction."

"And what does that tell you of the direction of the weapon?" Pugh inquired. Bevel had said north-south.

"It was swung in an east-west direction."

"Did you find anything else along the south wall?" Pugh asks.

"At maybe ten feet from Donnah Winger, there is a piece of tissue. It adhered to the wall and was traveling in an east-west direction. It could have gotten there by adhering to the hammer when it was flown in the backswing or from impact also."

"That would be consistent with the in-line stains upon the ceiling and on the south wall. It would also account for the piece of tissue. It supports my opinion that the hammer was swung in an east-west direction."

Laber then examined exhibits of the west wall, fourteen or fifteen feet from the impact area showing bloodstains. "As to the bloodstains, I can't say how they got there, but they are projected there, as some are airborne. Castoff or impact would be the only way they could have gotten there."

Zeroing in on Bevel, Pugh continued, "Mr. Bevel stated that they would have gotten there when Donnah Winger's shirt was thrown and flung in that direction. Would you comment on that?"

"As the shirt that was lying next to Donnah Winger for a period of time, if the shirt was thrown against the wall, it would not give this appearance. The drops of blood would not fly from the article, and the tissue would not fly up the wall. Furthermore, I am not aware of any testimony that the garment was thrown."

"Mr. Laber, looking at the pools of blood on the floor, how did these pools of blood occur?"

"The large pool of blood where Harrington was lying occurred when he was shot the second time. As to the small pool of blood, between the bullet hole and the small pool of blood, the distance was approximately sixteen to seventeen inches. It most likely was from a person lying in one position after being shot and then being rolled over or rolling over and shot a second time."

"Mr. Bevel stated that Roger Harrington was originally lying face down in the smaller bloodstain. Do you agree with that?"

"No, I do not. If you are lying on the side of your face or on the front of your face, I don't see any evidence that it was lying in that pool of blood. If he was lying on the side of his face I would expect to see matter in the hair."

Pugh then asked, "Did you examine the bloodstains on Roger Harrington's, Donnah Winger's, and Mark Winger's clothing?"

"Yes, after my initial examination of Donnah's clothing, I did not believe it came from gunshot wounds. They were large tissue stains, and the direction was inconsistent with coming from Harrington's wound. I asked for DNA analysis. I did the same with the jean shorts of Donnah Winger."

Laber continued, "On Harrington's shirt, there were bloodstains that appeared not to be mixed with any other bodily fluids, and there were bloodstains that were mixtures of a yellow-type fluid consistent with spinal fluid from the skull, a yellow fluid mixed with blood. I asked for DNA of these stains."

"After your examination of the clothing of the individual, what did you do?"

"We made a diagram of the clothing, and then using a magnification of 5x we marked off the stains. After we did that then we viewed the diagram as an entire pattern."

"Did you do that with the T-shirt of Mark Winger?"

"We found very large contact bloodstains consistent with holding somebody and coming into contact with a large body of blood. There are areas of transfer stains. The shirt was stained inside and out. There were not any patterns on Mark Winger's shirt consistent with impact."

"Did you remove any stains for closer examination?"

"I removed two stains."

"What about the stain from the right upper sleeve?"

"That stain came from the outside and landed on the shirt. It was an impact stain. In the region around the stain, I did not find any other impact stains, but all the stains were contact."

"Now turning the T-shirt inside out and looking at stain number eight, can you tell us what the stain is on the right sleeve?"

"Mr. Bevel said that the stain on the right upper sleeve was consistent with castoff, but I did not find any pattern consistent with castoff. In order to have castoff you have to have a pattern. I examined all four sides of the shirt Winger wore, inside and out. I found only contact staining."

"Did you examine Donnah Winger's denim shorts?"

"Yes, I made a diagram of them."

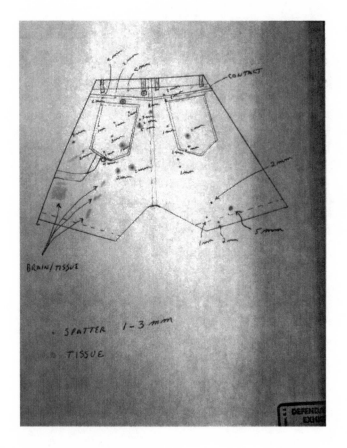

"What did the diagram show?"

"There were two different types of stains. They are all fairly small with the exception of one stain on the lower portion. Yellow fluid is mixed with the bloodstains, and there are other very small stains that show no evidence of tissue. There were stains above the pocket near the belt loop, and there are four stains on the back of the right leg. The areas of the shorts above the right pocket were impact. They were very small, the size of a tip of a pen. There was a large contact."

"You would have expected blood from Donnah Winger on Harrington's shirt if he was beating her over the head with a hammer. DNA analysis after Bevel's reports stated that none of Donnah's blood was on Harington's shirt. Bevel was wrong."

"Was Harrington's blood on Donnah's shirt?"

"Yes."

"Do you have an opinion on how Harrington's blood got on Donnah Winger's shirt?"

"It is consistent with blood spatter from the first shot to Roger Harrington's head when he was beating her with a hammer. This was confirmed by DNA analysis. It supports Winger's statement that Harrington was over Donnah when he was shot."

"Did you diagram Harrington's shorts after it was cut off?"

"Yes."

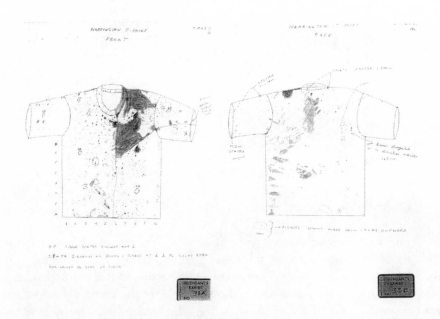

"Please describe what you found."

"There was a stain right below the belt loop. It contained yellow brain tissue. There are other stains with spinal fluid, elongated down the pant leg. There is an excess of twenty-five small stains, some mixed with tissue, which are impact stains. There are two sources of these bloodstains, Donnah Winger or Roger Harrington. There is a stain underneath the seam of Donnah's shorts. It is impossible for this stain to have come from Donnah Winger, as it had no tissue in it."

"Did you request a DNA analysis of that stain underneath the seam?"

"I did of several stains. This included the stain below the belt loop and the stain above the pocket and the stain below the pocket. The DNA test on those stains matched that of Roger Harrington. There were other stains in the same size and the same area."

"What is your opinion as to how those stains got on the back of Donnah Winger's shorts?"

"They were consistent with a gunshot to Roger Harrington when he was shot the first time."

"And what did Mr. Bevel say about these stains?"

"He said it could have been consistent with blood coming from the wound of the first shot as the second shot was fired into the forehead. I disagree."

"Did he mention that in his reports of 1999, 2001, 2002?"

"No, sir, he did not."

"Why do you disagree?"

"The distance between the locations of the large pool of blood and Donnah Winger is about six feet. Blood splatter would have originated very close to the floor. It does not have enough mass to travel six feet. The stains of less than one millimeter could not travel that distance."

"In reading Mr. Bevel's report about Harrington's shirt, what did he say?"

"Bevel said that none of Donnah Winger's blood was on Roger Harrington's shirt."

"And what did you find?"

"Small stain patterns on the front three inches of the sleeve. If you look at the back side of this sleeve there is no staining. The direction on the front of the sleeve is down the sleeve. There are many small stains that cover a large area of the front of his shirt. They are all over. They are not mixed with tissue. There are a number of other stains, tissue and bloodstains, which are traveling down Harrington's shirt. These are gravity or impact stains consistent to hammer strikes to Donnah's head."

"Could these stains have come from the gunshot wound to Harrington's head?"

"No. The direction of the stains, the number of the stains, and the physical amount of tissue is not consistent with coming from the forehead wound."

"You recommended that some of the stains be tested by DNA?"

"A stain was taken for DNA sampling from the inside of Roger Harrington's left sleeve, and the DNA matched Donnah Winger's."

"Were other stains DNA tested on Harrington's shirt?"

"The tissue stain on the back of Harrington's left sleeve had Donnah's DNA."

"If Mr. Harrington was swinging the hammer over his shoulder while hitting Donnah in the head, could that have deposited Donnah Winger's tissue and blood on his right shoulder?"

"Yes, and it was Donnah's DNA."

"Mr. Bevel testified that it was possible that the blood could have gotten there when Mark Winger struck Harrington in the chest with the hammer. Is that possible in your opinion?"

"No. Harrington was lying on his back. Striking him in the chest would not have deposited those stains on Harrington's back."

"Now let's take a look at the shorts that Harrington was wearing. Was the large tissue stain along the belt area above the right pocket DNA tested?"

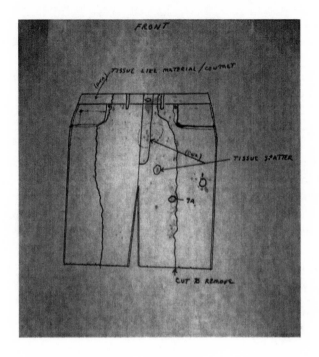

"Yes, and it was Donnah Winger's DNA."

"In examining Donnah Winger's shorts, did you find similar stains?"

"On the back side of Donnah Winger's shorts there was a large contact stain with tissue on the back left side. This is similar to the stain noted on the belt line of Roger Harrington's front right shorts."

"What else did you find on Roger Harrington's shorts?"

"Around the fly area there was a cluster of stains. They are a mixture of blood and have tissue and are perpendicular. DNA showed that these were Donnah Winger's blood, again consistent with Harrington leaning over Donnah."

"Moving down Harrington's shorts, was there anything else that you noted?"

"In an area marked 7A there are gravity stains and elongated. Essentially they are falling down the jeans. That stain was determined to be Donnah Winger's tissue from DNA testing."

"Mr. Bevel said these DNA samples of Donnah Winger were produced by the hammer strikes to the chest of Mr. Harrington. What is your opinion?"

"The tissue on Roger Harrington's shirt and shorts were not produced by that. It was not possible."

"Why?"

"The stains from the hammer blow would have been cessation or castoff. The tissue would continue and would be driven into the shirt, where it hit the shirt. On the hammer there was a lot of blood but very little tissue. The tissue was behind the claw of the hammer and not on the head. It is not going to cause a gravity stain. It would radiate from the strike and not be parallel or perpendicular to it. They could not have come from the hammer because of the direction in which they are deposited, the way they are located, their size. It simply could not have happened."

"Were the stains you found on Harrington's shirt and shorts consistent with the gunshot wounds to his head?"

"No. They had Donnah Winger's DNA on them."

"After examining the shorts and shirts of Mr. Harrington and of Mrs. Winger, do you have an opinion whether these stains were consistent with Mr. Winger's version of events?"

"Yes, and they were consistent."

"Your cross, Mr. Weinhoeft."

It was now three thirty-five on a Friday afternoon. Judge Zappa told the jury that they would remain in session until they finished with this witness. He didn't want Mr. Laber to stay over the weekend. They then took a short break.

After the break Weinhoeft started his cross-examination. There was clear conflict of opinion between Bevel and Laber.

"A lot of the analysis of blood pattern is subjective, is it not?"

"Yes, a lot is subjective. Different people can look at the same thing and come to different conclusions. That happens."

"Your opinion is that the physical evidence is consistent with the defendant's version of events that he told to Detective Cox."

"Yes."

"Winger told others different versions of what happened."

"I haven't seen those statements."

"You completed you report on May 12, 2002, the day before the jury was selected, did you not?"

"Yes."

"And in that report you requested DNA analysis, did you not?"

"Yes. I looked at the pattern and selected representative examples. I wanted to see whose blood and tissue they were. Bevel apparently did not think that necessary. When I requested DNA, Bevel also selected some stains for DNA analysis."

"Like Mr. Bevel you selected a small number of stains to select and test, simply because you can't test every stain."

"That's correct. We selected what we felt were the most important stains from the patterns."

"Looking at the south wall, you saw groups of stains that went from the floor to the ceiling, and you drew lines to connect them up?"

"That's not correct. I drew lines through the individual bloodstains, not through the groups of stains. I did not see any linear patterns. I did not see what I would call castoff. There were areas where you could line up four or five bloodstains, and some of those elongated stains were gravity stains."

"There were spots on the ceiling also, was there not?"

"Yes, the stains on the ceiling that were going east to west direction. The stains were smaller than a drop of blood. You cannot say that was blood."

"Yes."

"Assuming that that's blood, there are six stains that are lined up in a cast-off pattern in an east-west direction?"

"Yes."

"You also indicated that there was a piece of tissue halfway down the south wall?"

"Yes."

"You can't say that it was not blood?"

"No."

"If it was blood how did it get there?"

"It could have been either castoff or impact. There was no pattern so you couldn't determine which it was."

"And after the line of six stains, you don't find any other stains going toward the west wall, do you?"

"No, not on the ceiling or on the wall."

"If the attacker was holding a hammer facing an east-west direction he would be looking down the hallway, is that not correct?"

"That's correct."

"You did not find any stains on the carpet looking to the hallway?"

"Yes."

"Then isn't it likely you would find castoff in the hallway if the hammer was swung in an east-west direction?"

"I disagree. You have to take into account the position of the person or the position of Donnah. If someone is on the ground and you are making the swing, I would expect to find blood going forward. If you were bent down and you are raising the hammer straight up, there is no centrifugal to send the blood forward. It is different depending on the position of the body."

Weinhoeft then examined Laber on bloodstains that were on the chairs. "There are five bloodstains on one chair. If the killer was facing the south wall and swinging back with a hammer, this is the place you would find castoff, is that not correct?"

"Yes."

"If the killer was facing an east-west direction it is not where you would expect to find castoff, is that correct?"

"That's correct."

"But there was blood there, so do you have any opinion how it got there?"

"No."

"In your direct examination you said that the killer was facing an east-west direction?"

"Yes."

"You conclude that without being able to identify a single cast-off pattern facing the east-west direction?"

"None on the south wall. I did identify a pattern that's castoff on the ceiling, but I don't know if its blood. There wasn't a single stain at the scene that was treated for the presence of blood. We can see that they are the same color as blood."

"On the stains on the west wall there are roughly three, but you don't know what type of bloodstains these were, do you?"

"They could have been from impact or castoff."

"The tissue way down the south wall, you don't know if that's impact or cast-off stain?"

"There is no pattern."

"There is nothing in the east-west hallway that was castoff, was there?"

"The photographs aren't sufficient to show anything."

"As to the aspirated blood, Harrington had aspirated blood on his jeans, is that not correct?"

"I would not agree with that. I would characterize the blood on his jeans as back spatter, but we cannot eliminate aspirated blood."

"Are you aware that Donnah Winger was struck in a violent fashion at least seven times in the back of the head?"

"Yes."

"You are also aware that Winger hit Harrington in the chest with a hammer at least two times?"

"Yes."

Weinhoeft needed to show that Harrington's blood on Donnah and Donnah's blood on Harrington could have gotten there from these hammer blows.

"A cessation castoff was certainly possible to occur when Harrington was struck by the hammer?"

"In all likelihood it did occur."

"When Roger Harrington was shot the second time he was lying on his back. This shot could have caused spatter onto Donnah, right?"

"There is evidence that it did cause quite a bit of spatter, but it would not go far enough to reach Donnah."

"Because the hammer that struck Harrington in the chest had previously been used to hit Donnah Winger, it could have left castoff on Roger Harrington, is that not correct?"

"Yes."

"The fact that Winger went over and struck Mr. Harrington in the chest with the hammer after holding his wife would significantly affect the possibility of cross contamination on Donnah's shorts?"

"Yes."

"There was evidence of large pieces of tissue from Donnah on the shoulder of Mr. Winger, was there not?"

"Yes, on his left shoulder."

"That could be a result of cross contamination?"

"Yes."

"Blood and tissue spatter could have different characteristics?"

"To some extent, but in many crime scenes you will find blood and brain tissue in the same locations."

"The two stains you tested on Roger Harrington's shirt were described as fat with very little or any blood?"

"Yes."

"That is solid, is it not?"

"Not necessarily. We think of it as being solid, but when it is impacted, such as from a gunshot, it is not unusual to see tissue spatter. I examined it under a microscope, and there was tissue, not the presence of fat. Tissue has a different consistency."

"There isn't any research that deals with the analysis of tissue spatter against blood?"

"No, there is not. I made my conclusions based upon experience of hundreds of crime scenes where there has been tissue spatter. I have seen fat spatter where I have observed bloodstains and made comparisons. On tissue stains you can determine the directionality of the stain."

"There are a number of tissue stains on Harrington's shirt, are there not?"

"Yes, some of the stains could be contact smear."

"Let's take a look at the shorts of Donnah Winger again. You indicated there were twenty-five one—to three-millimeter impact stains on her shorts, is that not correct?"

"Yes."

"On the bottom of her shorts there is a rather large tissue?"

"Yes, that particular one is a contact stain."

"There are other tissue stains. Just above that was the DNA of Roger Harrington?"

"That's right. They are elongated in the direction of the pant leg. I characterize them as contact or possibly castoff or coming down from impact."

"As Harrington was originally lying on his stomach, it could be castoff?"

"It is very unlikely based upon the nature of the staining pattern."

"But possible?"

"I guess so."

"This crime scene was contaminated by the police, paramedics, the gunshots, the rolling over of the bodies of Donnah Winger and Roger Harrington, the attempts to resuscitate the victims, etc., was it not?"

"Yes."

Donnah's blood was found on the front of Harrington's shorts and his blood on the back of Donnah's shorts. It was consistent with Harrington leaning over Donnah when striking her. Breen and Pugh felt that they had created reasonable doubt. The defense rested.

The judge said, "Ladies and gentlemen, we need to work on the jury instructions over the weekend. On Monday, we will finish up. Closing arguments will be on Tuesday."

Laber's Exhibits

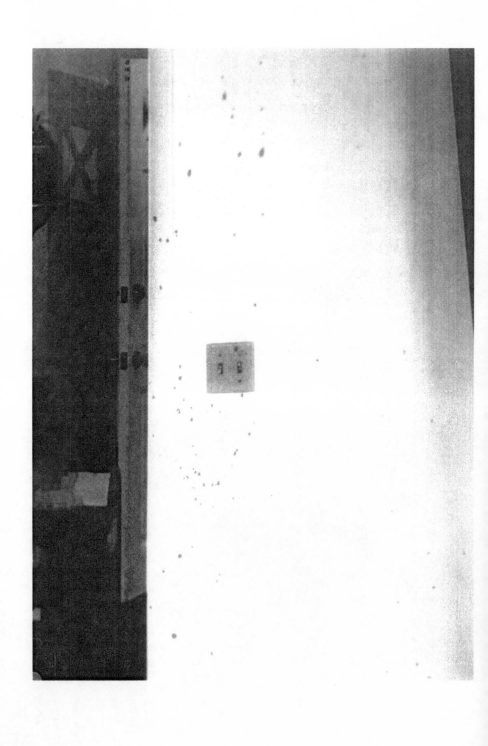

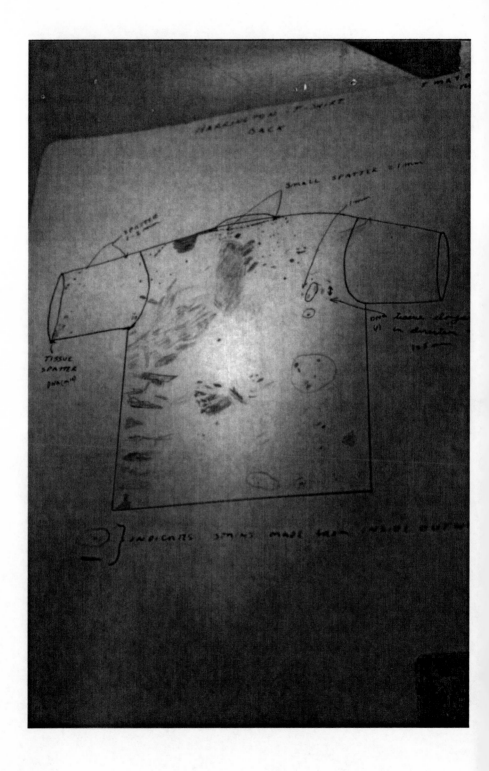

Harrington's Shorts

Front

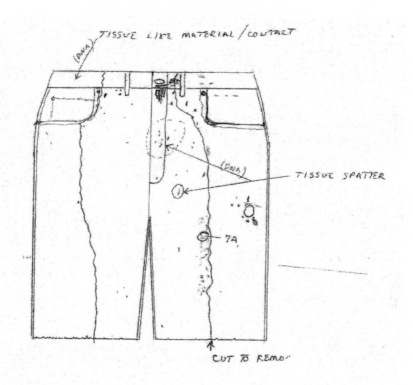

TISSUE LIKE MATERIAL / CONTACT

(DNA)

(DNA)

TISSUE SPATTER

7A

CUT TO REMO-

Donnah W.

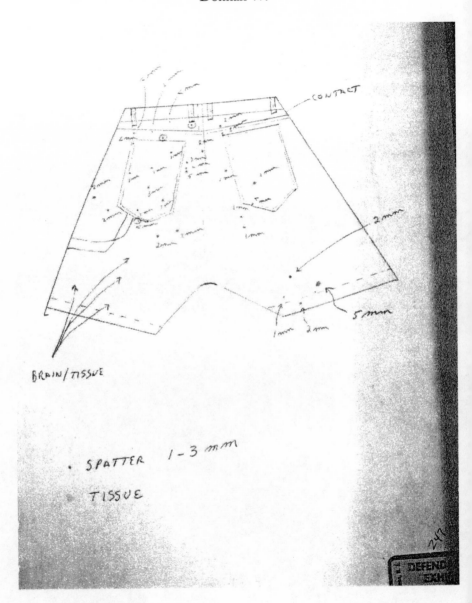

HARRINGTON T-SHIRT

FRONT

7 MAY 0
72

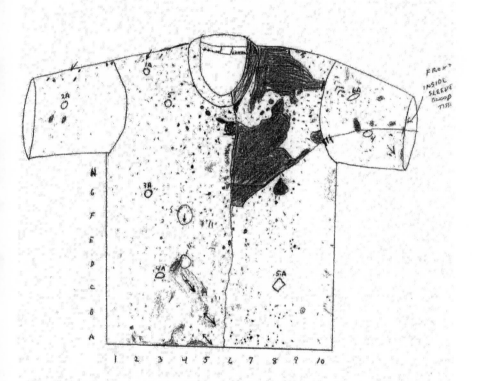

3-F   TISSUE SPATTER ANGULAR AND ⊥

3-B → 5A DIAGONAL of BLOOD & TISSUE AT L ⊥ TO WOUND AREA

DNA SHOULD BE DONE ON TISSUE

FRONT

TISSUE LIKE MATERIAL / CONTACT

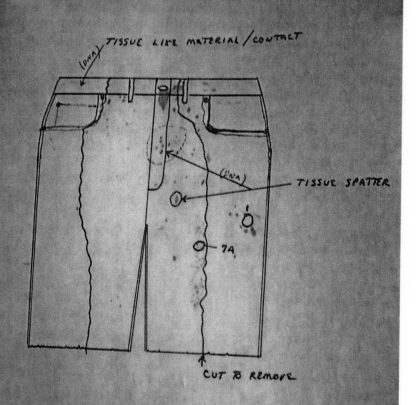

(DNA)

(DNA)

TISSUE SPATTER

7A

CUT TO REMOVE

Harrington's T-shirt

Front

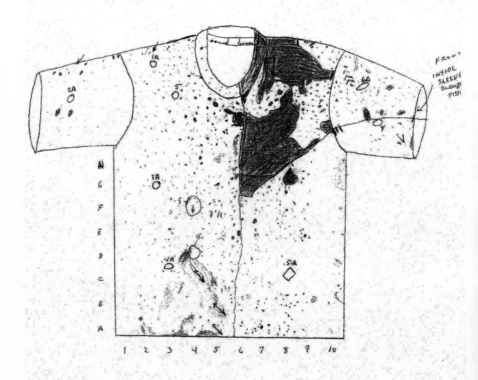

3-F   TISSUE SPATTER ANGULAR AND ⊥

3-θ→5A DIAGONAL OF BLOOD & TISSUE AT L ⊥ TO WOUND AREA

DNA SHOULD BE DONE ON TISSUE

Harrington's T-shirt

Back

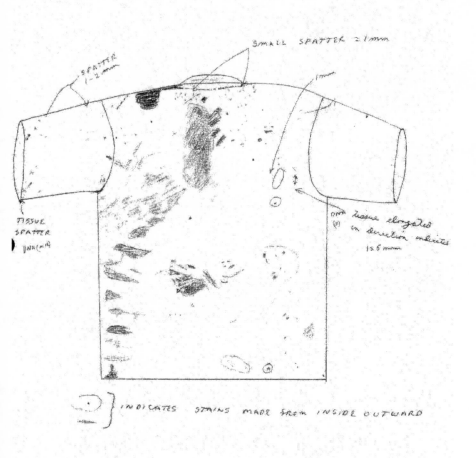

SMALL SPATTER ≈ 1mm

SPATTER 1-2mm

1mm

TISSUE SPATTER

DNA(mA)

DNA tissue elongated in direction indicated 12.6mm

INDICATES STAINS MADE FROM INSIDE OUTWARD

CHAPTER 23

The Closing Arguments
June 4, 2002

On June 4, 2002, the courtroom was packed, the atmosphere tense. The families of the Harringtons, Wingers, Browns, and Dreschers were all there. They were not looking at each other.

After the jurors were seated, Judge Zappa welcomed them back and said, "Ladies and gentlemen, both parties have rested their cases, and it is now time for the closing arguments; as the state has the burden of proof. It opens and closes. The defendant will make his closing argument after the state and the state will then make its rebuttal. At the conclusion of the arguments I will instruct you as to the law, and then you will retire to the jury room to decide the case."

Judge Zappa said, "Mr. Belz, are you ready?"

"Yes, sir."

Belz had been working all weekend on his closing. Not mincing his words, he started, "Mark Winger set up the meeting with Roger Harrington on August 29, 1995. He lured him into the kitchen, shot him, and then beat his wife to death. Donnah Winger heard the shot, put the baby down on the bed, and ran into the dining area. The defendant hit her over the head seven times with a hammer, and she died an awful death. He then called 911.

Hearing Harrington moaning he then hung up, rolled Harrington over again, and shot him in the head, execution style. That is what happened, and that is what the state has proved."

"Mark Winger and Donnah were married in 1987. John and DeAnn Schultz and Donnah and Mark Winger were good friends. They were such good friends that Donnah and DeAnn could talk together about any of their problems. DeAnn confided to Donnah that she and John were having intimacy problems and that she was thinking of leaving Springfield. Donnah told Mark of this conversation when he was in Chattanooga, Tennessee, taking the first course for updating his skills. Mark called DeAnn on July 17 and told DeAnn that he knew about her marriage and that he was having similar problems with his. Mark suggested that he and DeAnn meet in Mount Vernon, Illinois, over the weekend. She expressed reservations, and then in a series of telephone calls, she agreed to meet on July 20. Their affair started at that time. They had twenty-seven telephone calls during these two weeks. He told her that he loved her. She was getting the attention she craved. Passion took over."

"On July 29, Winger returned home. The affair continued. They could not get enough of each other. DeAnn said that she would divorce John. Mark said that it would be easier if Donnah just died. All she would have to do is find the body. DeAnn said, 'That is crazy. If anything happened to Donnah I would cease to be a vital person.' The passionate affair continued, in the parking lot of Jungle O Fun, in his truck, in her car, in motels, and, during the day, at their houses. He again told DeAnn that it would be easier if Donnah died. DeAnn said, 'I am going to divorce John. You do what you have to do.'"

"Donnah and John knew nothing about this affair. They continued going out together, eating together. Donnah and John were completely in the dark".

"On August 13, Winger had the second of his two training sessions in Chattanooga, and Donnah went to visit her mom and stepdad in Florida while Mark was out of town and took Cindy, their newly adopted child, with her. She went on August 19 and stayed there five days. She came back on the twenty-third. Mark's training ended on August 25. While Donnah was in Florida, Mark and DeAnn again met in Mount Vernon on August 20, continuing this passionate affair".

"In going to Florida, Donnah had taken a shuttle to St. Louis to catch a flight to Miami. The shuttle company, Bart Transportation, picked her up on her return on August 23. Roger Harrington was the shuttle driver. He met her at the airport. She got into the van in the front seat, and they headed to Springfield."

"Roger Harrington was weird. He talked of strange things and had a spirit, Dahm, that told him what to do. He drove fast, talked of using explosives, flying outside his body, smoking marijuana, living with an older woman, nude parties, etc. Donnah was concerned. He knew where she lived and that her husband was out of town."

"Upon arriving home, Donnah called DeAnn, and said, 'I have a patient for you.' DeAnn said he sounded schizophrenic and off his meds. DeAnn stayed with Donnah on Thursday and Friday nights until Mark Winger returned home on Saturday."

"On the twenty-fourth, there were telephone calls between Mark, Donnah, and DeAnn. Mark was told about the strange ride and that the driver could be schizophrenic and off his meds. Mark told her to call the police. Mark did not come home when the course was over at noon on Friday, August 25, even though others taking the course did. He said he was too tired. He waited until Saturday morning."

"Now I ask you, ladies and gentlemen of the jury, if you knew your wife had a ride with someone who was talking about killing people, smoking marijuana, sex parties, going around in the nude and your wife was concerned about her safety and that of her child, would you have waited until the next day, or would you have gone home as quickly as you could? He said call the police, yet he did not come back until Saturday. Why?"

"Late Friday, Mark Winger called the owner of Bart Transportation. He wanted to know Roger's last name. He said he should not be driving. The driver endangered his wife and child. They had a heated discussion. Duffy denied that Roger would say such things and refused to give him Roger's last name. Duffy said he will talk to Roger and find out what happened."

"Remember prior to the ride, in July and August, DeAnn and Mark had conversations about divorcing. DeAnn said she was going to divorce her husband and asked Mark if he was going to divorce Donnah. Mark said it would be better if Donnah died. 'I could be out of town, and all you would have to do is find the body.' DeAnn said, 'This is crazy. I don't want to have anything to do with that. I would cease to be a vital person.' He also told

DeAnn it would be nice if Donnah died because he didn't want Cindy to grow up in hot, humid Florida. All this time they were having passionate sex together."

"On the Saturday, August 20, trip back from Chattanooga with Candice Boulton, a co-worker, Mark asked her, 'What do you think would happen to Cindy if Donnah died?' Candice assured him there were many single fathers that had custody of the children. Why would he be asking her that?"

"Ladies and gentlemen, what do you think Mark Winger was thinking about at this time? He was thinking about his affair with DeAnn and getting rid of Donnah".

"We know that this affair was out of control. It was lust, passion. look at these telephone calls." With that Belz produced to the jury a blown-up list of the telephone calls."

"There were twenty-four calls from July 18 to July 28 between DeAnn and Mark Winger."

"He came back to Springfield, the affair continued. He went to Tennessee again from August 13 to August 25. The calls start again. There were thirty-four calls."

"Total calls—833 minutes in a little over a month, all long distance. We don't know how many local calls were made. This affair was out of control."

"It was not simply a roll in the hay. They could not get enough of each other".

"But Mark did not want a divorce, Cindy in Florida, support, alimony, loss of his friends, the Datzes. Donnah was popular in the Jewish community. It frowned on divorce. He wanted out—'better if Donnah died.'"

"Along comes Harrington, a perfect patsy. Winger thinks he is a smart guy—he can pull it off if he can get Harrington into the house. He can have DeAnn to himself, no messy divorce, no custody battle, no support payments."

"Did he want the insurance, $250,000? Did he want a family of his own? He learned Donnah could not carry a child in early 1995. He wanted his own family. Donnah had to die. Her death was inevitable. 'I have to get him in the house.' 'Dead men don't talk.'"

"Things had to appear normal. On that Saturday and on Sunday, August 26 and 27, Mark, Donnah, John, and DeAnn had cookouts with each other at their houses. Mark wanted everything to seem normal. On Monday Mark went back to work, and Donnah stayed off for the next couple days to be with Cindy."

"On Monday, August 28, Duffy had talked to Roger. Harrington was told that unless he got this matter straightened out with the Wingers he would not be getting any more rides. Harrington liked his job and wanted his job. He wanted to get this straightened out."

"Mark called for Harrington at 9:07 a.m. on August 29. He spoke to Susan Collins and asked to speak to Roger. Collins gave Roger the phone and saw him write down a note on a bank slip she gave him. We have the note that says 'Mark Winger, 4:30.' Mark set up the meeting with Harrington at his home at four thirty. This note proves it."

"On this very same day, August 29, about noon, Donnah brought Cindy to the defendant's office to show off Cindy. Mark's co-workers played with the baby. Mark and Donnah then went out to lunch. He wanted everything to appear normal. Donnah was on cloud nine and happy. She told her this was just the first of many adoptions. After lunch Mark went back to work, and Donnah went to have pictures taken of Cindy."

"Mark's story is that he got home first, and he was in the basement, he said, working out on his treadmill. He did not hear Donnah come in. He heard noise upstairs, heard the baby crying or something, ran upstairs and saw Cindy on the bed by herself, heard a noise in the dining area, got his gun, and ran to the noise. Donnah was kneeling. He saw Roger Harrington leaning over his wife facing him, beating her over the head with a hammer, swinging the hammer east to west. He shot Roger Harrington once. Roger rolled off two to three seconds later. He said he shot Roger in the forehead as he was trying to get up, that's what Mark said."

"He called 911. You heard the call. He said the baby was crying. He hung up on the 911 operator. Ladies and gentlemen, this telephone was a wall phone in the kitchen. It had a cord. In order to hang it up he had to get up and go into the kitchen and hang it up. He did not drop it and run to the baby. On the 911 tape Roger was groaning. You can hear it on the tape, but you cannot hear a baby crying. Roger was not dead. If he lived then Winger was in trouble. He shot him again execution style. 'Dead men tell no tales.' The 911 operator called back. He said he had shot an intruder who had been bludgeoning his wife. Ambulances, fire trucks, and police arrived on the scene. There was blood on the south wall, and there were three pools of blood on the floor, one underneath Donnah, one underneath Harrington, and one in between Harrington's blood. Firefighters, paramedics, and police officers were milling about. They were trying to save lives. The bodies were lying in the same direction, six feet apart."

"Detectives Charles Cox and Doug Williamson were downtown. They sped to the scene. On questioning defendant, he did not know who this man was. 'I was downstairs and heard some noise and came upstairs, the baby was crying, I got my gun, went into the dining area, and saw Donnah being hit over the head. I shot this man once and saw some blood fly from his head. He rolled off of Donnah. He then shot him again in the same motion because he was trying to get up.' This was what Winger told Cox. He was angry and hit Harrington in the chest with the hammer."

"Look at the position of the bodies. Could this have been true? That answer is no. It did not happen that way. If it had been true the body of Harrington would have been next to Donnah. Their feet would not be in opposite directions as Winger described. Look at this diagram where the body was found. His head was six feet from Donnah's head."

"What really happened—he shot Roger first in the head, Donnah came into the dining room hearing the shot, and he then hit her in the head with a hammer, not once but seven times, a brutal premeditated crime. He planned the meeting. He planned these murders. He had told DeAnn that it would be better if Donnah died. Blood spatter on the south wall, castoff from the swinging. Winger said the hammer was swung in an east-west direction, looking down the hall."

"Look at the location of the bodies and the blood spatter on the south wall. It could not have happened as Winger described."

Belz picked up the hammer and walked over to the jury box. He said to the jury, "Now I am Roger Harrington. This rail at the jury box is the south wall of the house. Donnah Winger is on her knees facing to the left, east, alongside of the wall with Roger Harrington leaning over her."

Belz swings the hammer seven times and falls down out of sight. As he falls he slaps his hand loudly against the jury box. It startles the jurors; what happened? Looking over the jury box, the jurors see Belz on the ground in the position as Winger described. Belz got up and walked the six feet east and lies down with his feet facing to the wall. He stayed there for a moment and then gets up. "This is what Winger said happened. He lied. Ladies and gentlemen, when I hit the jury box with my hand that was a shot that killed Harrington. How could I have ended up six or seven feet from Donnah Winger, when Winger said Harrington just rolled off of her? That is not possible."

Then Belz went over to the exhibits and picks up the watch and the ring of Harrington, and he lays them on the rail in front of the jury. "These were on Roger's right hand. He is right-handed. Look at them, there is no blood on them. There was none on them. Could someone striking someone with a hammer on the head seven times, crushing the skull, leaving blood all over the wall, not have any blood on the ring or the watch? Roger didn't do it."

"Winger tried to blame Roger Harrington. Sure, he had problems, but as Dr. Bohlen said, these problems were not related to violent behavior. He was schizotypal, and the only time he showed any evidence was in a domestic disputes. His ex-wife even said that he is a wimp. He talked in weird ways, but as Dr. Bohlen said, this was to try and impress people, get their attention, especially women. He did not do any of the things he talked about. He never threatened or attempted to harm anyone outside of a domestic situation, and that was years ago."

"So that leaves us with Mark Winger, a man who was having an affair with his wife's best friend, a man who said it would be better if Donnah died—all DeAnn would have to do would be to find the body. He wanted out but did not want a divorce."

"Roger was the perfect patsy. He lured Roger into the house and shot him. Donnah heard the shot, put down Cindy, and came running into the dining area. Mark grabbed her and shoved her down on her knees and beat her over the head with a hammer in a north-south direction, seven times on the head, fracturing her skull and spattering brain tissue on the south wall."

"He then called 911, went to the kitchen. Roger was still groaning. He was not dead. He hung up and shot him again."

"Lauralee Smith and the tape supported that it happened that way. Lauralee had just brought her children home, and they are in the process of getting out of the car. She was a next-door neighbor. Roger was still alive. You can hear him groaning on the tape, and Mark Winger couldn't let that happen, so he rolled him over and shot him again in the forehead. 'Dead men don't tell tales.' That is the shot Lauralee Smith heard. That is what happened. Defendant is guilty of premeditated murders."

"The evidence leaves no doubt that Mark Winger set them up and killed his young, attractive wife and blamed Roger Harrington for it."

"The blood spatter, the position of the bodies, the affair and the statements to DeAnn, the ring and watch, the one shot, and the gap in the 911 tape."

"Look at all this evidence, the facts. Mark Winger is guilty beyond a reasonable doubt of these murders."

Judge Zappa says, "Thank you, Mr. Belz; Mr. Breen, it is now your turn."

"Thank you, Judge. Ladies and gentlemen of the jury, Counsel."

"Mr. Belz never mentioned to you, ladies and gentlemen, that you took an oath not to ever, ever sign a verdict unless you, each one of you, believe the state has proven its case beyond a reasonable doubt. The state has failed and failed miserably."

"Donnah Winger was Mark's wife of seven years. She and Mark were adopting Cindy. The state wants you to believe beyond reasonable doubt that Mark Winger took a hammer to this lovely lady and bludgeoned her to death, just when they were adopting a baby, just four hours after they had lunch together."

"They had a good marriage. The testimony of Amy Jaffe, the Randlemans, the neighbors, all the people the investigators spoke to said it was a good and loving marriage. Sure he strayed. He was a jerk for having this affair and for what he did with DeAnn. It was a betrayal. It was an act of lust and he is ashamed. He made a mistake, but that does not prove he murdered Donnah".

"During voir dire I asked each and every one of you that if a man was having an affair, would that be proof that he murdered his wife? You all answered no. Why would he kill Donnah? Because he wanted to be with this lovely yet unhappy DeAnn? Because Donnah was not good enough for him and DeAnn was? No way."

"Did he want the life insurance? Friends called the insurance company, not Mark, to get the house cleaned up. They found that there was life insurance with the home owners. Mark Winger never knew of that insurance."

"What was the motive? Was there any motive proved by the state. Was there any motive at all? None, none that was shown. If there was no motive, why would he do such an act? No one would do such a horrible act without a motive. This murder was the act of a violent, crazy person, beating someone over the head with a hammer, seven times, splattering blood and brain tissue. Mark is not that person. Do you really believe that someone with no history of violence, no history of mental problems, could do this type of thing? Pick up a hammer and hit the head of his wife seven times? He just had lunch with her. They were just adopting a baby. This murder is the act of a disturbed, angry man, not of Mark."

"Isn't it ironic that four years later, after DeAnn is having her mental breakdown, after attempting suicide four times, she tells about her suspicions? These are just suspicions. She said as much. She never said he did it or confessed to her. She told her psychiatrist of her affair after he had threatened to drop her as a patient. She told him of her affair but not of these alleged statements."

"Mark had been able to put Donnah's death and the affair behind him and go on with his life. She could not. She was angry, mad, that he got on with his life".

"The statements seven years ago that Mark gave to Detective Cox were when he was in shock. He was in shock. He was sobbing and crying. He was shaking and rocking back and forth. He had just seen someone bludgeon his wife, and he had shot and killed that man. Now seven years later, they are going to go back and pick away at the statement he gave to Cox, statements that weren't videotaped, weren't written down verbatim, and were not signed by Mark."

"The police some seven years later looked for inconsistencies. If they had videotaped it you could hear exactly what he had said. They didn't do it, they summarized. Why did they not see these so-called inconsistencies then? They saw the bodies."

"They could have taken a swab of Roger Harrington's right hand. It would have been Donnah's blood on it, but they did not. They could have checked the DNA on the clothes. They did not."

"They could have gotten the telephone records of the two unknown calls to the Wingers' home, but they did not."

"Collins's telephone had caller ID on it, but they only copied one number. They didn't get the numbers of Bart calling Collins's home on Tuesday afternoon or on Monday for that matter. They could have done that but did not."

"Seven years later when those records are not available and when the swabs were not done, when there is no videotape, when there was no DNA taken, they are pointing the finger at Mark Winger. This is unfair".

"Let's go back to the twenty-third, the limo ride. This ride upset Donnah. DeAnn told Mark about the limo ride and gave an assessment that the guy was schizophrenic and off his meds."

"Mark called Duffy on Friday. He was angry. He asked Duffy not to let Harrington know of his call, as he was out of town. He called him several more times, but Duffy seemed to care less. On Monday Mark thought no one really cared. He talked to Duffy again and said that Harrington shouldn't be out there driving a van. He talked to the State's Attorney's Office, and as no crime had been committed there was nothing that could be done. He was concerned."

"Now look at Roger Harrington. Dr. Cavanaugh testified, after reviewing his medical records and the report of the ride, this guy is dangerous. He is a sociopath. He could be set off by events. He smoked marijuana, experimented with cocaine. He had delusions and had a spirit of Dahm who told him to kill people. He talked about parties in the country where they smoked marijuana and ran around naked. This guy was plain crazy. Cavanaugh said that. He was potentially dangerous. He had put a shotgun to his wife's head. He had tried to handcuff her. He had beaten her up. He stuck knives in the wall and trashed the house of someone that had been dating his sister. He had the potential for violence."

"Harrington said that torture, pain, and murder were his destiny. He was a cannon waiting to go off. He stopped being treated, and as DeAnn said, he sounded schizophrenic and likely was off his treatment. In fact, he had stopped seeing his therapist on December of 1994".

"Donnah was threatening his job. It was a job that he liked, the only one he had been able to keep for more than a few months. Duffy would not give him any more rides until he straightened this matter out. He was threatened."

"Look at the note found in the car. The top portion is written in pencil, 'Mark Winger.' Below are a street and a time in ink. There was never an appointment. This allegedly was written at 9:07 a.m., when Susan Collins and Tricia Ray were there with a five-week-old baby. The home had the aroma of marijuana. Tricia Ray was sleeping. Susan Collins testified she had been in custody in Sangamon County Jail. She was a crack addict. She made different statements to the police in August 1995 than she said in court. Somebody from work called on Monday, the twenty-eighth and talked to Roger. She didn't hear this conversation because he went into his bedroom."

"Tuesday morning, on the twenty-ninth, the caller ID showed a call from the state of Illinois, Mark Winger's office at 9:07 a.m. Tricia Ray in August said, 'I was in bed at 9:07 a.m.' The next call that Roger got was in the afternoon from his office, according to Collins."

"That supports what Mark Winger said to the police and in his deposition. He talked to Harrington on Tuesday morning. Winger did not set up a four thirty meeting. Roger Harrington wrote the note. He wrote it after he talked with someone from work. Did they tell him that this guy gets off work at three thirty and why don't you go by his house at four thirty? We don't know, but we do know Susan Collins said somebody from Duffy's office called that afternoon, and we know the note was written with two different types of instruments, one pen and one pencil, indicating that it was written at two different times. Two different telephone calls, one from Mark and the other from his office. We know that the police never checked on the other calls."

"The 911 call was at four twenty-seven, and the firemen arrived first and then the police. Jones and Filburn go into the house. They saw Mark over his wife, holding and cradling her. He had a towel trying to stop the bleeding. They ordered him to move away from his wife. Jones said he hesitated and then crawled away. Jones helped him up.

"Mark said after he shot Harrington, he rolled over, and Mark thought he was getting up and shot him again in the forehead. He thought the man was getting up."

"Murphy, Cox, Williamson, Young, Filburn, and Jones all saw the scene. Mark demonstrated what happened. They saw the position of the bodies. They had their police roundtable. There were no inconsistencies in 1995. Now in 2002 they say Harrington's body should have been somewhere else. Nothing has changed. Why didn't they accuse him then? The reason is obvious. The body was consistent with Mark's statement and descriptions."

"Once DeAnn came forward everyone got suspicious. They decided to review it again. She gives them a motive. They now focus on Mark. Consistent statements and evidence now become inconsistent. The state then developed a new theory, that Mark Winger shot Harrington and then beat his wife with a hammer and called 911. There is no evidence of that. The 911 call, the first call, Mark said there is a man with a bullet in his head. That is perfectly consistent because he shot him in the forehead. This is perfectly consistent."

"He hangs up because the baby is crying, and the dispatcher calls him back immediately. He says my door is open and unlocked. It was open. The police did not have to break in. This evidence supports that Roger Harrington wandered into the house, saw Donnah. He snapped. He then hammered her to death."

"The psychiatric profile of Roger Harrington fits that. Both psychiatrists testified that his behavior was delusional, psychotic, and inappropriate. He wandered in. He may not have knocked or he may have. He wandered in with his cup of coffee and his cigarettes. He puts them on the table, calls out, and Donnah is in the bedroom with the baby. Donnah goes to see who that is. She leaves the baby on the bed. He snaps when he sees her. She threatened his job."

"Did Roger go there with the purpose of killing someone? No, but as Dr. Cavanaugh said he has an explosive nature and could be dangerous. He was threatened. Donnah confronted him. Harrington grabbed the hammer."

"Now to the blood experts. Bevel was working for Bart's insurance company. Bevel's job was to put the hammer in Mark's hands, to defend the civil suit. That is what he was paid to do. He was a hired expert. On Mark's

T-shirt he finds three little spots and circles them and says that's proof that Mark wielded the hammer."

"Of course Donnah's blood was all over Mark's shirt. He was holding her. Bevel does not recommend DNA testing of any of the stains. He never looked at Donnah Winger's clothing. Bevel found no blood of Donnah on Roger Harrington's T-shirt. He found no blood of Donnah's on Harrington's clothes. That's how Bevel concluded his report. No blood of Donnah's on Harrington's shirt. 'Could not be if Roger was the killer,' Bevel said. He was wrong."

"We had the DNA testing done. This should have been done even before charges were filed. Harrington's blood was on Donnah's shorts. Donnah's blood was on Harrington's shorts. You know why? Because Harrington was standing right behind her, beating her with a hammer when Mark shot him. Harrington's T-shirt had Donnah's blood on it and tissue all over it. Donnah's clothes had Harrington's blood on them from when he was shot."

"On the south wall, it's not blood from being thrown from the hammer, not castoff, but it's blood as a result of the hammer hitting the skull and throwing blood and tissue out. Terry Laber finds what could be blood in the east-west direction on the ceiling—showing the hammer swung in an east-west direction. He has been doing this twenty-seven years as a scientist, a DNA analyst. He suggested the DNA testing. He determined that Donnah's DNA was all over Roger Harrington. The DNA was right here on Harrington's T-shirt. Donnah's DNA was found on the shorts that Harrington was wearing. Her tissue is on his shorts. The DNA results prove that Bevel's conclusions were based on false premises, an incomplete investigation."

"Now let's look at DeAnn. She has anxiety attacks, depression, and migraine headaches. She has a horrible marriage. She had an affair with Winger and she fell for him. Mark Winger broke up with her in February of 1996. She then sees him on October 16, 1998, with Barbara, his new wife. Cindy has been adopted, and they have three children of their own. This is the first time she has seen him in two and a half years. She asked Mark how he could live with this and how he could move on, and he replied 'I found Jesus Christ.' He was talking about the affair, not about the murder. She wanted to get even? Angry because her life had fallen apart? She calls Bart Transportation and says don't settle. Was it jealousy, anger, vindictiveness? All we know is that it happened after she learned that Mark had rejected her and remarried and had three more children".

"We know a week after Donnah's murder she was telling her psychiatrist, Dr. Shea, that her friend was murdered by a psycho and her friend's husband shot him. She maintained that all through 1995, 1996, and 1998."

"Mark has gotten his life in order, and she blames him for destroying hers."

"Roger Harrington went to the Winger home on the twenty-ninth. There was a confrontation. He didn't arrive to kill her. He wandered in, the door was unlocked. He wandered into the dining room. He called for Mark. Donnah heard him, put the baby down, and he sees her and flips. Perhaps she confronts him. Mark heard a noise and came upstairs."

"Laber is a scientist. He is a DNA analyst. He is a blood-pattern analysis guy. He is a serologist. He did not have the tunnel vision of Bevel. He was not here to defend Bart. He had not made up his mind until the DNA was done. He did not jump to conclusions as Bevel did. And what did the DNA show? Harrington's shorts had Donnah's blood and tissue on them. The front of his shirt had her blood and tissue on it. The back of Donnah's shorts had Harrington's blood on them. And what did Bevel do? He strode back and forth and talked about a piece of tissue, which he says is Donnah's on Mark's shirt. Well, surprise, this was an artifact, a dust bunny, on the blow up. These little things, none of Donnah's blood on Harrington, no DNA, dust bunny, all in Bevel's report, undermine Bevel. His conclusions were disproved by the DNA. This DNA proved that Harrington was over Donnah as he was hammering her to death."

"I am about out of time. There is a lot more I would like to say, but I have to leave this in your hands. This man's life depends on your decision. Mark Winger did not bludgeon his wife to death. He did not do it. He had no history of violence, a steady job, no psychiatric history. He did not kill his wife by hammering her seven times to the head."

"The judge will instruct you that the state must prove its case beyond a reasonable doubt. The evidence raises not only reasonable doubt but also clearly shows that Mark Winger did not—I emphasize not—kill his wife."

"Thank you for your attention."

Mr. Breen sits down.

Judge Zappa says, "Thank you, Mr. Breen." Directing his attention to the jury, Judge Zappa continues, "Ladies and gentlemen, as I have previously informed you, the state has the burden of proof, and therefore it has the right to open and close. Mr. Schmidt, are you ready for the rebuttal?"

"Yes, sir," Schmidt replies, standing up from the table.

"Ladies and gentlemen, I have the privilege to give to you the state's final argument. The judge then will instruct you as to the law, and you will retire to make a decision. Mr. Breen talked about proof beyond a reasonable doubt. That is the state's duty. The state recognizes its obligation to prove its case beyond a reasonable doubt. If we have not done so, you should dismiss the case and find for the defendant."

"I submit to you that the guilt of the defendant has been shown beyond a reasonable doubt. We have shown that on August 29, 1995, the defendant beat his wife to death with a hammer, and he shot Roger Harrington in the head with his gun."

"Mr. Breen talked about the fact that we did not obtain a DNA analysis of the blood on the various pieces of clothing. He asked that we do so right before trial and we did so. There is no fault here. He talked about a couple of the stains on Roger Harrington's shirt being from Donnah. If Roger was hammering her on the head seven times and crushing her skull, you would expect a lot of blood on Roger's shirt. You would expect it on his watch and ring. The blood would come directly at him. If he was beating someone with a hammer there would be blood all over him. DNA doesn't prove anything here about guilt. It just identifies the blood. It doesn't say how it got there or who got it there. There was blood all over the floor. Both Donnah and Roger were rolled over. Paramedics were walking from one to the other, cutting at clothing, treating them. There were many ways the blood from one could have ended on the other."

"Remember the blood spatter is subjective, meaning you can have two opinions on the same set of facts. You have to look at the evidence in its entirety. It is up to you to evaluate all of this evidence. Blood was everywhere, on the floor, on the chairs, on the walls, etc."

"So now let's look at the evidence, the cold facts which are not in dispute and are not opinions. One, from the first time the defendant spoke to the police, he lied. He initially denied knowing DeAnn Schultz's telephone number. He said, 'She is a friend of mine, and she is a friend of my wife. I know her husband's work number. I don't know her phone number.' He had called her some twenty times, and yet he didn't seem to know her number. He denied knowing who Roger Harrington was. Again he lied."

"The physical evidence proves that the crime could not have happened as Winger told Detective Cox. He lied again. Just because some of Donnah Winger's blood was on Harrington's shirt and shorts does not mean that Harrington did it.

"Harrington was right-handed, and his watch and ring that were worn on his right hand were produced. They did not have any blood on it. Roger Harrington did not use the hammer.

"Then there are the inconsistent stories about how this happened—the story to Andy Scar, the story to Cox, and the story in his deposition. He heard noise upstairs and got his gun. They are all inconsistent. Then there is the testimony of Candice Boulton, who was asked on the return trip what would happen if his wife died, what would happen to Cindy. The statements that he made to DeAnn Schultz that her death was inevitable, all she had to do was find the body, etc.

"Also remember the gaps in the tape and the testimony of Lauralee Smith. She was getting out of her car and unloading her kids. She heard one shot, only one shot. Winger said there were only two or three seconds between the shots. How come Lauralee Smith, who was in the driveway for many minutes, only heard one shot? The answer is simple—Winger heard Harrington groaning during the 911 call, hung up, and shot him again in the forehead.

"Why did Mark Winger shoot Harrington a second time? The first shot had not killed him, and if he wasn't dead, he maybe could say what happened. 'Dead men tell no tales,' he said. You can hear Roger groaning on the 911 tape. He said the baby was crying, but you can't hear the baby crying. The telephone was on a cord in the kitchen. He had to get up, go to the kitchen, and hang it up. He just did not drop it to check on the baby."

"What were the cigarettes and the coffee doing on the table? Why was the note found in the car? '4:30, Mark Winger.' Never was explained away. Harrington came to get his job back."

"DeAnn Schultz told him he sounded like a schizophrenic off his meds. That's all Winger needed. He thought he was the smartest guy in the room.

Mark Winger is smart, a college graduate, he is a nuclear engineer, but ladies and gentlemen, that doesn't prove he's not a murderer. Harrington was odd, he was strange, could not hold a job, but he never did any of these things that he talked about doing. He was not a danger to anyone. The psychiatrists and the social workers saw him twenty-four times and did not admit him, except for once when he talked about going down the river in the canoe. He was a danger to himself, not a danger to others."

"The most compelling bit of evidence was where Roger Harrington was found. He was found by the refrigerator. His feet were the same way as Donnah's. He was six feet from Donnah. He was rolled over and shot again in the forehead. You stand him up, and he would have been in the kitchen, not leaning over Donnah. Harrington did not just roll off of Donnah when shot as he told Cox and Williamson."

"Winger stated he was concerned for his wife's safety and his child's safety, yet he spends another night in Chattanooga. He thought he was smart. He wasn't so smart when he talked to DeAnn Schultz. He wasn't so smart when he asked Candice Boulton. He carefully planned these murders—cookouts with the Schultzes, calling Bart, leaving the hammer onthe table, having lunch on the day of the murder. It is just too pat."

"They tried to dismiss DeAnn Schultz as a lady with a lot of psychological problems. She at first could not believe that Mark Winger could have killed his wife, but after she started thinking about it after the emotions of the affair ended, she realized that was a real possibility. She felt guilty. She was scared. She fell apart. Could she tell her family, her friends? Finally, Dr. Lauer convinced her to come forward. That took courage and guts. She had to admit to the public, to her friends, to everyone who read the newspapers, that she was having an affair when Donnah, her best friend, died. It was an act of courage. She could have just walked away."

"Don't feel sorry for the defendant. I'm not asking for anything except justice. Those facts prove beyond a reasonable doubt that Mark Winger killed his wife and shot Roger Harrington and tried to blame him for the death. He almost got away with it. Don't let him get away with it. We want justice. It is not win or lose—it is justice, justice for Donnah, justice for Rob Brown and Sarah Jane Drescher, and it is justice for the Harringtons. Ladies and gentlemen, until today there has been no justice for the man that brought this pain to all of those families. This is his day of justice. This is the time that he will face you and he will face justice. Do your duty, look at the facts. Mark

Winger is guilty of these crimes. He carefully planned these murders. Don't let him get away with it."

John Schmidt looked the jury in their eyes and then walked over to his table and sat down.

Judge Zappa proceeded to instruct the jury. "It is your duty to follow the instructions. It is your duty to determine the facts and determine them only from the evidence produced in the courtroom.

"Only you are the judges of the believability of the witnesses and the weight to be given to the testimony of each of them. Only you are to determine what the facts are. Use your notes to refresh your memory.

Judge Zappa continued, "The defendant is presumed to be innocent of the charge against him, and this presumption remains with him throughout every stage of the trial and during your deliberations on the verdict. It is not overcome unless, from all the evidence in the case, you are convinced beyond a reasonable doubt that the defendant is guilty. The state has the burden of proving that the defendant is guilty beyond a reasonable doubt. The defendant is not required to prove his innocence."

The bailiff then took the jury to the jury room. The deliberations commenced at 12:34 p.m. on June 4, 2002.

About three hours later, the jury sent a question to the bailiff. The judge called the attorneys together. Winger was present. The jury asked for a copy of the deposition of Mark Winger. The court said, "No, it would unfairly highlight one of the statements the defendant gave during the course of seven years."

Again, the bailiff came back with another question. The jury would like a phone book to check area codes. The phone book was not entered in as evidence, and the request denied.

For a third time, the bailiff came back; they want to have the tape of the 911 call. The prosecution objected. The family of Donnah's was concerned— this tape showed a panicked call. The court responded, "I don't want the jury having the tape. What I am going to do is bring the jury back, play the 911 tape. They can listen to it again." The jury came in and listened to the tape, and then went back to the deliberation room.

At 10:00 p.m. the jury had not reached a verdict.

Judge Zappa called the attorneys together. "The jury has been out seven and a half hours. I suggest we call it a day and bring them back tomorrow morning at 9:00 a.m. Any objections?"

No one objected. The jury was dismissed until 9:00 a.m. the next day. The defense team felt relieved; the longer the jury is out, the better it is for the defendant.

At 9:00 a.m. the next day, the jury looked tired. They had not slept well. They felt the heavy burden. They were not looking at Winger or the prosecutors. They were led back to the jury room to further deliberate.

CHAPTER 24

The Jury Decides

One juror had fainted and another juror had a conflict; both were excused. Then right before the case went to the jury, a male juror's father had a heart attack, and the judge excused him. Three alternates would decide the case along with the nine original jurors. The alternates had sat through the trial, and they had taken thorough notes. They went back into the jury room to decide the fate of Mark Winger. The jury consisted of nine women and three men.

During the weeks of trial, the jurors had had become friends. They had eaten lunch together, talked about their families, their jobs, etc. They wanted to be careful in their decision. They read over the instructions and studied them. The conviction had to be beyond a reasonable doubt. What is reasonable doubt? They were glad it was nearing an end. It was a jigsaw puzzle, and now they had to put the pieces together.

A foreperson was selected; it was a woman. She suggested that they go around the room and take a straw vote to see where everyone stood. Nine were to convict, two were undecided, and one was for acquittal. They had to have a unanimous vote. A man and his family were at stake.

There were conflicting experts; how were they supposed to tell who was right and who wasn't? Bevel was hired by the insurance company to defend the civil case, and he might not be unbiased; Laber was hired to defend the defendant. Bevel never asked for DNA. There was blood all over the walls, on the floor, and clothes; there was also tissue and blood on the shirts. The DNA showed Donnah's blood was on Harrington and Harrington's was on Donnah. How did it get there? Much of what these experts said seemed to be based on conjecture.

Could Harrington be violent? Did you believe Bohlen or Cavanaugh? "We aren't the experts." Harrington talked about violence, torture, and death; but Bohlen said this was just to impress people, particularly young females. He was weird. He never acted upon these thoughts, but he was violent toward his ex-wife. He had serious psychological problems. Did he snap when he saw Donnah? Was there a confrontation? His ex-wife said he was a wimp. Was he crazy as Cavanaugh stated? Neither psychiatrist had examined him. It was guesswork. They cancelled each other out.

Everyone, including Donnah's parents, said Mark Winger had a good marriage. Donnah thought so, but Mark told DeAnn that he did not. Was he just manipulating her for sex? Donnah never expressed any concerns; Mark had never shown any violence. Was he a psychopath? A sociopath? Only that kind of person could bludgeon his wife to death and set up this murder. Once Winger heard about the ride, could he have acted that quickly to plan the murder? Why did he not come back on Friday from Chattanooga as the others had?

The telephone call at 9:07 a.m. Tuesday to Harrington, the note written in two different instruments—did that create reasonable doubt? Several of the jurors couldn't believe that someone with his education and his background could kill two people, just like that, after having lunch three hours before. Why was part of the note in ink and the other in pencil? Was there a call to Harrington on Tuesday afternoon from his office? Collins gave conflicting statements to the police.

What was his motive? It could have been that Donnah could not conceive; he wanted to have his own children, his own family; he was egocentric. He had three children in three years after Donnah's death. The timing fit.

They returned to exhibits and photographs of the crime scene. There were pools of blood on the carpet, photographs of the location of the bodies. Winger stated that when he shot Harrington he just rolled off and tried to get up again, and he shot him again a second time. Harrington was six feet from Donnah. How could that have happened? The pieces of the puzzle began to fall in place.

Why didn't he get a divorce? Was it the insurance money? Was it that Donnah was paying more attention to Cindy than him? He wanted out but did not want to pay alimony. The jury went around and around on this. Was it a combination? The foreperson stated that they did not have to find the motive, just that he committed the murder.

Could they believe DeAnn Schultz? There was no question about the affair, but if all those statements were true and she suspected he was involved in the murder of her best friend, why did she continue the affair? Why didn't she come forward right away? Was she blinded by the passion of the affair, by her love for Winger? Was she involved? Did she just block it out? Was she scared to come forward? Why did she need immunity if she was not implicated?

Winger had been remarried, had found Jesus, and put Donnah's death behind him, but she couldn't. Was she angry, vindictive, because he could put it behind him, and her life had fallen apart? She called Bart Transportation, saying, "Don't settle." Some thought that made her look vindictive. Why wouldn't she just talk to the state's attorney?

"What about this ride?" a juror asked. Harrington was obviously weird, his spirit of Dahm, the crazy talk—talks of torturing people, death was his destiny. Was this just talk? Was he really that violent? He had a serious psychiatric history. He never acted on these fantasies.

Several jurors said, "Let's forget the experts and look at the facts." They talked about the 911 call. One juror said, "I would sure like to hear that tape again to see if we can hear the baby crying as Winger said." They passed a note to the bailiff; the judge called the attorneys and heard their arguments for and against. He then brought the jury back into the courtroom. The attorneys and family were there. So was Officer Williamson. He was looking at the jury and seemed to be angry. "What is taking you so long?" The judge said they couldn't take the tape to the jury room, but he would play it again for them. The bailiff did. They could not hear the baby crying. They went back to the jury room.

The prosecution was concerned. The tape showed that Winger was panicked, supporting what he said happened. They did not know the reason why the jury wanted to hear the tape.

Was the second shot made during the break in the 911 call? That would be the only explanation for the neighbor hearing only one shot. He was not getting up; the second shot went straight through his head into the floor, execution style.

They examined the photos again. Harrington wouldn't be that far from Donnah if he had just rolled off her. He would not have fallen backward, not toward the kitchen. He would not be six feet away. Winger said Harrington just rolled off Donnah. The pieces of the puzzle began to fall into place. As Bevel said, if you rotated him onto his feet, he would be in the kitchen.

The three jurors were still not convinced that someone with Winger's background could bludgeon, close and personal, his wife, when they were just adopting a baby and just after having lunch together. He had no history of violence, no history of mental illness, no criminal record. They wanted to think about it overnight. How could someone sane do this—beat his wife to death with a hammer?

The story was too pat. He asked DeAnn to call the police; there was a .45 in the drawer in the bedroom and the hammer on the dining room table. He had just taken his wife to lunch on the day she was murdered; it was all too smooth. All too planned out.

A female juror had a friend who was divorced. Her husband was really likeable to others; he made a good impression on the people he met, but at home he was different. He was abusive. "You don't know what goes on behind closed doors!"

About that time there was a knock on the door. The bailiff asked if they were still deliberating at all. The forewoman said yes. The bailiff said it is getting late. Do they want to go home and come back in the morning? The jurors agreed that they would like to do that to think about it overnight.

Upon return the next day at 9:00 a.m., Winger and his attorneys were seated at the counsel table, the judge at his desk. The police officers and the families of both parties were present. The bailiff led the jurors back to the jury room; eleven voted to convict. One juror was still unconvinced. She asked for more time to look at notes and was told to take all the time she needed. She reviewed her notes while the rest of the jurors just talked about their families, plans for summer, etc. The juror got angry because they were talking about vacations and families while she was reviewing her notes and trying to make up her mind. They had made their minds up, and they were just waiting for this remaining juror.

This juror reviewed the pictures and her notes again. Finally she said, "Yes, I am convinced." No one had put any pressure on her.

The forewoman reminded them that thinking Winger did it was not enough. It had to be beyond a reasonable doubt. She polled the jury again. All voted to convict.

They knocked on the door at about 11:00 a.m. The lawyers were assembled; Mark Winger was sitting in his chair. None of the jurors were looking at him. Breen and Pugh knew that was a bad sign. Judge Zappa asked the bailiff to collect the verdict forms, and he brought them to the judge. The judge asked the defendant to stand, and Breen stood with him. He read the verdict. "Guilty of murder in the first degree of both Donnah Winger and Roger Harrington." Winger showed no emotion; it was like he was frozen. His family, his mother, cried out, "No!" Mark Winger was led back to jail for sentencing in sixty days. The Dreschers felt relieved, the Wingers devastated. Mrs. Harrington broke down. Her son was exonerated.

A. The Devil Is in the Detail

Many lawyers in complex cases feel the need to have experts explain and interpret the evidence. The jury, laypeople, is asked to evaluate this expert testimony. It can be in airplane collisions, forensics in criminal cases, physicians in malpractice, or technical experts in any field. They, the jurors, are asked to determine which expert is correct. In this case the jurors did not have to.

Judgment, common sense, and facts decided this case.

The devil is in the detail.

(a) The position of the bodies.
(b) Harrington's watch and ring—no blood.
(c) The break in the 911 tape,
(d) One gunshot heard by the neighbor.
(e) No baby crying on the 911 tape.

Facts, not opinions, decided the case. The pieces of the puzzle fit together. As to motive, it was never resolved. It did not have to be. It could have been passion, wanting out of the marriage, not wanting to pay support or alimony, Donnah not able to carry a baby and Winger wanting his own children; was it insurance, or all of the above. We will never know why. Mark Winger was smart, arrogant, and manipulative. He thought he was the smartest guy in the room. Well, he was not.

CHAPTER 25

The Sentencing

On August 1, 2002, Mark Winger was sentenced to two life sentences in prison for the first-degree murder of Donnah Winger and of Roger Harrington. The court had sent out questionnaires to the victims as to how their lives had been affected and what had occurred to their lives after the crime. Donnah's father, Cash Brown, talked about how he couldn't carry on with his business anymore and sold it. He doesn't watch any violent movies or television. He cries easily and is very sensitive. He has given up their religion and doesn't know if there is a God. Would any God have let this happened? He wanted Mark to be sentenced for the rest of natural life. Mark had murdered two innocent people brutally, including a wife who adored him. He hopes Mark Winger has a life full of misery, longing, and perdition. "The pain he has inflicted on us all is immeasurable. The pain and distress he should receive should be incalculable for the harm that he has brought."

Ira Drescher, Donnah's stepfather addressed Mark Winger. "I am one of the last in the family to believe your guilt. I cared for you greatly and stood by you to the end. I went to the house and picked out the dress for Donnah to be buried in."

Ira Drescher asked Winger directly, "How could you commit such a diabolical bloodthirsty crime? How could you hate her so much when she loved you so much? Your act is simply so incomprehensible, and you must be crazy to have performed this.

"You were so smart that you had beat the system, but through your greed, your intelligence eventually got you. You thought you would make millions from your civil suit, but you underestimated your adversaries and never thought DeAnn would turn you in."

He continued, "So now you have found Jesus Christ, and you say he has forgiven you. You can make up any excuse to satisfy what you want, just as all other convicts do.

"Mark, the most difficult thing I ever had to do in my life was telling Sarah Jane, while she was reading in bed, that her eldest daughter died, was murdered. You can't imagine how many times we have cried. The pain and hurt that you have inflicted on Sarah Jane is monumental. She was so wonderful to you, and the pain is so endearing to us both.

"Last time I saw Donnah was when she put Cindy on my bed next to me while I was sleeping on August 23. She then woke me up with joy and excitement and with her big smile while her baby Cindy was lying next to me.

"The only gratification I had is that I worked hard for the past few years with Assistant State's Attorneys Steve Weinhoeft and Doug Williamson. I have assisted them in gathering information."

A doctor who worked with Donnah Winger said that Donnah assisted him with many surgeries. "She was adorable, caring, smiling, and energetic. She lit up the room. My life has changed since your tragic and brutal murder because I am deprived of my friend, colleague, and protégé, whose only desire was to make others happy. Donnah Winger was a purity of soul, happiness, and giving."

Roger Harrington's sister belonged to the same church that Mark Winger joined. She was branded as the sister of a crazed murderer. She wanted to go to a doctor but was afraid that he would think she was crazy. She said, "Roger Harrington was a real person. He was a son, brother, uncle, cousin, nephew, and a friend to everyone who met him. Many did not understand him, but many loved him and believed in his innocence for many years. The loss we have had was unthinkable. Winger used Roger's weakness to his advantage, and for many years people were led to believe that my brother was a hateful, crazy killer. There is no sentence that is good enough or would bring back my brother to us."

Ralph Harrington stated, "Helen could not eat. I would pass out. I had open-heart surgery. I used sick time from work."

"Our routine changed. We both acquired part-time jobs. Helen would shut herself in the bedroom and cry for hours. I kept trying to relive Roger's footsteps at the front door."

They talked about seeing him bouncing up the steps to their home. They talked about Roger helping them out. "He would leave money on the table when he came over. He spent a lot of time with his nephews, going fishing with them whether they caught fish or not. Now everywhere we went, people stared at us. They would drive by the house and stop and stare. We would despise going to the store, going out to eat, or even sitting on the front porch. People at work tried to see our side, but we always felt that some had their doubts.

"During the trial, Mark's mother came over and spoke to us. She said, 'My son was innocent, and he loved Donnah. He has four little children to provide for.' Helen replied, 'Roger will never have any children, will he? We will never get Roger back, but at least he will get his name cleared.'"

Donnah's stepmother talked about remembering waking up at night and finding her husband, Donnah's father, sitting in the dark living room in the middle of the night. "Can't stop thinking of Donnah," he would say. She said she remembers feeling him shaking with sobs in the bed next to her. She talked about how she remembered Donnah.

Statements also came from those supporting Mark Winger; they believed he was innocent. He was a good student and received a nomination to West Point but chose Virginia Military Institute for a degree in physics. They talked about the marriage and how both were happy, and the child was an immediate joy. He was the victim of a deeply troubled DeAnn Schultz, who went to the police in 1999 to seek vengeance for his ruining her life.

Barbara Winger, Mark's wife, described him as a humble, kind, thoughtful, sensitive, and very attentive father. They were married in October 1996. They had four children. He was devoted to them. He treated her with respect, admiration, and love. Why should he grieve over the loss of Donnah? He was not a murderer. "These children were given the best daddy in the world, and now he is being taken away from them."

Andrea Parker testified how she watched Mark as he lost weight. Her husband was Mark's boss. She tried to console him and get him to eat after Donnah's death. They often spoke of Donnah. Most times they didn't see anything except for deep sorrow.

There were other letters both from church members and friends attesting to Mark Winger's thoughtfulness, gentleness, and his loving nature toward Donnah.

Judge Zappa asked Mark Winger if he had anything to say before sentencing. He got up and he spoke. He was a victim too, he didn't do the crime, and that he didn't kill Donnah. He denied making these statements to DeAnn Schultz. He said that Donnah had asked him to ask DeAnn to stay in Springfield, as she was one of her best friends, and she thought she would be making a mistake to move to Minnesota. He called DeAnn from Tennessee. He did not want to wait because Donnah had told him DeAnn was about ready to move. He suggested maybe they could talk it through, and they met halfway. There were no plans to spend the night, but he just wanted to talk to her. He said he was apologetic for having the affair, but he did not kill his wife. "I knew the affair was wrong. I should have stopped it, but I didn't. After I went to Africa I came to my senses, and I said this is wrong, this is something I should not be doing, and broke off the affair.

"All I can say is I am innocent. I loved Donnah and I did not kill her."

He sat down. The jurors, who had come in for the sentencing, sat in the back row and shook their heads in disbelief. How could this man claim to be innocent?

Judge Zappa sentenced Mark Winger to two life sentences in the penitentiary at Pontiac, Illinois.

EPILOGUE

The Pontiac prison is not a country club. It houses some of the worst criminals—gangbangers, rapists, murderers, pedophiles, etc. Many are psychopaths or sociopaths. It is an old prison, and many of the cells are small, two prisoners to a cell. The largest cells are eight feet by ten feet. Two cots, a stainless steel pot and sink. It has a total prison population of 2,504. It is crowded and noisy with inmates constantly screaming. It has a stench of sweat and urine mixed together. The inmates are confined to their cells except when they are working in the prison, have yard time, or meals. The only time they see the sun is when they get out for yard time. Infractions of the many rules commit a prisoner to a confinement cell for three to eight days, where he is only provided with bread.

The prison is ruled by inmates, black and Latino street gangs from Chicago and the drug dealers. It is intimidating to those who are not hard-core criminals or gang members. Most of the prisoners have to fight or die. It is not a pleasant place.

Winger was processed in the prison in August 2002. He was stripped, provided with prison clothes, showered, and then led shackled to to his cell. Prisoner's arms were hanging out of the cells, hands out reaching at him, threatening him, calling him names—fresh meat, etc. It was frightening. He was locked in with a cellmate whom he never knew before.

Some of the old-timers showed him the ropes. He continued to complain of his innocence—what else was new. Almost everyone contended that they were innocent, they were framed. He talked about DeAnn Schultz. "I would not have been convicted if that bitch had not lied." He wanted to get even.

After about a year, he struck up a friendship with a Terry Hubble, a bad dude. Hubble had been convicted of rape and murder of a fourteen-year-old girl and was serving a life sentence. He was a con with a record and looking for an angle, as almost everyone there was.

Winger kept complaining. He wanted to get DeAnn Schultz. Hubble initially blew Winger off, saying, "Everyone claims they are innocent. Everyone says they would like to get rid of a witness." But Winger persisted. Hubble began to take him a little more seriously. Winger said, "I have a plan. You have contacts on the outside, I will make it worth their while."

Hubble said, "Show me the plan." Winger produced a nineteen-page handwritten plan. DeAnn was to be kidnapped from her home but made to look like she was going on a trip. Then she was to write a long note to Winger's lawyer, his mother, and his brother and say she had lied and "I wanted to get even with Winger for breaking up with me, that he didn't kill Donnah, that I knew he loved her." He carefully scripted the details and directed them to make sure her fingerprints were on the notes and the letters. After DeAnn is forced to write these letters and to do a tape recording of her confession, she was to be killed.

Hubble said, "I have contacts on the outside. I talked to them, but I need to know how you are going to finance this." Winger told him they are to kidnap a friend, Jeffrey Gilman, who was worth millions. They were to threaten to kill Gilman's wife and children unless he paid a ransom. Once they got the money, they can use that as payment for taking care of DeAnn. Hubble asked what they should do with Gilman. After further discussion, Hubble said, "Well, here is the issue we have. They have no problem whacking the old boy and his lady. Kids, you know, I'm not saying they have a problem. They just don't really like it. They want it to be worth their while. They don't want to fucking do it for chunk change." They talked for over an hour, planning the kidnappings and the murders. They talked about how to get rid of the body and where to put it. Winger said, "I don't care where they deposit her."

Winger did not know that Hubble was wearing a wire. Hubble had gone to the FBI and the state police. Hubble was instructed to get Winger on the wire, and that's what he did.

The written notes and the recorded conversations were enough to charge Winger with solicitation of two murders, DeAnn Schultz and Gilman. He had a jury trial and was subsequently convicted in 2007, and his appeal of that conviction was denied. He was sentenced to two concurrent sentences of thirty-five years each for solicitation of murder.

Thinking that things could not get worse, they did. Winger was sentenced to a maximum security jail, Tamms. He is currently serving his time there.

Tamms was a C Max prison, a super max prison. It only has single cells—seven by twelve feet. There is no mess hall. Three walls of the cell are solid; a small window at the top is the only way to see outside. Contact with outsiders is sharply restricted. No conversations are allowed with fellow prisoners. Meals are served on a small tray in the cells. There are no inmate work details.

Initially, Winger was confined to his cell twenty-four hours a day. After filing and winning a federal suit he was allowed out of his cell for one hour a day in the yard, a twenty-by-thirty-foot enclosed area. No other prisoners were allowed in the yard at the same time.

Typically the prison is reserved for gang leaders and prisoners who have attempted to kill staff or who are extraordinarily dangerous or destructive.

This is where Mark Winger resided for five years, and except for an occasional letter from Ira Drescher, letting him know how good a meal he just had was and how nice the weather is in Florida, Winger has little or no communication with his family, his wife, children, and parents. Tamms was closed in 2012, and he was transferred to the maximum-security prison at Illinois. He remains there to this day.

With a loving wife, one has to wonder why. What kind of ego, what kind of arrogance, leads someone to such a brutal murder, and he almost got away with it, but he did not.

166C-SI-54668
06/13/2005
MARK A. WINGER
PMB/pmb

TRANSCRIPT

Updated on 06/09/2007

For approximately the first 30 minutes, non-pertinent conversation takes place between TERRY HUBBELL and various members of the law enforcement community and other inmates as HUBBELL walks from the identification room to "the yard", where he meets MARK A. WINGER. The following conversation takes place between TERRY HUBBELL and MARK A. WINGER approximately 30 minutes after the recording device is activated:

TERRY HUBBELL: I did talk to Old Boy though last night. Got a couple little issues. One was with DeAnn, like, uh . . . everything has to go according to the paperwork, right? Pretty well?

MARK A. WINGER: Pretty well . . . (UI), I mean the concept.

HUBBELL: Right . . . the call . . . give her a call from . . . the calls from her house is not going to be a problem; getting the note left at her house is not going to be a problem they don't think, but they're not sure they can get her to write that fuckin' note . . . immediately, that's the only thing . . . he, he's not sure, ya know . . . and I know the note's real important. He said, "Man," he said, "you know, you go in there and, you know, kidnap somebody . . . and try to force them to write a note immediately. He said it's gonna be tough, hard to get her to write it where it's not, you know, like, a panic, you know . . .

WINGER: Right.

HUBBELL: . . . where she's not gonna panic . . . so maybe . . .

333

WINGER: On, on that I would say . . . you would best . . . but that note's gotta get . . . to that house . . . within twenty-four, forty-eight hours.

HUBBELL: Or how about if she calls 'em?

WINGER: Calls 'em?

HUBBELL: Right?

WINGER: What makes you think that, that's gonna go over . . . (UI)

HUBBELL: (UI) They'd have time, uh, time, you know, because the initial shock, right? And they don't want to be there, for (UI) you know

WINGER: Here, here's the problem with this . . . now I understand their problem (UI), and I agree it's gonna be hard, but . . . if she's gone, even if they, you know, they got her bags packed and everything, it looks like, you know, she's lost . . . but there's no note because of the special circumstances of her being a witness in my case . . . they will . . . they might not treat it . . . as some, larger, larger ring, and they might immediately start tape recording her cell phone calls . . . or the home phone, whichever, ya know, maybe both probably . . .

HUBBELL: Right.

WINGER: And so, if, let's say, then they got her to talk . . . and authorities are taping it, if she stutters, and, and says like wha, wha, ya know, anything, anything out of the fuckin' ordinary . . .

HUBBELL: Right, yeah, I understand, but I'm, I'm just tellin' ya, that's the only concern they had.

WINGER: Yeah, I don't think she should be makin' any . . . calls, after, after, after . . . until after the break . . . so she can't leave a note, she's gonna have to mail . . . unless . . . here's another option . . . if they can . . . do all this early enough . . . so when they have a couple a hours with her after the hooch.

HUBBELL: Yeah.

WINGER: They, they do that . . . and drive it up the same day . . . and just drop it in a box, well, you know, everyone else, however . . .

HUBBELL: Did you think that . . . you thinkin' the note should be mailed, could be mailed from Springfield?

WINGER: No . . . if they can find the time drive it up there . . . what I was thinkin' was that, let's say they got her say at eight in the morning. And by noon, they got her to the point where she could write a note. I don't know how, and don't tell me, but I don't know how long it takes to get from where they're gonna be keepin' her, to her house, but if they could get back by then . . . the note . . . either put it in the mailbox or just walk in the house, put it in the house, but then her fingerprints on it. Ah, that happens where, but mailing it and have to mail it from out a town (UI) because it has to be done, like, immediately, because see the thing about the note . . . is . . . it makes police have to stop and check other things out, you know, the affair, her husband . . . you know, makes me . . . even though she wrote my name in a note, it still makes me third priority . . . on the suspicion list . . . initially . . .

HUBBELL: Well . . . I, still, I don't think they're gonna come see us quick as you think they are. I don't think they're gonna . . . I don't know . . . I don't know, you know, that much about your case. I just don't see 'em, you know, thinkin' that you (UI) seem to think.

WINGER: Well . . . I gotta be conservative about it. If I, if I were givin' suggestions, I would, I would say . . . try to get her away from her family. If she doesn't, whisk her away. Make her write the note. Umm, you know that day. Try to get it back that day. Put it in the mailbox . . . or put it in her house and if that, baring that, you gotta mail it . . . within another day . . . from out a town.

HUBBELL: But you know, the thing . . . you know I told you they was concerned about you being so clean in all this shit, right?

WINGER: I'm really not.

HUBBELL: Well, you know, it, they're, you know, I'm just goin' by what they're tellin' me, you know, they feel that you're . . . way clean, way cleaner than any of us, you know.

WINGER: Um-hmm.

HUBBELL: Their concern is they don't want to bury her . . . in my property, it's like you (UI) were sayin', how they'd be out on my property lookin', right? They say, well, so, they want to bury her somewhere else . . . any suggestions?

WINGER I don't think . . . I could care less . . . as long as it's fuckin' thirty feet, you know, I mean . . . here, here's the thing . . . I . . . my opinion is . . . I'm trustworthy because . . . look at all I did . . . in all my own handwriting . . . there's things that only I would be able to (UI) in this whole thing, you know, these notes and others . . . okay? And it's so intricate, the only one who stands to gain . . . is me. It all points to me, it's all intrical . . . any, either you or them get, get ah, busted . . . I get busted right along with you. There's no way that I would not be implicated . . .

HUBBELL: Right, you know, they're just tryin' . . .

WINGER: . . . and then, and then, if that did happen . . .

HUBBELL: Right.

WINGER: . . . there's no way that I could like . . . make a deal . . . because I'm tryin' to get out of a situation.

HUBBELL: Right, well, you know, they're just out lookin', trying' to look out for me too, you know, that's, that's their only concern, you know.

WINGER: The, the thing is . . . where, where they bury her . . . has never been a concern.

HUBBELL: Right . . . but I wanted to bring that up to you.

WINGER: Because the other thing is I don't know where your property is.

HUBBELL: Yeah, I know, but still, you know . . . it come down to me if it ain't, he buries her out on his property, they're gonna be comin' down there a long time (UI) if they (UI) . . .

WINGER: The thing is . . . what, what does that assure me? That assures me of not getting another life sentence?

HUBBELL: (UI) I'm just, I'm just tellin' . . .

WINGER: And it, it'll cap my fate on being here, forever . . . I, I understand, I'm just, I'm just . . . reasoning my, my . . . perspective . . . there's no fuckin' way, if ever . . . and, and on top of that . . . (UI) . . .

HUBBELL:	And they had a couple questions about Gelman. One, they want to know . . . for sure . . . how much you think . . . that they can get outta him? Because they (UI) early in the year, ya know, they found a little shit, but maybe, but they ain't really had the time either, to set into lookin', ya know, so they gonna go solely on what you, you said.
WINGER:	Well . . . I don't KNOW anything. I only know what I've been told and . . . and what I've seen. And what he told me . . . was that he has a hundred million in the bank. What he told me is that he does invests in (UI) and banks (UI), that's all I know, you know, I don't really know, I only go by what he says, but what I've seen . . . is him make a phone call and say, "Hey, set these people up here," and in this building, and, and the guy jumps through his fuckin' ass to make accommodations for me and my wife and one of our kids at one really fancy condo high-rise in Chicago . . . and in another, another (UI) . . . and . . . I saw his fuckin' penthouse which is the entire top floor of a fuckin' building with a walk-around balcony, you know, I mean, and a wave pool, I mean, you can't have all that without having some, some leverage.
HUBBELL:	He told you he had a hundred million in the bank?
WINGER	In fact, he told me, he said his first year in business after he sold his heavy machine company, ah, construction company, he said first year he made fifty thousand dollars. Second year they made five million, and the third year they grossed fifty million.
HUBBELL:	Wow, was he in business with somebody else . . . got partners and shit?
WINGER:	Umm.

HUBBELL: Is this solely his business?

WINGER: It's, it's, it's him . . . and two or three guys, but I think it's his business. He just hired them. They might be his partners. There may be one, there might be . . . umm, but what they do is, is they arrange to buy a building and then they make a bid on . . . eh, they estimate how much it would cost to, ah, renovate it, as luxury condos, and they bid it out and let someone else do all the work, and then, then, they sell it . . . sell the units and ah, they usually left, you know, with a bunch of leftover units, and from that it's all profit . . . not, not including the profit margin he makes from his process with uh, with the (UI) you know, so ah, and he, often contracts, ah, the Walsh Construction Company . . . ah, 'cause he set me up with an interview with one of their head guys, and they hired me, they offered me a job, but I couldn't take it. But, ah, you know and I was on the phone with, with Jeff after the interview, after they offered me the job, and they said it was a standing offer, whenever I sell my house, whenever I had to do and, and, ah, in the conversation, Jeff said something, yeah, so-and-so ah, been buggin' me because I owe him, ah, forty million dollars, but I'm not gonna pay him until he finishes something, you know, so I know (UI) the transaction fly back and forth. He told me he was (UI) he told me he bought his mom and dad a house. He told me he has a big, ah, luxury RV thing.

HUBBELL: Right.

WINGER: So those are, you know, I've never been to his house. I've never seen his house, except his condo, his luxury penthouse, ah, and, ah, there's a guy I went to college with who happens to, who lives in Chicago who knows him and knows my girlfriend out in, ah, California. Because she actually, she was at a bar one time, and there's this guy named Jim Chaney who's about six foot eight, real big guy . . . and she, he was tryin' to pick her up, because she was a fuckin' ten, and ah, they were talking, said where you from and, and she said a little town outside Cleveland, Elyria. Cleveland, really? You know, I knew a guy from Elyria, Ohio. He was the baddest motherfucker I've ever known. He goes, he had, he would scare the shit out of me when I was in college because I'd be, like, right in his face, but I'm like at his chest . . . fuckin' college kid, you know, and, and he goes, I wonder if you know him, and, and she goes, well, um, what year did he graduate from college? And he said '85, and, and she goes . . . is it Mark Winger? Right as she was sayin' it, he said Mark Winger (laughs) and she's like, oh, you know, he's a sweetheart. He's like, he's the meanest motherfucker, you know, all this shit. He goes, that motherfucker scared me. But he liked me because afterwards, after his rat year, you know, I stuck up for him, on a couple things, but anyway, ah, so I call him, and ah, this was when the job description, and, and I had worked on pumps and stuff, and that's what his family makes, is pumps, and ah, he was tellin' me that he was good friends with Jeff and that Jeff was doin' really fuckin' good. So you know, the bottom line there is that from another circle, I get that Jeffs, ah, wealthy. But as, as far as the real truth, I don't know. All's I know is, from what I've seen . . . if I had a (UI) and I descended upon his fuckin' family and squeezed them for every nickel I could get . . . I know it'd be in the millions.

HUBBELL: In the millions . . . yeah (UI).

WINGER: I know, because, under, under the arrangement that we already made (UI).

HUBBELL: (UI)

WINGER: But even if it turned out . . . let's say even if it turned out that they could only squeeze the one buck, one million . . . even for them, that's a pretty big chunk . . . for a small . . . I know, I know the risk . . .

HUBBELL: Well, here's, here's the issue they have . . . you know, they got no problem whackin' old boy and his old lady. But the kids . . . you know? I'm not sayin' that they're havin' problems or they had a problem, they don't . . . it's kinda like . . .

WINGER: They prefer not to.

HUBBELL: No, they want it to be worth their while, you know, they don't want to fuckin' do it for, you know, chump change . . . see what I'm sayin'?

WINGER: Um-hmm, well, not . . . the only thing I could suggest . . . is to research the piss out of it.

HUBBELL: Well, they're goin' to. But I'm just sayin' they figured you probably know . . . a little, you know, and . . .

WINGER: I know . . . I know what I know . . .

HUBBELL: Because . . . they go to research and they really don't come up with . . . what you're lookin' for . . . it may be because he's got it somewhere they ain't lookin', ya know?

WINGER: Umm-hmm.

HUBBELL: And they want to make . . . have an idea what they're lookin' for . . .

WINGER: Well, well, I know that . . .

HUBBELL: Because of the amount of money is gonna make 'em look in different places . . . you know.

WINGER: Right . . . I wouldn't be surprised if he's got some money in the Caymans . . . I wouldn't be surprised if he's got some money spread out to Vegas. He goes out there a lot, and I know he told me he's gonna be opening a office out there. I don't even know the name of his company. I asked him once, he told me, but I didn't catch it.

HUBBELL: Uh-huh.

WINGER: It's not Gelman Industries or anything . . . you know?

HUBBELL: Right, right . . . and then the other thing, they said . . . that when they get 'em . . . you don't really know his wife though, do you?

WINGER: No, I just know that she's a petite ballerina.

HUBBELL: You know the kids?

WINGER: I don't know anything.

HUBBELL: (UT) just him.

WINGER: Just him, and I haven't seen 'em . . . literally, since the late nineties . . . since 1981?

HUBBELL: No shit? When was the last time you talked to him?

WINGER: Um, like 1999 . . . no, 2000, no, no, no the last time I talked to him was 2001. See what happened was . . . minding my own business . . . got a phone call out of the blue . . . hadn't spoke to the guy in twenty years . . . and he said he was somewhere and my name came up and he was curious about what I was doin' so he thought he'd give me a call.

HUBBELL: Uh-huh.

WINGER: I thought he was callin' because all the shit that was in the newspapers.

HUBBELL: Right.

WINGER: But he didn't know anything about it . . . in fact, the reason my name came up . . . was he had just learned that my wife had died back in '95 . . . so, and years had gone by . . . seven, eight years, so, so . . . and, ah, so he thought he'd give me a call, so he made contact and from, from there, I said, told him, you know, the situation that I got remarried, and I told him the new situation . . . and man, didn't know any of that, so that's when he was like, well, let me, you know, you and your wife need a getaway, why don't you let me set you up in one of my, ah, condos, and that's when that started happening.

HUBBELL: Well, the reason they asked that, 'cause they were kinda wantin' to see what you thought about, as far as separating them, like, you know, separating the mom from the kids, the dad from the kids, or would they work better if they were kept together, you know, cause some people, if you separate 'em from the kids, they (UI) up, you know what I mean? . . . refuse . . . and it takes forever to get 'em to do shit, but if you keep 'em together, let 'em see each other, ya know, things tend to work a little better.

WINGER: I think that the same technique the (UI) uses and they, they need incentive . . . (UI)

HUBBELL: And are you sure on the way we spelled his name? Are, you're pretty sure that's how it's spelled?

WINGER: G-e-l-m-a-n.

HUBBELL: Yeah.

WINGER: About 99.9 percent.

HUBBELL: Yeah. (UI) Anything you want, huh? Well, I'm talkin' to 'em tonight.

WINGER: (UI) I just want everything as far, as far as that. From everything I know, from what he told me . . . (UI) know for sure (UI) and you know, plus other people have told me (UI) and not only that, you know, when he says, he knows, ah, Jesse White real well. Then I meet Jesse White, and I ask, hey you know Jeff Gelman? Yeah, I know Jeff. So . . . to ask.

WINGER: Right, and that's fine, and, and you know . . . I've had . . . numerous acquaintances, close acquaintances (UI), but only . . .

HUBBELL: And I'm sure that if you was to, ever get to them . . . you can get a deal 'cause they, you know, these motherfuckers they would probably love to happen, you know?

WINGER: I don't know anything about it.

HUBBELL: Yeah, exactly.

WINGER: Yeah, I don't know anything about it.

HUBBELL: Exactly, but I'm just sayin' that if it came down to that . . .

WINGER: I can understand 110 percent their concern . . . both for themselves and for you.

HUBBELL: Right

WINGER: Because I'm a guy they don't know . . . they're goin' on your word vouchin' for me.

HUBBELL: Right.

WINGER: And then they see the shit on the Internet and they say, "What the fuck?"

HUBBELL: Yeah.

WINGER: And I'm not a piece a shit.

HUBBELL: Yeah, well, they wouldn't give a fuck if you was guilty or not, you know, I mean how . . . who are they to judge somebody, you know.

WINGER: But you know, I look at it . . .

HUBBELL: They would probably give you brownie points for being guilty, you know?

WINGER: Well, I look at it like this . . . (UI) they're only out for (UT) trust established by your loyalty, and and I'm hopin' that one day, I'll be able to prove my mettle with them, you know, because, it's my intentions . . . (UT)

HUBBELL: (UT) Tell me that. Believe me, you're gonna, you know, I'm gonna see, I'm gonna see if, you know, what I do for you comes back there to me. You know. If you help me in return.

WINGER: Oh yeah, without a doubt.

HUBBELL: (UT)

WINGER: (UI) I mean, (UT) I don't, like, you know, touchy-feely, mushy shit. I'm just sayin' (UI).

HUBBELL: Right.

WINGER: (UT)

HUBBELL: Yeah, it's your freedom, you know . . . you can't put a price on freedom.

WINGER: No, and . . . in addition, everything in addition (UT) who in the fuck'n' world would ever do that for me? You know, 'cause, I know that's (UI). I've never met anybody I've needed.

HUBBELL: Right.

WINGER: (UI) You know . . . (UI) bad enough . . . (UI)

HUBBELL: Yeah.

WINGER: To some extent . . . you know, a lie . . . and I only know what . . .

HUBBELL: Yeah, you only know what you've told me (clears throat).

WINGER: Getting back to DeAnn, er, the note . . . I'd say try . . . you know, do it right there on the spot. Probably get it back up to there later that day. They know the schedule, they know (UI), just . . . given hypothetical . . . if you can do that the fallback is to have it mailed from out a town that night or the next night.

HUBBELL: That'll work.

WINGER: I wish there was a better way with, with Gelman, you know, and I'm sure . . . given enough time . . . probably figure out a plan that would . . . somehow get those kids in a camp or something . . . or some trip they, their folks are sendin' them on, you know, where they're chaperoned by, by a group that doesn't know any of them . . . in the meantime you got, you got (UI) but like you said, those guys are free thinkers . . . ahm, ahm, they're, they're free to come up with any plan they want.

HUBBELL: And they will. But they're just tryin' to get, you know (UI).

UNKNOWN MALE: **Nonpertinent conversation**

HUBBELL: I just hope all this shit works out. I'm so, I'm so over this shit, you know? Let's get it done and be done this is the, this is the last time . . .

WINGER: Oh man, I'm sick last night, I'm still sick from that fuckin' meat sandwich last night.

HUBBELL: Yeah, this is the last time I'm gonna talk about any of this shit. They kinda got a . . . they kinda got a laugh out of that last part though, that bubba shit.

WINGER: (Laughs.)

HUBBELL: Yeah, I don't what you to take offense or nothin' . . . but . . . they, you know, they've read every fuckin' thing there is to read on your case, you've . . . everything, and then they kinda thought you was guilty, then they read that fuckin' shit about . . . tell Bubba, whatever fuck it says, I don't remember how it says it now, they said that the, they believe she was involved in that shit too, you know, but that's just their opinion.

WINGER: Yeah.

HUBBELL: So . . . it don't, it don't matter one fuckin' way or another, you know? But when we get out a here, you will meet these guys . . . they will meet you.

WINGER: As far as I'm concerned it don't . . . to me, it doesn't matter at this point. If guilty or (UI). Only thing that matters to me is getting out and doing things right by you, and startin' over and havin', havin' good fuckin' career and shit, opportunities with you . . . that's all, that's all I want to do, man. I remember readin' that fuckin' Harley Davidson Motorcycle book. It's fuckin' great, man. It's got me psyched, that's all I want to . . . Hey, why do they have, ah, on some models . . . a cross member between the two exhaust manifolds?

HUBBELL: To equalize the back pressure . . . that's usually on dressers and shit like that though.

WINGER: Umm-hmm.

HUBBELL: Dressers you don't . . . you don't ride them as hard as you would, say, ah, you know, barhop . . . what I call bar hoppers. You know, bar hoppers, you just . . . usually start barhoppin' then . . . where cruisers, you're just cruisin', you know, and it gets better mileage, and it runs smoother if you equalize the back pressure.

WINGER: When I get out, you know, if they're ever on a job . . . they need me, I'd do it for room and board. They got it planned out . . . stayin' out a jail like they (UI) . . . I'd do it (UI) for room and board . . . because you know, I'm, I'm done with all that shit. You know, when I graduated, when I graduate, before I graduated from college, I really wanted to be a CIA hit man or work for the FBI or some fuckin' black group. Not because I was into the law and shit like that . . . but because I wanted to do some fuckin' (UI) coldhearted fuckin' shit . . . you know? That, that's where I was. It didn't work out that way, but . . . but I know I can pull a trigger.

HUBBELL: Huh?

WINGER: I know I can pull a trigger.

HUBBELL: Yeah.

WINGER: Without question . . . man, I don't take offense about little things. I look at it like this . . . when I was talkin' to DeAnn back then . . . and she said that to me . . . I had talked . . . I had . . . always talked to my brother . . . and he . . . he saw that she was comin' on to me, shit, and he knew there was something goin' on, and he's like, man, you were just involved in a fuckin' homicide. He goes, it's over with, it's behind you . . . she is the fuckin' red herring in all of this shit. He goes, you need to dump this bitch. You can't see her anymore . . . and then . . . almost the same time . . . when I saw her . . . she said that . . . my wife's sister had been talkin' to her . . . sayin' that, and I don't know if it's true, what she was tellin' me or if she was just . . . tryin' to fuck with me, she said that Michelle told her that something's wrong and that Donnah's screaming to her from the grave . . . and then that, coupled with, with ah . . . what my brother said. I was like, man, I got to thinkin' like . . . we can't be seen together (UI) like, couple weeks later, me and her got busted, almost fuckin' by (UI), and so then it was like, that's it, you know . . . so I took her home and stormed outta the house, and then I took her home and, ah, and then my ex-wife, she was just my nanny at the time, she was startin' to think kids . . . because she thought we, DeAnn and I, had an affair together, so she got suspicious. So all this is coming down, so I had a talk with DeAnn one (UI) . . . boom . . . this don't look good. We can both get fuckin' in trouble. They'll, they'll look at both of us. And, and, ah, then some time after that, where she had, we were talkin' again, she had talked to her brother (UI) said something about, don't fuck Bubba for no one . . . so that's what she repeated to me . . . and like, and, but it was under . . . in the context of . . . okay, we agree not to see each other, we agree not to ever talk about the affair or (UI) and so, even though, it didn't happen like the impression that they got . . . there was still that talk between she and I, that look, that we don't look good (UI), you know . . . and I took her for her fuckin' word, I trusted her, she said, I won't fuck Bubba for nothin' . . . and then she fuckin' does.

HUBBELL: So you'd been better off if you just kept fuckin' her.

WINGER: Yeah . . . just like Ira said, "You dumped her big time."

HUBBELL: Who? . . . Oh . . .

WINGER: (UI) Piece of shit . . . you know, I'd been better off whackin' . . . you know . . . and the thing is . . . for two, three, four years . . . I had every opportunity (UI), you know . . . and if I was . . . guilty and paranoid and everything, I would have whacked her. You know, but I just thought (UI) it's over, we had an affair, bad timing, let's forget, bad shit happens, but it's over, but, man, it wasn't over with her. I didn't realize how much she had been fuckin' obsessin'. I had no idea.

HUBBELL: 'Cause it was a few years . . . between time you quit fuckin' her and she did this, right?

WINGER: Yeah, it was, she came forward in . . . basically February of '99, that's you know, almost four years . . . . I'd like to cut her fuckin' tongue out, quietly.

HUBBELL: I know you said that once before. Throw it in a jar.

WINGER: Yeah . . . in a jar, and every time I got like a, an ounce of crack butter, wipe my ass with that tongue and put it back in the jar.

HUBBELL: (Laughs.)

(NONPERTINENT OR UNINTELLIGIBLE CONVERSATION TAKES PLACE FOR APPROXIMATELY ONE MINUTE AND TEN SECONDS.)

HUBBELL: But ah, as far as the scheduling of this thing, callin' anymore . . . so . . . that's why I say if there's anything you gotta say, say it now . . . because . . .

WINGER: The only thing I gotta say is my . . . concerns about . . . (UI) time to (UI) that note . . . that first note, and ah, and, and then the other possibility that her phones are gonna be recorded . . . her cell phone and her home phone (UI) be a short period of time, I don't even know what her husband does, he's probably a lawyer.

HUBBELL: I don't know.

WINGER: I know he does pretty well. Whatever. I know he's real religious . . .

UNKNOWN MALE: **Background conversation, not related to WINGER and HUBBELL'S conversation.**

WINGER: Again, I don't care where they . . . deposit . . . her just as long as . . . it will never, ever, ever (UI) . . . I never wanted to know, really.

HUBBELL: Right . . . and there's no specific date that this has to be done by, right? . . . I mean it ain't like . . . I mean it's gonna happen soon, but I mean it's not like . . . it's got to happen . . . tomorrow or . . .

WINGER: No.

HUBBELL: Just . . . be good if we can get it all before they hear your post though, right?

WINGER: Yeah . . . (UI) I figured that was all up to them.

HUBBELL: Right, right.

WINGER: As long as they wait for more time (UI).

HUBBELL: Right, yeah, they don't want much spend much (UI).

WINGER: (UI) I mean I was kinda . . . I, I guess just assuming . . . because they didn't want you (UI).

HUBBELL: (UI) And that could be, I don't know, you know, they just, just (UI) . . .

WINGER: They know, they know to do it (UI).

HUBBELL: They, they might . . . that's in Springfield, right?

WINGER: Yeah . . . two o'clock . . . (UI) I think . . .

STATEMENT OF

MARK WINGER

Your Honor; Mr. Morgan; Mr. Luckman;

I am glad to have this opportunity to make a brief statement to the court and to others present. I would first like to thank my public defender, Mr. Morgan, for his efforts. We did not always see eye to eye on every issue, but what defendant ever does? Without question, Mr. Morgan is one of the more decent and honest people that I've encountered in a long while.

Your Honor, I have humiliated myself among my family and friends, in my foolishness and gullibility. Soon, my shame will become my entire family's shame as a major TV network prepares itself to once again line their pockets and boost their ratings on one blood of my late wife, Donnah Winger, and on my own grief and poor judgment.

I am consumed with remorse for the state of hopelessness that my actions have left my parents in. This trial, this conviction, was a sudden reversal of fortune for many, as there was little doubt in anyone's mind (including the prosecutors in Springfield) that my wrongful conviction of the 1995 murders of my wife and of the lunatic who actually killed her was about to be overturned and sent back for a new trial on the merits of my very strong and irrefutable postconviction petition.

Prior to my wrongful conviction in 2002 I was not a tough guy or a tough talker. Anyone who knew me back then can tell you that I was kind and compassionate. I was neighborly and showed hospitality to strangers. I was a loving husband and doting father of four beautiful children. I worked very hard in my employment so that my wife could be a stay-home mom. And although our family of six lived paycheck to paycheck I was charitable and managed to tithe a full 10 percent of my income each month and donate my time and my skills to my community.

I was raised in a loving and supportive home by the best parents a boy could wish for. My parents taught me to be nice to others and to be honest in all my dealings. We believed that only bad people got punished and that the police were the good guys. These were some of the cornerstones of my belief structure, my cherry view of the world around me.

All of that was shattered in the year 2002, when I was wrongfully convicted of a double murder, one of those victims being my beautiful wife. Your Honor, I have never struck a woman in my life. Certainly not my wife. Not once. Not ever!

But my foundation was put asunder as I witnessed the detectives in that trial and their uniformed brethren lie one after another. Some of whom have recently been fired from the police force for lying and cheating in other drug and murder cases, while yet others of them scurried off to early retirement to avoid a similar fate.

I came to prison dismayed, ashamed, perplexed, depressed, and frightened but, most of all, innocent.

I soon learned from some of the old-timers that now my innocence or guilt no longer mattered and that the reviewing courts have long lost any compassion, and all that matters now is whether or not I got a fair trial.

But I learned even quicker that one had few options in how to survive in a maximum—security prison in Illinois. As the saying goes, "Fight, Fornicate, or Die" (I cleaned up the language a bit for the court).

Pontiac Correctional Center and the other maximum-security prisons in Illinois are not only warehouses of men, but they are insane asylums. As I testified at trial, I am convinced that I've lost a measure of my sanity as a result of my incarceration.

You may believe that yourself, having been a part of the criminal justice system for so long, that you can to some extent empathize with me. But I promise you, Your Honor, you cannot. Until you have spent any time on the inside you cannot fully appreciate what you subject men to once you pronounce sentence.

The constant yelling and screaming and arguing. The continual din of voices. The sound of a neighbor being beaten down by his cell mate or, worse, raped. The stench of dirty bodies and the suffocating heat and stale air. Sadistic guards who delight in provoking inmates to violence or tears. The myriad other aspects that often exceed cruelty, all of which contribute to the psychological destruction of an inmate.

With that appallingly understated description is a backdrop, Your Honor—there am I. Everything I had and everything I was taken away from me, the tangible and the intangible alike. The only things remaining between the extremes of hope and hopelessness were anger and frustration.

I sank into my base thoughts and fantasized what it would be like if witnesses simply told the truth. Or to confess their lies. Or to suffer in the same manner as they have mercilessly left me to suffer. These were fantasies, Your Honor, nothing more. I did not tell any lies on the witness stand.

I am exceedingly sorry for my foolishness in sharing my fantasies with Terry Hubbell. And I regret that my incarceration has so affected my judgment that I would write down my fantasies as a diversion and then be idiotic enough to trust those writings in the hands of Terry Hubbell. I rue the day I met the man. By the way, I did not know until after all of this came to light that Hubbell was a child-killing pedophile. He represented himself differently to me.

I am ashamed of myself for actually finding amusement in these fantasies that I shared with Hubbell. I hate that my heart has been swept away to such a dark place, often illuminated only by my base emotions.

There is no question, Your Honor that I am an educated man. But smart people get fooled every day. No one dared claim that I was street-smart. Terry Hubbell tricked me. He used me from the start. He's no dummy. He is certainly skilled in construction and welding and other civil engineering—related activities. That was a big part of our relationship and our discussions. He's a sly fox, Your Honor.

He fooled me into believing that he would help me financially upon my release from prison, thus belaying many of my fears. Later, he pulled a classic, the bait and switch, and had me convinced that my children and my parents were in grave danger if I did not give him some information

Jeff Gelman. Then he tricked me yet again into engaging him in a conversation that was, in my belief and Mr. Morgan's belief, illegally recorded. He knew when he would be wired up, and he primed my pump over the course of the one and a half weeks leading up to that recorded conversation. Had you had the opportunity to hear the conversations leading up to the one of June 13, 2005, we would not be here today, Your Honor.

I am terribly sorry for my language and my behavior that my jury and the court had to endure when listening to an edited version of the tape. There is a logical explanation, one that does not include any intent that any murder be committed. And that leads me to my final regret, Your Honor.

I truly regret that the tape ever found its way into my trial, as you can well imagine. Not just because of its horrid content but because of the manner in which it came to be part of my trial in the first place.

I am not the only educated man to find himself fooled, Judge Frobish. FBI agent Peter M. Buckley sat in that witness chair and pulled the wool over everyone's eyes. First, claiming to have entered the case weeks before it was humanly possible, and you said later that you believed him. All the while Mr. Luckman sat silently, letting the false testimony to go uncorrected because it was to the state's advantage. Then Agent Buckley testified about the FBI's two-tier procedure to obtain approval for the intercept of oral communications, which is in fact a three-tier procedure requiring a judge's review. And you said you believed him. And Agent Buckley testified that he couldn't show us the FD-759, the document used to apply for authorization of the overhear, because it contained sensitive information, a fact that is simply not true. I read a copy of my neighbor's FD-759 just last week, Your Honor. There's nothing sensitive about it. But you said you found the agent credible, and so the tape was in and fairness was out. Everybody was impressed with the FBI agent, except me, Your Honor—because I knew he lied just like the detectives did in my first trial.

But this trial, unlike what Mr. Luckman said, was not about seeking the truth. Otherwise, Mr. Luckman would have corrected Agent Buckley's pretrial testimony or later in trial, when the agent gave a different answer to the same question—still equally false but different.

This trial was far too important to too many powerful people here and especially in Springfield to lose, Your Honor. One must ask themselves "Why would the state spend a quarter million dollars on a trial for a guy serving a life sentence to nail him for a crime that could in no way have occurred?" Or "Why would a prosecutor from my 2002 trial, an officer of the court, testify in this trial in direct contradiction to testimony that his own prosecution team put to my jury in the 2002 trial on the exact same question?" And "What is so important about Mark Winger that an FBI agent would dare lie under oath and then obstruct to prevent the defendant from obtaining discoverable material?" And finally, "Why would the prosecutor remain silent during all of these happenings?"

Remember, Your Honor, I told you that my conviction was about to be overturned. That's a strong motive and answers a few questions.

My word means nothing to anyone anymore. But the record speaks for itself. I only ask that you look at the record and the facts and check them against each other and against the state and federal statutes.